Women's Everyday Lives in War and Peace in the South Caucasus

Ulrike Ziemer
Editor

Women's Everyday Lives in War and Peace in the South Caucasus

palgrave
macmillan

Editor
Ulrike Ziemer
University of Winchester
Winchester, UK

ISBN 978-3-030-25519-0   ISBN 978-3-030-25517-6   (eBook)
https://doi.org/10.1007/978-3-030-25517-6

© The Editor(s) (if applicable) and The Author(s) 2020
This work is subject to copyright. All rights are solely and exclusively licensed by the Publisher, whether the whole or part of the material is concerned, specifically the rights of translation, reprinting, reuse of illustrations, recitation, broadcasting, reproduction on microfilms or in any other physical way, and transmission or information storage and retrieval, electronic adaptation, computer software, or by similar or dissimilar methodology now known or hereafter developed.
The use of general descriptive names, registered names, trademarks, service marks, etc. in this publication does not imply, even in the absence of a specific statement, that such names are exempt from the relevant protective laws and regulations and therefore free for general use.
The publisher, the authors and the editors are safe to assume that the advice and information in this book are believed to be true and accurate at the date of publication. Neither the publisher nor the authors or the editors give a warranty, expressed or implied, with respect to the material contained herein or for any errors or omissions that may have been made. The publisher remains neutral with regard to jurisdictional claims in published maps and institutional affiliations.

Cover image: © Getty/Oleh_Slobodeniuk
Cover design by Ran Shauli and Frido Steinen-Broo

This Palgrave Macmillan imprint is published by the registered company Springer Nature Switzerland AG
The registered company address is: Gewerbestrasse 11, 6330 Cham, Switzerland

Acknowledgements

I am indebted to many individuals, on multiple levels, for support and assistance during researching and writing this book. First of all, I would like to express my gratitude to all research participants who shared their knowledge with me and the contributors in this edited volume. I am also enormously grateful to the authors in this edited volume for delivering on time and putting up with my endless comments and requirements.

A book like this one can be done only with the support of many different institutions. I am indebted to the University of Winchester and the USC Institute Armenian Studies, whose generous research support facilitated my fieldwork trips to the region. This book also benefited from the quiet and stimulating research environment I found during my research stay at the Aleksanteri Institute of the University of Helsinki.

In the course of my research trips, I met many inspiring women, female scholars, politicians and activists, some of whom have become good friends. It is impossible to express my indebtedness to all those women who warmly welcomed me during my research trips, dedicated their valuable time and answered my never-ending questions so that I could gain some treasured insights into their lives. In particular, I would like to thank Gohar Shahnazarian, Lara Aharonian, Gayane Hambardzumyan, Karina Shahnazarian, Inga Shahnazarian, Pervana Mammadova, Avnik Melikian and Olya Azatyan. I also would like to thank Eve Richards for her technical support and Jo Laycock and Armine Ishkanian for their motivational support.

I would like to thank my parents, Susanne and Christian Ziemer, for their support and patience. Last but not least, thank you, Sean, for keeping me whole and grounded throughout this endeavour, for reading, listening and caring, as well as for keeping up with my long absences.

Contents

1   Introduction: Women's Everyday Lives in the South Caucasus   1
Ulrike Ziemer

Part I   Women, Tradition and Social Change

2   Women as Bearers of Modernity and Tradition   23
Melanie Krebs

3   'Supra Is Not for Women': Hospitality Practices as a Lens on Gender and Social Change in Georgia   43
Costanza Curro

4   Women Against Authoritarianism: Agency and Political Protest in Armenia   71
Ulrike Ziemer

viii   Contents

Part II   Experiencing War and Displacement

5   Between Love, Pain and Identity: Armenian Women
     After World War I   103
     Anna Aleksanyan

6   'We Are Strangers Among Our Own People': Displaced
     Armenian Women   129
     Shushanik Ghazaryan

7   Vulnerability and Resilience: Women's Narratives
     of Forced Displacement from Abkhazia   155
     Nargiza Arjevanidze

8   The Politics of Widowhood in Nagorny Karabakh   179
     Nona Shahnazarian and Ulrike Ziemer

**Part III   New Beginnings and Old Challenges: Feminism
             and Women's Identities**

9   Invisible Battlefield: How the Politicization of LGBT
     Issues Affects the Visibility of LBT Women in Georgia   205
     Natia Gvianishvili

10   Exploring Two Generations of Women Activists
     in Azerbaijan: Between Feminism and a Post-Soviet
     Locality   225
     Yuliya Gureyeva Aliyeva

11   Feminism in Azerbaijan: Gender, Community
     and Nation-Building   253
     Sinead Walsh

Index   277

Notes on Contributors

Anna Aleksanyan is a doctoral candidate at the Strassler Center for Holocaust and Genocide Studies at Clark University, Worcester, Massachusetts. Before starting her Ph.D., Anna worked at the Armenian Genocide Museum-Institute as a scientific researcher for seven years.

Nargiza Arjevanidze is a doctoral student in the programme of Sociology at Tbilisi State University, Georgia. She teaches at the Institute for Gender Studies at Ivane Javakhishvili Tbilisi State University.

Costanza Curro is a Postdoctoral Research Fellow at the Aleksanteri Institute in Helsinki. She received her Ph.D. from the School of Slavonic and East European Studies, University College London (SSEES-UCL) with a thesis on the transformation of hospitality practices in post-Soviet Georgia.

Shushanik Ghazaryan is a doctoral candidate and researcher at the Institute of Archaeology and Ethnography, National Academy of Sciences.

Notes on Contributors

Yuliya Gureyeva Aliyeva is a doctoral candidate in Social Anthropology at the National Academy of Sciences of the Republic of Azerbaijan. She is currently Hubert Humphrey Fellow at Maxwell School of Citizenship at Syracuse University.

Natia Gvianishvili is a lesbian feminist activist and researcher from Georgia. Currently she works as Advocacy Programme Manager at RFSL (The Swedish Federation for LGBTQ Rights) and studies for an M.A. in Global Politics and Societal Change in Sweden. Until July 2017, she worked as a director of the Women's Initiatives Supporting Group (WISG) in Georgia.

Melanie Krebs received her Ph.D. in Central Asian Studies at Humboldt University Berlin. Currently, she works as a development consultant for peace, gender and rural development in the South Caucasus.

Nona Shahnazarian is a social anthropologist and a Senior Research Fellow at The Institute of Archaeology and Ethnography, National Academy of Sciences, Yerevan, Armenia. She is also affiliated with the Center for Independent Social Research, St. Petersburg, Russia.

Sinead Walsh received her Ph.D. on women's activism from Trinity College in Dublin. She is currently affiliated with the Gender, Culture and Society Programme at the University of Limerick.

Ulrike Ziemer is a Senior Lecturer in Sociology at the University of Winchester. Her publications include numerous journal articles and book chapters on the Armenian diaspora in Russia, as well as on gender issues in Armenia and Nagorny Karabakh.

1

Introduction:
Women's Everyday Lives
in the South Caucasus

Ulrike Ziemer

At the beginning of the twenty-first century, a number of major political developments have helped propel the South Caucasus to international attention. In April 2018, political protests in Armenia resulted in the toppling of Serzh Sargsyan's semi-authoritarian regime.[1] This largely unexpected development saw former journalist and leader of the protest movement, Nikol Pashinyan, elected by lawmakers to the post of Prime Minister in May 2018, concluding this relatively peaceful, but no less surprising transfer of power. Ten years earlier, in August 2008, it was Armenia's neighbour, Georgia, that focused the international community, this time in the context of a five-day war with Russia over the separatist region of South Ossetia. This event was closely preceded by Georgia's own high-profile domestic political struggle that saw yet another transfer of power in the context of Georgia's 2003 Rose Revolution. Fifteen years later, and Georgia's domestic political scene, like Armenia's, remains vibrant. In December 2018,

---

U. Ziemer (✉)
University of Winchester, Winchester, UK
e-mail: Ulrike.Ziemer@winchester.ac.uk

© The Author(s) 2020
U. Ziemer (ed.), *Women's Everyday Lives in War and Peace in the South Caucasus*,
https://doi.org/10.1007/978-3-030-25517-6_1

1

Salome Zurabishvili was inaugurated as Georgia's first female president, becoming the first female head of a state in the South Caucasus.[2] Her inauguration comes at a time of institutional transformation, as Georgia implements constitutional changes ahead of a planned transition from a presidential to parliamentary republic by 2024. In contrast, Azerbaijan has experienced little notable domestic political turbulence under the long-standing leadership of President Ilham Aliyev, in what appears to be a relatively consolidated authoritarian system. However, in April 2016, hostilities between Azerbaijan and Armenia flared, taking the international community by surprise, as the two countries resumed their conflict over the disputed Nagorny Karabakh[3] region for four days.

Given these political developments it is no surprise that themes of transition, ethnic conflict and security, often subsumed under the umbrella of 'geopolitics' take priority in scholarly and media debates on the South Caucasus region. However, parallel to these high-profile concerns and operating at the societal level, the lived experiences of its inhabitants, especially the experiences of women in the region remain largely under-elaborated and unexplored. This is despite the by-no-means inconsequential link between macro political outcomes of the type previously mentioned and the often slower-moving and subaltern issue of 'social change'. It is with this in mind that this edited volume seeks to restore some balance to current debates by focusing on the everyday challenges faced by women living in the South Caucasus, their everyday struggles and their contributions to the region's history, societal life and politics.

As such, the original research underpinning the collection of essays in this volume helps redress the prevalent geopolitical focus to consider social change in the South Caucasus and in particular the role of female agency. In short, a focus on women does so much more than offer a better understanding of women's lives. Not least, it can show us how 'discursive power functions by concealing the terms of its fabrication' (Brown 2001, p. 122). The chapters in this volume offer a rich array of women's experiences during peace time, as well those times characterized by conflict, struggle and war. The approach taken in the chapters that follow is interdisciplinary, including essays written by sociologists, anthropologists, historians and feminist activists. By exploring the richness of women's experiences, this edited volume takes the view that gender is a category constructed by the social world, embracing the famous words of Simone de Beauvoir (1997): 'one is not born, but rather becomes, a woman'.

Diversity and Similarity: State Socialism's Legacy on Gender Relations

One of the ironies of the current focus on geopolitics in the South Caucasus, often at the expense of broader issues of social change and the role of women, is that the South Caucasus remains a highly 'inflexed' region in the sense that it has experienced a great deal of historical juncture relating to both change and gender. During nearly seventy years of communist rule, the Soviet government oversaw a revolutionary change in nearly every aspect of life. At its core, this revolutionary change aimed to create a qualitatively new Soviet man and woman, in part by freeing women from bourgeois patriarchal oppression by means of educating women and fully incorporating them into the paid labour force. Bolshevik leaders, such as Aleksandra Kollontai, the head of the Party's women's division until early 1922, thought that the family was the site of women's oppression (Ashwin 2000, p. 5). In other words, it was believed that industrialization and economic development would liberate women from the traditional confines of the family (Lapidus 1978, p. 55).

The Soviet government's commitment to equality between the sexes was demonstrated by the introduction of policies that officially guaranteed, for example, education equality, equal pay, the right to abortion and the reorganization of domestic labour and childcare (Buckley 1989). Women were supported by generous maternity and childcare benefits enabling them to develop their professional careers. Nonetheless, a wealth of publications has shown that in reality these policies did little to challenge traditional gender divisions. Male domination in the public sphere remained largely unquestioned and women continued to face a so-called 'double burden' of work and home life (Corrin 1992). For example, while women were gradually qualifying for more education and had largely achieved parity with men in terms of enrolment by 1991, they were still concentrated in educational fields leading to careers with lower wage returns—mostly in education, the social sciences, the humanities, medicine, law and economics—while men tended to concentrate on more remunerative fields, such as skilled manual work and engineering (Ziemer 2018, p. 481). Hence, the formal structures of socialist society formed by the state as well as by the geographical separation of public and private spheres, heightened traditional gender identity as a cultural resource for both survival and resistance (Watson 1993, p. 472).

The end of the Cold War did not just erase East–West antagonism, but heralded a radical change in people's everyday lives. However, the political, economic and social transitions which followed the collapse of the Union of Soviet Socialist Republics (USSR) led to a region-wide decline in welfare provision and dramatic changes in the economy affecting the living standards of every former Soviet citizen. The South Caucasus was not immune from these changes but experienced the additional impact of ubiquitous interethnic conflict and secessionist wars: the Nagorny Karabakh war being the first, dragging Armenia and Azerbaijan into a complex conflict from 1988 onwards, but followed in 1991–1993 by war in Georgia's breakaway republics of South Ossetia and Abkhazia.[4] In addition, 1988 witnessed a powerful earthquake in the North of Armenia that killed more than 25,000 people and destroyed tens of thousands of homes. Three decades later and this region is yet to fully recover from this disaster. As such, the combination of human-made and natural upheavals, in particular in Armenia and Georgia, renders poverty an enduring fact of life across the region. In 2017, The Asian Development Bank estimated that 21.9% of Georgians and 25.7% of Armenians live in poverty, contrasted with 5.9% of the population in Azerbaijan. In Nagorny Karabakh, according to the Republic's National Statistical Service (2017), 23.3% of the population are destitute, with 6.2% experiencing extreme poverty.[5]

As in other parts of the world, poverty, unemployment and labour market participation in the South Caucasus display strong gender patterns. According to a report by the International Labour Organization in 2018, Armenia has the highest female unemployment rate among all post-Soviet countries with 17.3% of women aged above 25 unemployed (Mkrtchian 2018). In Georgia, the unemployment rate for women stands at 7.7% and in Azerbaijan, this figure drops to 4.8% (ibid.). In terms of labour force participation,[6] gender patterns also reveal problems of unequal access. According to the United Nation Development Programme (UNDP) (2019b), 62.9% of women and 69.5% of men in Azerbaijan are active in the labour market. However, gender disparities in both the Georgian and Armenian labour markets are much more pronounced. In Georgia, 57.9% of working-age women are in employment, compared to 78.8% of Georgian men. In Armenia, 51.4% of working-age women are present in the labour market, compared to 70.6% for men.

These figures are placed against a backdrop of a particular demographic situation in the region, where each of the three South Caucasus republics have more women than men—below the global average of 101 men to 100 women (CIA World Factbook 2019). The sex ratio for Armenia in 2018 was estimated at 94 men for every 100 women. For comparable statistics in Georgia and Azerbaijan, as of 2015 this figure stood at 91 and 99 men for every 100 women respectively. Currently, the population of Azerbaijan is just over 10 million, of which 49.5% are male and 50.5% are female (Countrymeters Information 2019b). Georgia has an estimated population of 3.8 million people of which 47.1% are male and 52.9% are female (Ibid. 2019c). In Armenia, the population stands at just over 3 million people of which 46. 5% are male and 53.5% are female (Ibid. 2019a).

Nonetheless, due to sex-selective abortions, these countries have highly skewed sex ratios at birth. In Armenia (117 boys for every 100 girls), Azerbaijan (116 boys for every 100 girls) and Georgia (121 boys for every 100 girls)[7] the sex ratio favouring boys is much higher than in other post-Soviet states (Michael et al. 2013). In 2010, the number of girls born in Armenia and Georgia was 10% lower than expected, consistent with 1972 sex-selective abortions in Armenia and 8381 in Azerbaijan (ibid., p. 97). This phenomenon is a result of societal patriarchal features, including preferences for sons, in a context of low fertility and the possibility of prenatal sex selection by means of easy access to ultrasound screening and induced abortion.[8]

Domestic violence is also a pressing issue in the South Caucasus, disproportionately affecting women, in particular as in each of the three states in question domestic violence is considered both a private and family matter.[9] Globally, domestic violence accounts for a significant proportion of all violence directed against women, with figures from 2013 revealing that 38% of female victims were murdered by so-called 'intimate partners' (World Health Organization 2013). In Georgia, a 2017 study on violence directed against women (UN Women 2017) found that approximately 14% of partnered women in the 15–64 age range had experienced physical, sexual and/or emotional violence by an intimate partner. In 2014, 25 women were killed by their husbands or partners in Georgia, although this figure is likely to be higher due to the non-systematic recording of violence against women (Lomsadze 2014).

In Armenia and Azerbaijan, the situation is equally dire. According to Armenia's Coalition to Stop Violence against Women,[10] at least four women were killed by their partners or other family members in the first half of 2017, and at least 50 women in the period 2010–2017. The Coalition received 5299 reports of domestic violence from January through September 2017 (Ishkanian 2017). According to statistics from Azerbaijan's Ministry of Internal Affairs, January 2011–November 2013, there were a total of 4053 reported cases of domestic violence (Manjoo 2014, p. 3). Noteworthy here is that, according to the Azerbaijan Human Development Report, the prevalence of intimate partner violence among women IDPs (internally displaced persons) and refugees who had to flee their homes as a consequence of the Nagorny Karabakh conflict in 1990s, is 7% higher than in other environments (ibid., p. 4).

Part I: Women, Tradition and Social Change

Social change is universal to all societies. Yet, societies differ in terms of their structures, functions, institutions and processes. For some societies, change can be sudden for others it can be incremental—a slow-moving process that may be difficult to ascertain or even imperceptible. While modernization is associated with progressive change, tradition is often viewed as static and hostile to change. However, for a community or nation the notion of tradition can embody an expression of survival and order, thus becoming a key stronghold for national belonging in times of uncertainty. In this way, women often play active roles as both enablers and inhibitors of change, as well as passive roles as beneficiaries and, more often, oppressed victims of change.

Research has shown that the demise of the USSR prompted a re-evaluation of gender politics, which for many newly independent societies in the post-Soviet space has led to a certain 're-traditionalisation'; that is; the (re)appearance of traditional notions of gender as a way of dealing with the allegedly 'distorted' Soviet past (Ashwin 2000; Shahnazarian and Ziemer 2014; Ziemer 2018). From one perspective, the demise of old Soviet structures created new opportunities for women's self-realization (Turbine and Riach 2012). Conversely, so-called post-Soviet 'democratising processes' have simply transformed women into domestic goddesses or 'heroines of survival' (Bridger et al. 1996). In short, the explicit and implicit contradictions between traditional gender roles and emancipation continue to dictate women's lives in the South Caucasus—a theme explored in detail in the first three chapters (Part I) of this volume.

In Chapter 2, Melanie Krebs begins the discussion of women and social change by examining the case of city dwellers in Azerbaijan's capital, Baku. Her chapter explores how pre-revolutionary and Soviet approaches to modernity continue to dominate the public gender discourse, manifested in notions of appropriate and inappropriate gender behaviour in Baku's urban spaces. Following the collapse of the USSR, Azerbaijan witnessed a process of urbanization, as men and women relocated from rural areas to larger population centres. Older, established city dwellers often perceive these new arrivals as uncultivated and 'unable' to live city life, but with a common gendered bias: in Baku, public discourse depicts these newcomers as male, while female newcomers are almost invisible. This reflects an older idea shared by many Azerbaijanis that their country lies somewhere between 'East and West', with women and their public treatment signifying the hybridity of a nation that 'takes the best of both worlds', mixing the 'West's' political rights with 'the East's' traditional respect for women.

Chapter 3 draws on ethnographic fieldwork data and media and film analysis to continue the discussion of women and social change, as Costanza Curro examines the case of *supra* (the traditional Georgian feast). Georgian women and men are valued as 'proper' people when they embody and perform traditional gender identities and roles, which are then articulated as 'natural'. Gender divides are epitomized by the rigid structure upon which the *supra* rests. While women's contribution to the '*supra*' is fundamental to this cultural tradition, the female role envisages a passive presence in a male-dominated event. For this reason, the *supra* is regarded as a practice from which women are excluded. For this reason, modernization narratives, emerging after Georgia's 2003 Rose Revolution began to question and reframe traditional practices as expressions of backwardness serving to hinder or delay the country's 'Westernisation'. As a display of masculinity, the *supra* is contrasted with progressive ideas of gender equality. Costanza Curro's chapter shows how this process is entwined in the inherent tension between the internalization and exposure of 'traditional' gender divides, as well as between the private reproduction and public reappropriation of hospitality practices.

In the spring of 2018, protests aimed at changing the government of Serzh Sargsyan swept Armenia. In Chapter 4, Ulrike Ziemer explores women's roles and activism during these protests. While women and men participated in the protest movement in near equal numbers, for women, the events of April 2018 represented the first opportunity to enter political spaces previously reserved for men since the country's last wave of sustained protests in 2008. In 2018, women engaged in a range of active roles as leading figures of the protest movement, but also strategists, organizers and 'rank and file' protesters. The empirical analysis explores three facets of women's agency during the protests. First, while some leading female figures play the 'female card' by using gendered 'instruments of protest' or highlighting existing gender inequalities in their speeches, others underplay gender differences in order to remove the 'male' connotations associated with public speaking. Second, some women use their respectability as mothers to challenge the government. The third facet this chapter examines is how women use their bodies as sites of resistance in street protests. By exploring women's agency, this chapter adds new insights to the growing literature on women's creative activism during political protests in the post-socialist space.

1 Introduction: Women's Everyday Lives in the South Caucasus

Part II: Experiencing War and Displacement

The chapters comprising Part II of this volume examine women's experience of war, conflict and displacement. In terms of gender relations and war, many scholars have suggested that patriarchy and militarism are not only essential for war-making, but that patriarchy is exacerbated as a result of conflict (cf. Cockburn 2010; Enloe 2000; Golan 1997; Segal 2008; Sharoni 1999; Waller and Rycenga 2004). This has particular resonance in the South Caucasus, as both war and forced displacement have been defining features of the region for much of its history. From a shorter-term perspective, the armed conflicts emerging in Nagorny Karabakh, Abkhazia and South Ossetia at the twilight of the Soviet period resulted in an enormous displacement of civilians, with up to 1.5 million people fleeing their homes (UNHCR 1996). As of December 2018, Azerbaijan counted 393,000 internally displaced persons as a result of the conflict in Nagorny Karabakh (IDMC 2018a). In the same year, and according to the International Displacement Monitoring Centre (IDMC 2018b), there were 289,000 registered IDPs in Georgia, most of whom had been displaced for more than fifteen years having fled secessionist conflicts in the two breakaway regions of Abkhazia and South Ossetia in the early 1990s. A second wave of displacement hit Georgia in August 2008 following armed hostilities with Russia over South Ossetia. For Armenia, data regarding displaced persons is neither readily available nor accurate, but it is estimated that 300,000 refugees fled Azerbaijan to Armenia as a result of the Nagorny Karabakh war in the 1990s, with 72,000 displaced people currently living in Armenia (IDMC 2018c).

From a longer-term perspective, displacement and violence against women were a central feature of the Armenian genocide. Although the Armenian genocide is well documented in academic literature, only recently has scholarship begun to explore women's experiences during this important event, including women's emotional responses and moral obligations—a hitherto neglected area in the genocide literature. In Chapter 5, Anna Aleksanyan addresses questions of love and identity by exploring the destinies of Armenian women who were abducted and, in many cases, forcibly married to Muslim husbands as part of the genocidal campaigns of 1915–1920. In the aftermath of

World War I, international organizations, such as the Near East Relief and the League of Nations, but also Armenian individuals and national organizations, attempted to locate those Armenian women who had survived the genocide in order to rescue them from slavery and forced marriage. Many of these organizations worked tirelessly to this end, yet some girls and woman, once discovered, refused to return to their Armenian community. The reasons were diverse. Some were afraid they would not be accepted, if they returned to Armenia. Others knew that none of their family members had survived the genocide and were fearful of a future life with an unknown Armenian family. Some, however, refused to return because they had fallen in love with their Muslim husbands and did not want to abandon their children. Thus, they were forced to choose between love and their Armenian identity. Based on records of Armenian women from various Armenian sources, including the Armenian National Delegation Archives in the Nubarian Library in Paris and the National Archives of Armenia in Yerevan, this chapter explores the emotional and moral complexities behind these choices.

Chapter 6 returns to a more recent war by analysing the narratives and challenges of displaced women from Azerbaijan. Shushan Ghazarian examines the impact of displacement on Armenian women forced to flee Azerbaijan and resettle in Armenia in the wake of interethnic violence in the 1990s. Her interview participants relocated from Baku and still live in temporary dormitories in Armenia's capital city, Yerevan. This chapter explores the barriers to their integration into Armenian society, including language difficulties and broader social differences that set these immigrants apart from the host society in terms of appearances and dress style but also their practical problems in gaining employment.

In Chapter 7, Nargiza Arjevanidze focuses on the lives of women forcefully uprooted from Abkhazia as a result of the armed conflict that emerged at the beginning of 1990s. Based on ethnographic research and life-story interviews, this chapter listens to women's voices as they reflect on their lives during and after the conflict, while living a period of prolonged displacement. This chapter explores how these women's past experiences and memories of armed conflict are linked to their present circumstances and to their lives in peaceful times, distanced from past violent events, yet characterized by the uncertainty caused by the protracted nature of their displacement. In particular, this chapter traces how these women have coped with extremes of change, and how the violent events of their past lives have become an inseparable part of the everyday by their *descent into the ordinary* (Das 2006). Although they were naturally vulnerable to *crisis*, it was the forms and tactics of everyday resilience during and after the armed conflict that allowed individuals to cope with and survive these traumatic events (Vigh 2008). By allying with the scholars who challenge the construction of human beings as either resilient or vulnerable/passive, this analysis attempts to offer new ways of conceptualizing this dichotomy through and exploration of internally displaced women.

In Chapter 8, Shahnazarian and Ziemer explore the everyday challenges of widows in Nagorny Karabakh. Widowhood is an under-recognized, albeit significant aspect of life in every region and in every country. However, the scant literature dealing with contemporary narratives of widowhood among women as a consequence of conflicts indicates that this aspect of lived experience remains underexplored. Although loss is integral to life in Nagorny Karabakh, it is often overlooked because of the unsettled politics in the region. The long-standing conflict over Nagorny Karabakh has generated and continues to generate severe consequences for society—sporadic clashes along the border with Azerbaijan remain common to this day. Thus, for women married to soldiers, confronting death is part of life. The purpose of this chapter is to examine the everyday experiences of women in the region, understanding and reworking the concepts of widowhood. In this way, this chapter is intended stimulate discussion on the relatively neglected subject of widowhood, both in the region and in broader comparative terms.

Part III: New Beginnings and Old Challenges: Feminism and Women's Identities

As highlighted above, in many aspects of women's lives, old structures and challenges have persisted. This becomes particularly evident when analysing the difficulties of women's activism. Across the region, women's organizations continue to face many obstacles, in part because of their tendency to position themselves as feminists and thus as 'challengers' to the traditional patriarchal family (Shahnazaryan 2011). As a consequence, these woman's organizations and their staff often become targets of hostile public discourse (Abrahamyan et al. 2019; Roberts and Ziemer 2018). Furthermore, LGBTI activism in the South Caucasus has been the object of sustained hostility in recent years marking it a major human rights concern in the region (Mijatović 2019; Human Rights World Report 2019). In Armenia and Georgia, for example, survey results from the PEW Research Center (2017) revealed that 97% of Armenian respondents and 93% of Georgian respondents thought that homosexuality was morally wrong. In addition, traditional views on gender roles continue to persist. According to the same survey, 82% (Georgia) and 71% (Armenia) of respondents thought that women had a societal duty to bear children.

In Chapter 9, Natia Gvianishvili addresses the challenges faced by sexual minorities in Georgia. In contemporary Georgia, homosexuality and broader LGBTI issues are employed as a political tool by a range of actors to discredit opponents and mobilize voters, with media monitoring revealing a notable increase in hate speech directed against LGBTI persons, in particular during election periods or other important political events. In this way, Georgia's 2016 parliamentary election and the wave of state-sponsored homophobia was no exception, nor the notable absence of figures from Georgia's political elite ready to raise the issue of rights for lesbian, gay, bisexual and transgender persons. This chapter explores the politicization of sexual minority issues and how it affects the lives and well-being of LBT women in Georgia.

The meaning of feminism is a widely debated topic, not only in the South Caucasus but in a broader comparative context. In Chapter 10, Yuliya Gureyeva Aliyeva considers this question in the context of Azerbaijan. Her chapter explores two different 'waves' of engagement with gender equality and women's rights issues in post-Soviet Azerbaijan. The first wave relates to the scholarly engagement with Western gender studies and feminism that ensued following the collapse of the USSR, in the period 1990–2010. The second wave relates to the 'new' feminist activism visible in twenty-first-century Azerbaijan. Although the 1990s

1 Introduction: Women's Everyday Lives in the South Caucasus   13

saw the promotion of gender equality and women's emancipation by the academic community in Azerbaijan, many avoided identifying themselves with the global feminist movement. In contrast to these 'hesitant' feminists, a group of young activists in twenty-first-century Azerbaijan is more open about self-identifying and can be seen as belonging to the second wave of women's empowerment within the country. Born for the most part in the 1980s and early 1990s, these women belong to a generation which has grown up in independent Azerbaijan. As Gureyeva Aliyeva shows, they symbolize a new class of empowered women (and men) who have developed strong personal ambitions and greater confidence.

In contrast and in complement, in the final chapter of this volume, Sinead Walsh addresses the question of whether there are any real feminists in Azerbaijan. Research on women in post-Soviet Azerbaijan highlights the contradictory nature of gender politics in this secular/Muslim society, while mostly steering clear of the term 'feminism'. This mirrors a tendency in society as a whole, including the women's advocacy sector to relegate feminist viewpoints to the margins. Nevertheless, since the 1990s, some Azerbaijani women have been claiming the term for themselves and seeking to apply its concepts and theories to the local context. This trend is advancing with the global spread of information technologies and the coming of age of the post-Soviet generation. This chapter looks at the phenomenon of Azerbaijani feminism from two angles. First, it considers how critical feminist discourses offer alternative forms of protest in the tightly controlled sphere of public dissent. Second, it explores the conciliatory aspect of feminist activism and its efforts to pre-empt social conflict and polarization. Taken together, this suggests the existence of an alternative political community at the grassroots level, which can be distinguished from the NGO sphere occupied by women professionals. This disparate network is unlikely to lead to a full-blown social movement. However, the transformation of everyday gender politics provides an important insight into some of the social changes affecting Azerbaijan.

A prime aim of this introduction chapter has been to highlight a number of common patterns and regularities which need to be understood through the prism of diversity. To conclude this introduction, I would like to return to the original idea and aim that inspired this edited volume: to shift the pre-occupation with geopolitical analysis in the region and to share new empirical research on women and social change in the South Caucasus. This collection of chapters is a collaborative venture of women scholars and activists from the region and beyond, exploring the region's complexities through a gendered lens by examining women's everyday struggles and their contributions to the region's history, societal life and politics. The chapters in this book discuss a broad range of topics, each relating to women's every day challenges during periods (past and present) of turbulent transformation and conflict, thus helping make sense of these transformations as a whole, and in doing so add new empirical insights to larger questions on life in the South Caucasus.

Notes

1. In 2018, Freedom House classified Armenia's political system as a 'semi-consolidated authoritarian' regime with a democracy score of 5.43 out of 7—with 7 being the least democratic (Freedom House 2018). In comparison, Georgia received a 2018 score of 4.61 out of 7, receiving a classification of 'hybrid regime'.
2. Although a milestone, it should be noted that Zurabishvili was sworn into office amid continued allegations of electoral violations by opposition figures (rferl.org).
3. Following a constitutional referendum in February 2017, the unrecognized Nagorny Karabakh Republic was renamed the Republic of Artsakh. However, this edited volume uses the more common 'Nagorny Karabakh'.
4. Three decades on, and most of these conflicts remain stubbornly unresolved. The Minsk Group has thus far not achieved a normalization of relations between Armenia and Azerbaijan, while the 2008 Russo-Georgian war placed both Abkhazia and South Ossetia firmly outside Tbilisi's control.
5. There is no available data on poverty in either Abkhazia or South Ossetia.
6. As defined by the International Labour Organization (2018), labour force participation is the percentage of a country's working-age population that engages actively in the labour market, either by working or

1 Introduction: Women's Everyday Lives in the South Caucasus   15

looking for work. It provides an indication of the relative size of the supply of labour available to engage in the production of goods and services (UNDP 2018).

7. Biologically, the sex ratio at birth is approximately 105 boys for every 100 girls, an imbalance believed to be an evolutionary response to the elevated probability of death in childhood among boys (Michael et al. 2013, p. 97).

8. In 2016, Armenia, for example, introduced a law to ban sex-selective abortions. Under this new law, a woman seeking an abortion must attend a counselling session with her doctor and then wait for three days for the procedure. The government says this is to allow doctors to pass on information about the dangers of abortion. This law, however, has been criticized by women's rights activists for placing women at risk (Low 2016).

9. According to a UNFPA (2010) survey on domestic violence in the South Caucasus, 78% of women in Georgia consider domestic violence a private matter that should remain within the family (Chkeidze 2011).

10. In Armenia, in October 2017, the government redrafted a proposed law on preventing domestic violence, presenting it for public discussion. This development can be attributed to the persistent advocacy and lobbying efforts of Armenian women's rights organizations, which have worked on this legal initiative since 2006 (Nikoghosyan 2017). In 2010, the Coalition to Stop Violence against Women was formed in response to the murder of 21-year-old Zaruhi Petrosyan by her husband. Since then, the campaign to raise awareness of domestic violence has gained momentum, yet it is still considered a taboo issue and one that should not be discussed publically. In the period 2012–2013, the Women's Support Center NGO dealt with two high profile cases that led to a further breakthrough in ending the silence and taboo surrounding this topic. As a result, the media has started to report more cases of domestic violence, with an average 20–30 news items a month appearing in the Armenian press (Matosian cited in Ishkanian 2017).

References

Abrahamyan, Milena, Pervana Mammadova, and Sophio Tskhvariashvili. 2019. "Women Challenging Gender Norms and Patriarchal Values in Peacebuilding and Conflict Transformation across the South Caucasus."

Journal of Conflict Transformation. February 1. http://caucasusedition.net/women-challenging-gender-norms-and-patriarchal-values-in-peacebuilding/.

Agenda.ge. 2018. "New Constitution of Georgia Comes into Play as the Presidential Inauguration Is Over." *Agenda News*, December 17. http://agenda.ge/en/news/2018/2674.

Artsakh Republic National Statistical Service. 2017. "Poverty and Social Panorama of the NKR." November 17. http://stat-nkr.am/en/publications/756--2017.

Ashwin, Sarah. 2000. *Gender, State, and Society in Soviet and Post-Soviet Russia.* London: Routledge.

Asian Development Bank. 2017a. *Poverty in Armenia.* https://www.adb.org/countries/armenia/poverty.

———. 2017b. *Poverty in Azerbaijan.* https://www.adb.org/countries/azerbaijan/poverty.

———. 2017c. *Poverty in Georgia.* https://www.adb.org/countries/georgia/poverty.

Bridger, Susan, Rebecca Kay, and Kathryn Pinnick. 1996. *No More Heroines? Russia, Women and the Market.* London: Routledge.

Brown, Wendy. 2001. *Politics out of History.* Princeton, NJ: Princeton University Press.

Buckley, Mary. 1989. *Women and Ideology in the Soviet Union.* Ann Arbor: University of Michigan Press.

Chkeidze, Ketevan. 2011. "Gender Politics in Georgia." *Heinrich Boell Stiftung, Gunda Werner Institute: Feminism and Gender Democracy*, February 7. https://www.gwi-boell.de/en/2011/02/07/gender-politics-georgia.

CIA World Factbook. 2019. *Global Gender Ratios.* https://www.states101.com/gender-ratios/global.

Cockburn, Cynthia. 2010. "Gender Relations as Causal in Militarization and War: A Feminist Standpoint." *International Feminist Journal of Politics* 12 (2): 139–157. https://doi.org/10.1080/14616741003665169.

Corrin, Chris, ed. 1992. *Superwomen and the Double Burden.* London: Scarlet Press.

Countrymeters Information. 2019a. *Armenia.* https://countrymeters.info/en/Armenia.

———. 2019b. *Azerbaijan.* https://countrymeters.info/en/Azerbaijan.

———. 2019c. *Georgia.* https://countrymeters.info/en/Georgia.

Das, Veena. 2006. *Life and Words: Violence and the Descent into the Ordinary.* Berkeley: University of California Press.

1 Introduction: Women's Everyday Lives in the South Caucasus

de Beauvoir, Simone. 1997. *The Second Sex.* London: Vintage Classics.

Enloe, Cynthia. 2000. *Maneuvers: The International Politics of Militarizing Women's Lives.* Berkeley: University of California Press.

Freedom House. 2018. "Nations in Transit 2018—Country Report Armenia." https://freedomhouse.org/report/nations-transit/2018/armenia.

Golan, Galia. 1997. "Militarization and Gender: The Israeli Experience." *Women's Studies International Forum* 20 (5–6): 581–586. https://doi.org/10.1016/S0277-5395(97)00063-0.

Human Rights World Report. 2019. "Country Report: Georgia." https://www.hrw.org/world-report/2019/country-chapters/georgia.

IDMC. 2018a. "Azerbaijan." *International Displacement Monitoring Centre.* http://www.internal-displacement.org/countries/azerbaijan.

IDMC. 2018b. "Georgia." *International Displacement Monitoring Centre.* http://www.internal-displacement.org/countries/georgia.

IDMC. 2018c. "Armenia." *International Displacement Monitoring Centre.* http://www.internal-displacement.org/countries/armenia.

Ishkanian, Armine. 2017. "Heated Debates Around Domestic Violence in Armenia." *OpenDemocracy*, November 3. https://www.opendemocracy.net/en/heated-debates-around-domestic-violence-in-armenia/.

Lapidus, G. W. 1978. *Women in Soviet Society: Equality, Development, and Social Change.* Berkeley. University of California Press.

Lomsadze, Georgi. 2014. "Georgia: Confronting Domestic Violence." *Eurasianet*, December 3. https://eurasianet.org/georgia-confronting-domestic-violence.

Low, Florence. 2016. "Law to Cut Sex-Selective Abortions in Armenia 'Putting Lives at Risk'." *The Guardian*, October 21. https://www.theguardian.com/world/2016/oct/21/law-to-cut-sex-selective-abortions-in-armenia-putting-lives-at-risk.

Manjoo, Rashida. 2014. "Report of the Special Rapporteur on Violence Against Women, Its Causes and Consequences, on Her Mission to Azerbaijan (26 November–5 December 2013)." United Nations. http://evaw-global-database.unwomen.org/-/media/files/un%20women/vaw/country%20report/asia/azerbaijan/azerbaijan%20srvaw.pdf?vs=3212.

Michael, Marc, Lawrence King, Liang Guo, Martin McKee, Erica Richardson, and David Stuckler. 2013. "The Mystery of Missing Female Children in the Caucasus: An Analysis of Sex Ratios by Birth Order." *International Perspectives on Sexual and Reproductive Health* 29 (2): 97–102. http://www.jstor.org/stable/41959961.

Mijatović, Dunja. 2019. "Report on Armenia." *The Commissioner of Human Rights of the Council of Europe.* https://www.coe.int/en/web/commissioner/-/report-on-armenia-recommends-measures-to-improve-women-s-rights-protection-of-disadvantaged-or-vulnerable-groups-and-establishing-accountability-for-p.

Mkrtchian, Anush. 2018. "Armenia Has Highest Female Unemployment Rate Among Post-Soviet Countries." *Radio Free Liberty/Radio Liberty.* https://www.azatutyun.am/a/29089151.html.

Nikoghosyan, Anna. 2017. "The Paradox of Armenia's Domestic Violence Law." *OpenDemocracy,* November 22. https://www.opendemocracy.net/en/odr/paradox-of-armenia-s-domestic-violence-law/.

Pew Research Centre. 2017. *Religious Belief and National Belonging in Central and Eastern Europe: Social Views and Morality.* May 10. https://www.pewforum.org/2017/05/10/social-views-and-morality/.

Roberts, Sean, and Ulrike Ziemer. 2018. "Explaining the Pattern of Russian Authoritarian Diffusion in Armenia." *East European Politics* 34 (2): 152–172. https://doi.org/10.1080/21599165.2018.1457525.

Segal, Lynne. 2008. "Gender, War and Militarism: Making and Questioning the Links." *Feminist Review* 88 (1): 21–35. https://doi.org/10.1057/palgrave.fr.9400383.

Shahnazaryan, Gohar. 2011. "Challenging Patriarchy in the South Caucasus." *Global Dialogue* 1 (2). http://globaldialogue.isa-sociology.org/challenging-patriarchy-in-the-south-caucasus/.

Shahnazarian, Nona, and Ulrike Ziemer. 2014. "Emotions, Loss and Change: Armenian Women and Post-Socialist Transformations in Nagorny Karabakh." *Caucasus Survey* 2 (1–2): 27–40. https://doi.org/10.1080/23761199.2014.11417298.

Sharoni, S. 1999. "Gender in Conflict: The Palestinian-Israeli Conflict Through Feminist Lenses." *Signs: Journal of Women in Culture and Society* 24 (2, Winter): 487–499. https://doi.org/10.1086/495348.

Turbine, Vikki, and Kathleen Riach, 2012. "The Right to Choose or Choosing What's Right? Women's Conceptualization of Work and Life Choice in Contemporary Russia." *Gender, Work and Organization* 9 (2): 166–187. https://doi.org/10.1111/j.1468-0432.2009.00494.x.

UNDP. 2018. Human Development Reports: Statistical Update. http://hdr.undp.org/en/2018-update.

———. 2019a. Human Development Report: Armenia. http://hdr.undp.org/en/countries/profiles/ARM.

———. 2019b. Human Development Report: Azerbaijan. http://hdr.undp.org/en/countries/profiles/AZE.

———. 2019c. Human Development Report: Georgia. http://hdr.undp.org/en/countries/profiles/GEO.

UNHCR. 1996. "UNHCR Publication for CIS Conference (Displacement in the CIS)—Conflicts in the Caucasus." *United Nations High Commissioner for Refugees*, May 1. https://www.unhcr.org/publications/refugeemag/3b5583fd4/unhcr-publication-cis-conference-displacement-cis-conflicts-caucasus.html.

UN Women Georgia. 2017. "National Study on Violence Against Women, Summary Report." http://www2.unwomen.org/-/media/field%20office%20georgia/attachments/publications/2018/national%20study%20on%20violence%20against%20women%202017.pdf?la=en&vs=957.

Vigh, Henrik. 2008. "Crisis and Chronicity: Anthropological Perspectives on Continuous Conflict and Decline." *Ethnos* 73 (1): 5–24. https://doi.org/10.1080/00141840801927509.

Waller, Marguerite, and Jennifer Rycenga, eds. 2004. *Frontline Feminisms: Women, War, and Resistance*. London: Routledge.

Watson, Peggy. 1993. "Eastern Europe's Silent Revolution: Gender." *Sociology* 27 (3): 471–487. https://doi.org/10.1177/0038038593027003008.

World Health Organisation. 2013. "Global and Regional Estimates of Violence against Women Prevalence and Health Effects of Intimate Partner Violence and Non-Partner Sexual Violence," June. https://www.who.int/reproductivehealth/publications/violence/9789241564625/en/.

Ziemer, Ulrike. 2018. "Opportunities for Self-Realisation? Young Women's Experiences of Higher Education in Russia." In *The Palgrave Handbook of Women and Gender in Twentieth-Century Russia and the Soviet Union*, edited by Melanie Ilic, 479–494. London: Palgrave Macmillan.

Part I
Women, Tradition and Social Change

2

Women as Bearers of Modernity and Tradition

Melanie Krebs

We do not have gender problems in Azerbaijan, you know. We are not a Muslim country. We are Muslims, yes, but being modern is more important for us. It always was. Men and women have the same rights here. Azerbaijani women were the first ones in the Near East who were allowed to vote. That is why we do not have gender problems in Azerbaijan. (Azerbaijani woman, 39, Baku)

Apart from the unusual phrase 'gender problems' this interview excerpt of a university teacher in Baku shows many attitudes towards gender, Islam and modernity that are common within the Azerbaijani society. Whether it was in Baku, where most of my field research took place, or in the smaller Azerbaijani towns or villages: when it came to the legal situation and everyday problems of women in Azerbaijan today, women and men of all ages assured me that in Azerbaijan for a long time women had rights equal to men's and therefore there was not the same need to discuss women's rights in contemporary Azerbaijan as there was

---

M. Krebs (✉)
Humboldt University of Berlin, Berlin, Germany
e-mail: melanie.krebs@berlin.de

© The Author(s) 2020

U. Ziemer (ed.), *Women's Everyday Lives in War and Peace in the South Caucasus*,
https://doi.org/10.1007/978-3-030-25517-6_2

in other Muslim countries. The most quoted evidence of Azerbaijani women's rights was that women had gained all political rights long ago in the first Azerbaijani republic (1918–1920), often together with the information that this Azerbaijan had been the first Muslim country to give them these rights. For nearly all of my informants, women's rights are associated with the political participation of women or with the fact that most women in Azerbaijan work outside the house[1] and many of them are well-educated.[2] Equal rights in family law such as divorce, child custody, a ban on domestic violence or reproductive rights were never among the first examples cited of achieved—or even important—women's rights. At the same time, respect for women, particularly mothers and elderly women, was also claimed to be crucial to Azerbaijani culture and often set in contrast to what other cultures could show, especially modern Western states where the speaker assumed that family values were less important than in Azerbaijan. Many Azerbaijanis describe their country as 'somewhere between East and West' and the situation of women is sometimes used as sign that the country takes the best of both worlds: from 'the West' the political rights and from 'the East' the traditional respect for women. Often the argumentation sounds very close to official statements such as the one that Mehriban Aliyeva, wife of the current president, delivered in her opening speech at the III Congress of Azerbaijani women in Baku 2008, from which the following words are quoted:

> Women have a played a great role throughout history in the protection of our culture, native language, religion, traditions, national values … Woman, mother has always been much respected in Azerbaijan … [the country] that established the first democratic republic in the Moslem East gave women the right of electing and being elected.[3]

Women as protectors and bearers of tradition and the liberated woman with the same rights as men to political, economic and social participation as the symbol of modernity are the lenses through which women and their role in society have been discussed in Azerbaijan since the beginning of the twentieth century. The debates about women's rights have been closely interlinked with the debates on 'modernity'

2 Women as Bearers of Modernity and Tradition   25

and 'backwardness', on 'belonging to the West' and 'belonging to the East' (often also associated with 'being Muslim'). The subject of women's rights as criteria for 'being Western' is not limited to Azerbaijan but was in the late nineteenth century a typical subject for debate in the Middle East and the Ottoman Empire (Göle 1995, pp. 64–72). This orientalist view of the passive 'oriental' woman who needs at least the example, more likely active support, from the West to achieve her rights was often accepted by Muslim intellectuals of the time. That did not necessarily mean they aimed for a Western-style society in general, but rather a modernized Muslim society that could keep up with Western colonizers. For Azerbaijan, the activities of the Jadids, Muslim reformers writing mostly in Turkish languages within the Russian Empire around 1900 (Khaleed 1998) were especially important. The problematic connection of 'modernity' and 'orientation to the West' and the role of women as symbols and actors of change still affect feminist movements in Muslim states today (Göle 1997).

This chapter follows these discourses on women's rights during different political regimes. What were the political aims behind these discourses and in what ways did they affect the everyday life of women in the cities as well as in the countryside? How are the different approaches and policies perceived today by different social groups? Concentrating on the idea connecting the achievement of women's political and economic rights with desired modernity, I found my focus was on another discourse on modernity and backwardness: The perception of long-standing city dwellers in Baku of their city and lifestyle as much more modern and 'cosmopolitan' than they were in the rest of Azerbaijan. In particular, women born and brought up in Baku used to point out that they lived a much freer and more independent life than women in the countryside and usually to link this to the more 'cultivated' life of the city. I refer to this group among my interviewees as *Bakintsy*, a term that most of them use to distinguish themselves from the newcomers who moved into the city after Azerbaijan became independent. Most of the Bakintsy families have lived in Baku for at least two generations and usually set their identity as 'people from Baku' higher than their belonging to the nationality indicated in their former Soviet passports.

The relationship between Baku and Azerbaijan as well as the nostalgic mourning of the long-standing city dwellers of Baku for their lost 'cosmopolitan' city is widely researched (Sayfutdinova 2009; Grant 2010; Rumyansev and Huseynova 2011; Darieva 2011; Krebs 2013). The gender dimension in this discourse on urban and rural life, as well as its modernity and tradition, is hardly reflected. In the present paper, I connect the debates about women's rights as part of a necessary modernization process especially in the first half of the twentieth century, with the ongoing debates on the way in which Baku and Azerbaijan in general should appear as a modern country. How are the perceptions of modernity and women's rights still shaped by their pre-Soviet and Soviet origins?

Several studies have been written on modernization projects in Muslim areas of the Russian Empire (Massell 1974; Northrop 2004) and Azerbaijan (Adam 2008; Fenz 2008) but, despite the claims for women's rights that always appear in these studies, the focus is elsewhere. Early Soviet policies concentrating on Muslim women are central to two studies dealing mainly with Uzbekistan (Massell 1974; Northrop 2004). These studies also show a shift in the evaluation of women and women's rights activities during the pre-Soviet and early Soviet eras. While Massell concentrates on the violations of women's rights before the region was included in the Soviet Union and highlights the liberation of women through Soviet policies, Northrop explores to a wide extent the pre-Soviet attempts made by the women's liberation movement. Heyat in her study on women in Azerbaijan from the late nineteenth century until the early 2000s takes a critical look at the often quoted use of Muslim women as the 'surrogate proletariat' in Central Asia and the Caucasus in the first decades of the Soviet Union. She describes it as a colonial and orientalist depiction of Muslim women which neither respects the demands for women's rights in pre-Soviet times nor the activities of Muslim women during the 1920s (Heyat 2005, pp. 110–111). The shift to a higher recognition of these movements came with the emerging historic awareness of the newly independent republics and affected the whole population, not just its academic discourses. While elderly people among my interviewees often still advert to the importance of the Soviet policies for the liberation of women, younger ones are much more likely to take pride in 'national' traditions and pre-Soviet movements.

My fieldwork was done in four research periods of two to four months in Baku between 2010 and 2012 and two shorter visits made in 2014 and 2015. The observations, informal conversations and interviews quoted in this paper were held between August 2010 and May 2012. Those of my informants who identified themselves as Bakintsy were between 35 and 75 years old and came from Azerbaijani, Russian and Armenian backgrounds. The interviews were always conducted in Russian, because that was the language my informants preferred (often it was the only language they felt confident in). Most of my elderly interviewees were women, because they approached a younger female researcher freely and were often eager to share their stories and concerns about the changes to 'their' city. For them, it was important to make sure that I got Baku 'right' and appreciated the city that they remembered more than the new one from which they feel increasingly excluded. They gave many examples of clashes between 'uncultivated' young men from the countryside and 'cultivated' (often but not necessarily elderly) urban women to demonstrate the downfall of the city after independence. Men from the same urban, mostly academic background also complained about the changes to the city but while women tended to illustrate their point with many personal experiences with (usually male) newcomers, men had more general complaints about the new Baku: less (well paid) work, problems with traffic and public transport or the new skyscrapers changing the outlook of the city and destroying old neighbourhoods. Even if they also tended to blame the 'Azerbaijanis' (i.e. the non-Bakintsy) for these problems they usually did not claim to have the same personal problems with them as the women did.

Towards Modernity—Liberating Women and Liberated Women from the Late Nineteenth Century to the Soviet Union

The debate about women's rights in Azerbaijani society began in the late nineteenth century when Azerbaijani intellectuals started to promote these rights as part of the modernization and nationalization of the new society to which they aspired. Their aim was to create an Azerbaijani national consciousness that should lead to an independent nation with close ties to other Turkish nations instead of the traditional ties to Persia.

Probably the most important voice of this movement was the satirical magazine 'Molla Nasreddin', published by Jalil Mammadguluzadeh in Tbilisi between 1906 and 1917.[4] 'Molla Nasdreddin' addressed issues such as the veil and polygamy, but, as Fenz points out, its respect for women was mostly respect for the mother as a bearer of Azeri traditions, especially the mother tongue, in this case Azerbaijani Turkish, whose improvement and reassessment as a cultural language was one of the most important points for Mammadguluzadeh. Educating women would also help to educate children better and at an earlier age (Fenz 2008, p. 53). No women contributed to the magazine (at least, so far as is known) even if Mammadguluzadeh's wife Hamideh Javanshir was very active as an advocate of women's political rights and also in many kinds of welfare work for women (Heyat 2005, pp. 89–92). The argument that women have to play a role in the awakening of the nation and that well-educated women make better 'mothers of the nation' and the mixture of political demands and welfare work mostly carried out by groups of well-off, urban women was also typical of first-wave feminism in Turkey (Tekeli 1986).

Other still well-known artistic expressions of the changing awareness of the negative effects of tradition on men and women alike were the works of the composer Uzejir Hajibeyov. For 'Leyli and Majnun' (1908), the first opera written by a Muslim, he used the tragic love story which had already been used for a poem by the twelfth century poet Nizami Ganjavi and by Fuzûlî in the sixteenth century. The opera followed the version of Fuzûlî, in which Leyla and Qais (who later becomes 'Majnun', the crazy one, crazed with love for Leyla) fall in love with each other but are forbidden by their relatives to marry and finally die unfulfilled. In two later operettas, Hajibeyov also criticized arranged marriages but with far more positive outcomes. 'O olmasın, bu olsun' ('If not this one, that one', 1910) and 'Arshin Mal Alan' ('The cloth peddler', 1913) show young men fighting for their love against elderly relatives and fathers paying their debts by selling their daughters. But in Hacibeyov's

2 Women as Bearers of Modernity and Tradition 29

operettas the roles of active men and passive women are still fixed. Even if the woman also falls in love with the man and demands to marry him and him alone, their only way out of a situation where they are forced to marry someone they do not love is suicide. Men continue to be the main actors in these plays. They arrange the meetings in the first place ('Arshin mal alan') and organize the solution ('O olmasın, bu olsun').

Hacibeyov's operettas have urban settings and were staged in the cities, 'Molla Nasreddin' was published in Tbilisi and its distribution was also limited to urban intellectual circles. The publication must certainly have inspired other satirical magazines in Muslim countries. But it is hard to be sure how far its influence went, especially when it came to substantial changes in women's lives. The gap in the lifestyle and aspirations grew between the elite in the urban centres—mainly Tbilisi and Baku, but also Shusha in Karabakh where 'Arshin Mal Alan' is set—and the people in the countryside, starting at least from the beginning of the twentieth century. Heyat describes the differences between the well-off urban upper-class orientated on a European lifestyle brought to Baku and Tbilisi by oil millionaires and Russian colonial officials, on the one hand, and the rural population, on the other. The modern lifestyle and the traditional one were never entirely separated but varied according to space and time: some women might wear Western clothes in Tbilisi, but not in Baku, or in both Baku and Tbilisi, but not in the countryside or in the presence of elderly relatives (Heyat 2005, pp. 93–95). Modern and traditional lifestyles could also be restricted to certain ages—it might be perceived as appropriate to send daughters to schools with a Russian curriculum but not to let them choose their husbands themselves. Umm-El-Banine Asadullayev, born in 1905, was the granddaughter of the Azerbaijani oil-billionaire Musa Naghiev and daughter of the progressive politician Mirza Asadullayev who held the position of a Minister of Industry and Trade in the First Azerbaijani Republic. In her memoirs (published under her penname Banine), she recalls a childhood with German nannies, piano lessons and European clothes, a life not different from girls in Europe, except for the visits to her grandmothers in country houses where the 'old Azerbaijan' was still *de rigueur*, but which she already perceived as pretty exotic (or at least described it like that for the European reader). But despite this

'European' upbringing and the women's rights granted under the First Azerbaijani Republic for which her father worked, Banine agreed at the age of fifteen to marry a man she despised because of her father's obligations (Banine 2008).

'Molla Nasreddin' and Hacibeyov's operas, as well as the already cited early electoral rights for women serve today to show that Azerbaijan did not need the Soviet Union to become a 'modern' and 'Western' state but was, on the contrary, interrupted on its way to becoming a 'European' state by the Soviet invasion in 1920. In fact in their campaigns for women's rights in the first years of the Soviet Union, the Communist Party saw the previous attempts to liberate Muslim women mainly as concurrent with their own attempts (Northrop 2004, p. 168). Given that the demand for women's rights, the nationalist consciousness and the pan-Turkish movements were closely interlinked in Azerbaijan (Adam 2008, p. 36; Fenz 2008, pp. 52–54), they were right to be cautious over including in their own campaigns the pre-Soviet figures and artistic expressions of the case for women's rights. For the Bolsheviks, women's liberation was not just about improving the lives of women and including them in the Soviet workforce but was also regarded as a tool with which to implement Soviet ideas and repress Islamic institutions and traditions, as inconsistent with communist ideals.

The veil in particular became a symbol of gender inequality but also of Islamic traditions. When in 1927 the Communist Party of the Soviet Union (CPSU) started the *hujum* (in Turkish, 'attack'), a campaign directed at veiled women to persuade them to show their faces, the main aim was the repression of Islam rather than freeing women from their families' pressure. The main area for the *hujum* was Uzbekistan, but Sattarov also mentions incidents not only on the streets of Baku but also in smaller towns when members of the Komsomol pulled down women's veils without preamble (Sattarov 2009, p. 50).

Leaving aside these rather violent actions, again the theatre, opera and soon also the cinema became important media for transmitting the new ideas: In the new plays, women were far more active than in Hacibeyov's operettas (which nevertheless became highly successful films in the 1940s and 1950s) and became the bearers of modern ideas while men remained more loyal to tradition. Most famous among these

Soviet heroines in Azerbaijan and beyond was Sevil, the heroine of a play with the same name by Cafar Cabbarli written in 1928. Sevil is a young woman hemmed in by tradition who obeys her husband, while he is in love with another woman. Sevil accepts the power that her husband has over her until he divorces her and gets the custody of their son. Thrown out of the house she takes off her veil and finally goes off to study in Moscow. While Sevil starts as a 'typical traditional (or "eastern") woman' in Soviet eyes, and becomes the new Soviet woman not entirely by her own choice but through her husband's rejection; the heroine of 'Almaz', Cabbarli's other play of 1928, is already a new woman as the action begins. As a young teacher she comes back to her home village, where she fights with the backward-looking religious and traditional authorities. In contrast to Sevil, Almaz has put off the veil and now encourages other women to do the same. 'Almaz' was also made into a movie in 1936 but never became as successful as 'Sevil'. The latter gave rise to movie versions in 1929 and 1970, was turned into an opera in 1953 and was staged all over the Soviet Union.

The dichotomy between the already Sovietized city with its modern urban women and the backward countryside is clearly visible in 'Almaz', while in 'Sevil' the hierarchy of places is obvious in another way: Sevil comes back from Moscow to Baku, which here represents the remote place that has yet to develop.

Debating Modernity—Urban Women and Rural Men in Independent Baku

As shown in the lifestyles of the contemporary Azeri upper class, the cultural dichotomy between Baku and the countryside dates back at least to the time of the first oil boom in the late nineteenth century. Even if the Soviet policy addressed women in the rural areas as well as in the cities, the gap between the women in Baku, on the one hand, and women in small towns and villages, on the other did not shrink—at least not in the perception of the inhabitants of Baku.

These differences are still emphasized by women from the former Soviet intelligentsia in Baku who draw a strict line between 'us' and 'them', between the old Bakintsy and the Azerbaijanis from the country-side—regardless of whether they still lived 'in the regions' or had moved to Baku more than twenty years ago. For the Bakintsy 'old Baku', meaning the city of the first oil boom as well as the Soviet city—was a city clearly distinct from its country surroundings by virtue of the 'modern' and 'cosmopolitan' lifestyle of its inhabitants. Today the differences between the capital and the countryside are blurring, much to the discontent of the old city dwellers. Elderly women in particular—whether or not they define themselves as Russian, Azerbaijani or even as members of the former Armenian minority—complain about the newcomers from the countryside. When they describe the 'typical *kolkhozniki*'[5] who make them feel affronted in the streets every day, they always describe a man: 'He' wears a black (fake) leather jacket, speaks too loudly, listens to 'horrible' music from his phone, spits—in short, behaves in a completely 'uncultivated' way and is 'unable to live in a city'. Of the typical woman from the countryside, my interviewees mostly provided examples from the private or semi-private sphere of the apartment blocks and yards; they complain of neighbours who throw dirty water or left-overs out of the window without looking to see who might be passing beneath, let their children play outside with running noses and dirty clothes and in general have too many children—and not because they do not know about family planning, but because 'they care nothing about education at all', as I was told more than once. When I asked if there were no female '*kolkhozniki*' in Baku's public spaces I was told that among 'these people' women had to stay at home and were therefore not visible to the public gaze.

They are right about the gender imbalance in streets and squares, but in the restaurants and tea gardens of rural towns (though not in villages) it is often striking, as well. The public space is dominated by men who spend their time outside the house. Women do not necessarily stay at home but are nevertheless far less visible than men because they do not use public space as men do: instead of lingering around, women cross it intent on particular errands. Couples or families are an uncommon sight, while in the centre of Baku and along the seaside promenade it is usual for families, young couples and groups of women to use the space for leisure and entertainment on summer evenings. But even there men outnumber women; women and children without men tend to stay in their gardens or the small parks close to home. Darieva found the withdrawal of Bakintsy from the seaside promenade—the Bulvar—to be connected also with the presence of newcomers there (Darieva 2011). My interviewees, however, who also told me they no longer went there (or much less than before) explained it as the result of rising prices and the small salaries or pensions which made it just too expensive to have a drink there or to buy a toy or a ride for the children on the carousels.

The elderly women complain about the behaviour of the young *kolkhozniki* not only in interviews with me but also often loudly in the streets when they witness something that they regard as inappropriate behaviour. These women consider themselves to be defenders of the 'old', in this case Soviet, Baku, acting as the bearers of tradition that women are acclaimed to be and teaching their children and grandchildren (as well as occasional foreigners) about the virtues of the old times. They try to restore the old rules and when they see security guards also punishing 'uncivilized' behaviour they feel accepted by the new order. But even if no 'official' steps into support the claim of the elderly women, in all the cases I witnessed their public rebukes were successful, the reprimanded ones stopped what they were doing, at least for the time being, and accepted the authority of the bearers of Baku's tradition.

Another reason why the typical new-Bakuvian is described as male by the Bakintsy may be that young women seem to be much more eager to avoid confrontation with these champions of social norms and urban traditions than their male counterparts and try to blend in with the urban crowd. My female interviewees who came from outside Baku all emphasized their efforts not to show any 'rural' behaviour. They gave several reasons for their attempts: some adopted the view of the Bakintsy that the rural population was less cultivated and tried to become an 'urban person'. This ambition was mostly considered also as an improvement in terms of greater personal freedom through the anonymity of the city. While managing to avoid the attention of either the elderly Bakintsy or the omnipresent police or security guards through following all the written and especially the unwritten rules they find a space where they can act much more freely than in their rural communities. Others of my younger female informants, who see their roots in the countryside even if some of them were born in Baku, criticize the attitude of the Bakintsy as 'not accepting their own people' and stress that the real strength of the Azerbaijani people lies in the countryside where an original culture is preserved. Nevertheless, they take pride in the fact that they can behave like Bakintsy and like 'real Azerbaijanis' at the same time. Their reaction shows an approach to the question of the urban–rural relationship in Azerbaijan that is not mentioned explicitly by the Bakintsy but nevertheless plays an important role in the debates.

But even with the official and unofficial keepers trying to defend the 'right behaviour' in the city centre, the anonymity there and the freedom connected with it were also often mentioned in conversations with students, females as well as males, from an urban background. They emphasized that the police and security guards are not a problem for them 'because they do not know you'. In their interviews, the Bakintsy did not mention this problem so often. This is mainly because most (even if not all) of them were elderly and therefore not so often subjected to control as younger ones; in fact, they were more often the person who actually felt obliged to restore control over appropriate forms of behaviour in public spaces. Younger Bakintsy sometimes reacted as if offended when I asked if they felt controlled. They emphasized that there was no need to control them because they knew how to behave properly. Another reason is that nearly all of them, due to the rapid building developments in Baku, had experienced at least once the destruction of their original neighbourhood and resettlement somewhere else in the city. Therefore they perceived their new neighbourhoods often also as rather anonymous. The only elderly Bakintsy who ever mentioned this to me as a good thing was an Armenian woman married to an Azerbaijani, who commented that she did not care that their neighbours consider them to be Russians but was happy for her daughter and granddaughter.

Even if the level of social control in the public sphere is fairly high, especially for younger people, there is a strong sympathy with the desire for privacy when it comes to the violation of women's rights in the domestic sphere. Domestic violence, and arranged and under-age marriages[6]—things already addressed in 'Molla Nasreddin' or Hacibeyov's operas—or the high rate of abortion of female foetuses[7] are viewed mostly as 'family matters' and not something requiring social control or help from neighbours or even politicians in order to improve women's lives. Asked about domestic violence, a student answered 'Yes, it happens. But, you know, our people do not talk about such things. We consider it a family thing. The family will solve such problems, not the state' (Woman, Baku, 22). She made clear in further communication that she considers the silence a problem but also sees it as something hard or even impossible to change. On this point all my interviewees regardless of age or urban/rural origin seemed to agree. It was striking in talks with the Bakintsy that the same woman who had just criticized the behaviour of a young male 'kolchozniki' in public and sharply retreated from him, used the same phrase to describe male dominance and violence within the family as the young women who referred to their own rural background. Suddenly it was not a case of 'us' and 'them', but 'our people' who are still enmired in tradition and need time to get used to new ideas. They might emphasize that arranged and under-age marriages or domestic violence was not a problem to them in particular, but rather to uneducated, non-urban families and if it happened in Baku then the main actors or at least their parents would have come from the countryside, but still there was an understanding, for anything other than appropriate behaviour in public spaces, that it takes time for these people to adjust to the idea of women's rights, especially when they are poor and have no access to information. This is what the Bakintsy suppose, because they generally assume a lower level of education among people from the countryside.

Again, even critics of the Azerbaijani government sound at this point very close to official statements where gender-based violence is rather seen as exceptional and due to political and economic hardship. Solving these problems will also end violence against women without addressing it as such:

Domestic violence, woman traffic, women rights violation is of great importance today among the women problems in the world.

Unfortunately, such cases exist in our country too, even if they are less. The Karabakh war, difficulties of transition period have caused some negative cases not specific to our society. It is linked mainly to the fact that people do not know their rights and have difficulty in getting adapted to new market economy. Our duty is to help people find adequate way to get out of these situations.[8]

At least none of my interviewees denied that there were problems of violence against women in private as well as the public sphere; nearly all linked them to traditions that were hard to overcome. Except for two who remained indifferent all my informants made it clear that they condemned any form of domestic violence, which is surprising because statistics show a pretty high acceptance of gender-based violence.[9] The discrepancy may be due to my sample and the context in which my informants had the feeling that condemning gender-based violence in general might be the right thing to say on this occasion to a researcher—and a woman—from Europe.

While the Soviet policies hardly ever addressed domestic violence, granting the right to divorce for women was an important part of the struggle against traditions and religion. As soon as it was granted, it became a right that was widely used by Muslim women (Northrop 2004, p. 268). But even if divorced parents, siblings and divorce were mentioned fairly often as part of their own biography by my interviewees this, still does not mean that divorce is widely accepted[10]—especially for women who usually have no other choice than moving back to their parents.

These double standards according to which women should play an active role within the Soviet society and economy but without equal rights to men's within the family were established especially firmly within Muslim areas of the Soviet Union. Here families demonstrated their devotion to the Soviet ideology through giving their daughters the education to become professionals in prestigious occupations, but also showed their acceptance of traditions and criticism of the Soviet system by preserving on values such as virginity and subordination to the will of parents and parents-in-law (for Uzbekistan Ghamvamshahidi 1997, pp. 158–160).

Challenging Modernity—Islam, Tradition and Urban Culture

Interestingly, none of my interviewees mentioned Muslim women's clothing in their descriptions of contrast to women from Baku presented by typical women from the countryside. When asked explicitly about Muslim clothing and especially the headscarf, they emphasized that it was of course not part of Baku's society but also explained that it was not much worn in Azerbaijan at all, even outside Baku. If a woman wore one, it was mainly for practical reasons such as the sun or the dust. Associations with Muslim clothing or Islam in general were nearly always connected with former generations and began with phrases like 'You know, my grandmother…' or 'I don't know … I should ask my grandmother about this'—interestingly, it was always—as in Banine's memories from the early twentieth century (Banine 2008)—a woman, a grandmother or an elderly aunt who was mentioned as the one knowing about religion and tradition.

My research participants in Baku mentioned religion or Islam often as synonyms for 'tradition' and 'being Muslim' was mentioned as part of Azerbaijani national identity. Bedford explains this also as a Soviet heritage dating back to the 1920s and 1930s when 'national' customs and traditions were created in the Central Asian and Caucasian Soviet republics, those newly created political entities, and many Islamic traditions merged into these 'national customs' (Bedford 2009, pp. 84–85, 94–95; also Motika 2001).

Despite this connection of many urban Azerbaijanis of Islam with a less modern and more traditional contemporary Muslim life, regarded either as negative (because backward) or rather positive (because it symbolized national values)—all the aspects of a modern Muslim movement can be found in society. Vazirova who analyses a long-standing controversy about the wearing of a headscarf on passport pictures, states that mostly well-educated young women from an urban secular background started to cover their hair in the 1990s (Vazirova 2011, p. 157). This corresponds with the findings of Göle about the background of veiled students in Turkey in the 1990s where turning towards Islam and starting to wear a headscarf was common among daughters of rather secular families looking for another meaning in their lives (Göle 1995, p. 119). Both groups, in Turkey as in Azerbaijan, were aware of the ongoing debates on feminism and Islam (women's) liberation and secular modernity, and their historic dimension also and both considered themselves a new generation able to reconcile antagonisms that seemed insuperable.

Most of my interviewees—especially the elderly ones—were unaware of the headscarf as a statement of contemporary Muslim life, even if some younger ones, in their early and mid-20s mentioned women of their age who had started to cover their hair as part of a new interest in Islam.

Another strand in the attitude to Islam among Azerbaijanis in general, and Baku's urban middle class especially, is the growing fear of an 'Islamization' of the country. As often observed in European countries also, the headscarves worn by numbers of women are seen as an indicator of such ongoing Islamization. When I started my fieldwork in 2010, veiled women were hardly ever seen in Baku's public space—at least, not in the comparison I was making with Berlin's public spaces.[11] For Azerbaijani colleagues such as Sergey Rumyantsev and Sevil Husseinova, who compared the presence of Islam in Baku of the 1970s and 1980s with the presence after 2000, the increase was disturbing. Their paper *Between the Center of Jazz and the Capital of Muslim Culture* shows the fear among the former Soviet middle class of Baku of losing their cosmopolitan city to groups more oriented to Muslim ways of life and belief (Rumyansev and Huseynova 2011). They quote a woman complaining about a friend who actually hired a veiled woman for a position that required contact with the public: 'She is in fact like a *matryoshka*. She wears it loose overall with flowers, and there are flowers on her kerchief, too' (Rumyantsev and Huseynova 2011, p. 224). The description of the veiled woman that the interviewee gave is notable because she compares her with the wooden *matryoshka* doll, which is neither a frightening nor particular exotic association that might be expected in a context where Islam is seen as a threat to an established lifestyle—a lifestyle that is connected with the dark business costume most elderly female professionals wear, not only for work but in general when they leave the apartment for more than a short walk to the grocery store, or the tight and colourful clothing with

Western brand names that young women wear—whether as expensive originals from the new malls or as cheap copies bought in the outskirts of Baku.

The debates on how modernity and Islam, urban and rural Azerbaijan, women's rights in the public as well as in the domestic sphere can and should be connected will continue. In these debates the role of women as the bearers of tradition and modernity still plays an important part, but the definitions of modernity and tradition are different for different social groups and lead to even more questions than answers: Are the Soviet values of women's participation in the economy and the public sphere the same as contemporary modernist ideas or are they old-fashioned ideas which should be replaced by new feminist ideas or by the 'return' to traditional Azerbaijani values? Is the 'return' to Azerbaijani values a step back, to overcome tradition, a new way to build the Azerbaijani nation or simply tying in the Soviet concepts of national traditions in their republics? And where is the place of Islam on this scale between tradition and modernity?

Notes

1. According to the Gender Inequality Index in 2015, 61.9% of all women over 15 work outside the house compared with 68.3% of men in Azerbaijan (UNDP 2015).
2. The school life expectancy was the same in 2014: 13 years for both genders (CIA World Factbook 2019).
3. For the period 2005–2015, at least 93.9% of women had at least some secondary education (for men: 97.5%) (UNDP 2015).
4. 'III Congress of Azerbaijani Women opened in Baku'. September 26, 2008. English quotation by an unnamed author. http://heydar-aliyev-foundation.org/en/content/view/59/1593/III-Congress-of-Azerbaijani-Women-opened-in-Baku.
5. A few numbers of 'Molla Nasreddin' were also issued in Tabriz, Iran, in 1921, by Mammadguluzade and from 1922 to 1931 in Baku, but gradually lost influence.
6. The fact that most of my interviewees used the Russian *kolchozniki* instead of Azerbaijani terms like gəlmələr (newcomers) or kəndçiler

(villagers) shows more than anything the limitation of my sample: because most of my fieldwork in Baku was conducted in Russian and with people who felt equally comfortable in Russian or Azeri, or even more so in Russian, I draw mostly on the perception of a special group with strong ties to Soviet ideas.

7. UNICEF (2004) declares that there are no valid data because child marriage is illegal in Azerbaijan, but still not uncommon in rural areas.

8. According to the CIA World Fact Book (2019) the sex ratio at birth in Azerbaijan was 111 boys to 100 girls in 2016, while the normal rate is 100 girls to 105 boys.

9. 'III Congress of Azerbaijani Women opened in Baku', September 26, 2008. No author mentioned. http://heydar-aliyev-foundation. org/en/content/view/59/1593/III-Congress-of-Azerbaijani-Women-opened-in-Baku.

10. Katy Pearcy (2016) quotes the 2011 CRRC Social Capital, Media, and Gender Survey that only 66% of women disagree that there are times when a woman deserves to be beaten and only 46% of men.

11. According to the Caucasus Barometer (2014), 48% of Azerbaijanis indicate that divorce can never be justified. Not surprisingly, Azerbaijan has one of the world's lowest divorce rates, which is especially interesting, because other former Soviet republics are among the countries with highest divorce rates.

12. In my field diary from 2010 I noted that, of the seven veiled covered women I saw in Baku's city centre or at the Bulvar over a month, only one was speaking Azeri, two Turkish and two Arabic. I did not register the language of the other two. According to my notes, the number of covered women increased significantly between 2010 and 2012, but because it was not part of my main research, in my later fieldwork I stopped counting.

References

Adam, Volker. 2008. "Literarische und ideologische Strömungen unter der Herrschaft des Zaren: die Anfänge einer neuzeitlichen aserbaidschanisch-türkischen Identität." In *Aserbaidschan - Land des Feuers*, edited by Ingrid Pfluger-Schindlbeck, 15–19. Berlin: Reimer.

Banine, Umm el Banu Assadullaeva. 2008. *Kaukasische Tage*. Frankfurt am Main: Verlag Hans Jürgen Maurer.

Bedford, Sofie. 2009. *Islamic Activism in Azerbaijan: Repression and Mobilization in a Post-Soviet Context*. Stockholm: Stockholm Studies in Politics.

Caucasus Research Resource Centres (CRRC). 2014. "Divorce Rates in Azerbaijan." June 9. http://crrc-caucasus.blogspot.am/2014/06/divorce-rates-in-azerbaijan.html.

CIA World Fact Book. 2019. Middle East: Azerbaijan. May 14. https://www.cia.gov/library/publications/the-world-factbook/geos/aj.html.

Darieva, Tsypylma. 2011. "A 'Remarkable Gift' in the Postcolonial City: Past and Present of the Baku Promenade." In *Urban Spaces After Socialism: Ethnographies of Public Places in the Eurasian Cities*, edited by Tsypylma Darieva, Wolfgang Kaschuba, and Melanie Krebs, 153–178. Frankfurt am Main and New York: Campus.

Fenz, Hendrik. 2008. "Zwischen Fremdherrschaft und Rückständigkeit: Die Satirezeitschrift Molla Nasreddin als Medium der Aufklärung im Südkaukasus." In *Aserbaidschan - Land des Feuers*, edited by Ingrid Pfluger-Schindlbeck, 41–60. Berlin: Reimer.

Ghamvamshahidi, Zoreh. 1997. "Die Entstehung des Nationalstaates und die Geschlechterideologie in Usbekistan." In *Feminismus Islam Nation*, edited by Claudia Schöning-Kalender, Ayla Neusel, and Mechthild Jansen, 139–165. Frankfurt am Main: Campus.

Göle, Nilüfer. 1995. *Republik und Schleier: Die Muslimische Frau in der Moderne*. Berlin: Babel-Verlag.

Göle, Nilüfer. 1997. "The Gendered Nature of the Public Sphere." *Public Culture* 10 (1): 61–82. https://doi.org/10.1215/08992363-10-1-61.

Grant, Bruce. 2010. "Cosmopolitan Baku." *Ethnos* 75 (2): 123–147. https://doi.org/10.1080/00141841003753222.

Heyat, Farideh. 2005. *Azeri Women in Transition*. Baku: Cashioglu.

Khaleed, Adeeb. 1998. *The Politics of Muslim Cultural Reform: Jadidism in Central Asia*. Berkeley: University of California Press.

Krebs, Melanie. 2013. "Negotiating Cosmopolitanism in Baku." In *Caucasus Conflict Culture*, edited by Stephane Voell and Ketevan Khutsishvili, 225–242. Marburg: Curupira.

———. 2015. "The Right to Live in the City." *International Journal of Sociology and Social Policy* 35 (7–8): 550–564. https://doi.org/10.1108/IJSSP-10-2014-0088.

Massell, Gregory J. 1974. *The Surrogate Proletariat: Moslem Women and Revolutionary Strategies in Soviet Central Asia: 1919–1929*. Princeton: Princeton University Press.

Motika, Raoul. 2001. "Islam in Post-Soviet Azerbaijan." *Archives de sciences sociales des religions* 115: 111–124. https://journals.openedition.org/assr/18423.

Northrop, Douglas. 2004. *Veiled Empire: Gender & Power in Stalinist Central Asia*. Ithaka: Cornell University Press.

Pearcy, Katy. 2016. "Gender-Based Violence in Azerbaijan." December 14. http://www.katypearce.net/gender-based-violence-in-azerbaijan/.

Rumyansev, Sergey, and Sevil Huseynova. 2011. "Between the Centre of Jazz and the Capital of Muslim Culture: Insights into Baku's Public and Everyday Life." In *Urban Spaces After Socialism: Ethnographies of Public Places in the Eurasian Cities*, edited by Tsypylma Darieva, Wolfgang Kaschuba, and Melanie Krebs, 227–246. Frankfurt am Main and New York: Campus.

Sattarov, Rufat. 2009. *Islam, State, and Society in independent Azerbaijan: Between Historical Legacy and Post-Soviet Reality*. Wiesbaden: Reichert.

Sayfutdinova, Leyla. 2009. "Baku and Azerbaijan: An Uneasy Relationship." *Stadt Bauwelt* 183 (36.09): 36–41.

Tekeli, Sirin. 1986. "Emergence of the Feminist Movement in Turkey." In *The New Women's Movement: Feminism and Political Power in Europe and the U.S.*, edited by Drude Dahlenrup, 179–199. London: Sage Publications.

Unicef. 2004. "Child Marriage." https://www.unicef.org/azerbaijan/protection_10022.html.

United Nations Development Programme. 2015. "Gender Inequality Index." http://hdr.undp.org/en/composite/GII.

Vazirova, Aysel. 2011. "Freedom and Bondage." In *Changing Identities: Armenia, Azerbaijan, Georgia*, edited by Heinrich Boell Foundation. Berlin.

3

'Supra Is Not for Women': Hospitality Practices as a Lens on Gender and Social Change in Georgia

Costanza Curro

The protagonists of the 2014 Georgian film In Bloom (*Grdzeli Nateli Dgheebi*) are two fourteen-year-old girls, Ek'a and Natia, growing up in the shattered context of early 1990s Georgia, in which the country, after gaining independence, was plagued by poverty, endemic corruption, organized crime, ethnic conflict and civil unrest (Manning 2009; Shelley et al. 2007; Dudwick 2004). One scene of the film shows Natia's wedding, which, as it usually happens in Georgia, is celebrated with a big *supra*, a festive meal involving the copious consumption of food and drinks in the occasion of life cycle events or of more mundane gatherings among relatives, friends and neighbours (Curro 2014; Altman 2011; Mühlfried 2006, 2007; Chatwin 1997, see below). Natia's wedding *supra* is set in a small overcrowded flat, with women rushing busily between the kitchen and the table, which is laden with food. Following the toasting and drinking structure called *tamadoba* (see below), men drink wine from horns, making several toasts, including, 'To our women! What would our life be without them?'

C. Curro (✉)
Aleksanteri Institute, Helsinki, Finland

© The Author(s) 2020
U. Ziemer (ed.), *Women's Everyday Lives in War and Peace in the South Caucasus*,
https://doi.org/10.1007/978-3-030-25517-6_3

43

The toast, 'To women!' ('*Kalebis gaumarjos!*', of which there is an old-fashioned but possibly more popular version using the term *mandilosani*, 'ladies'—literally 'those who wear headgear'), is pivotal to the *tamadoba* drinking structure. In many *supra*s, only men take part in this (and other) toasts. Most of the time women stay in the kitchen, emerging to bring out food. When a toast is said in their honour, women are sometimes invited to have a glass and sit down for a bit. Yet, even when they take part in hospitality events, sitting and eating with the men, women are largely excluded from traditional toasting, and, in general, from the active making of gestures, narratives and meanings at *supra*.

Gender and cultural studies specialists, as well as anthropologists and sociologists, have broadly highlighted the resilience of strict gender norms and ascribed gender roles in Georgian society (Curro 2012; Rekhviashvili 2010; Lundkvist-Houndoumadi 2010; Sumbadze and Tarkhan-Mouravi 2003, 2006). Georgian women (but also men) are valued as 'proper' members of their community to the extent to which they embody and perform what are perceived as 'traditional' gender roles, which common narratives articulate as 'natural' attributes of all 'normal' human beings.

Gender divides are epitomized by the rigid structure upon which the traditional Georgian *supra* rests. The female contribution to hospitality events is fundamental, not only for the great effort and the amount of time which women invest in cooking, preparing the table, serving guests, cleaning and tidying up, but also because the female figure is essential in the imagery of *supra* and of society at large (see below). However, women's role is that of passive presence in a male-dominated event. For this reason, *supra* is largely regarded by local people as well as external observers as a practice from which women are excluded (Curro 2014; Tsitsishvili 2006).

Modernization narratives emerged after the Rose Revolution questioned traditional practices as expressions of backwardness which hindered the country's 'Westernisation'. In politics, academic discourse and everyday life *supra* has been object of ambivalent evaluations. On the one hand, material and non-material elements of traditional hospitality practices—such as wine, food, singing and dancing, as well as Georgian people's warmth and friendly attitudes towards outsiders, or *supra*'s ability to establish and cement ties of friendship and reciprocity—have been celebrated in various ways, as a specific feature of Georgian identity and distinctiveness, a fundamental practice in people's everyday social life, as well as one of the country's resources to appeal visitors from abroad (Curro 2017; Frederiksen and Gotfredsen 2017). On the other hand, the vertical structure of *supra* and its drinking ritual, *tamadoba* (Tuite 2005; Manning 2003, see below), the irrational spending of time and money in hospitality practices, the celebration of harmful behaviour, such as getting drunk and overeating, and the role of *supra* as a hub through which informal networks and deals developed (Manning 2003; Chatwin 1997; Mars and Altman 1983, 1987) contrasted with the image of the country and its citizens which the post-revolutionary government wanted to give to outsiders: a young democracy which has got rid of negative legacies from the Soviet era and is rapidly modernizing following Western political and economic models. Such a critique of *supra* offered a potential framework for women to negotiate and challenge their marginalized position.

This chapter investigates social change in post-Rose Revolution Georgia focusing on gendered practices and narratives which surround traditional hospitality. After a brief overview of my research methods and my fieldwork experience, the interplay of gender dynamics and traditions of hospitality in Georgia is introduced. *Supra* is analysed as a social practice which, while largely unfolding in the private sphere of the house and the family, encapsulates social norms and dynamics which have a public relevance, including identities and roles attached to men and women and the regulation of interactions between genders. Subsequently, the problematic coexistence between 'tradition' and 'modernity' emphasized by post-revolutionary political narratives and practices will be delineated as the framework within which Georgian women negotiate changing roles and identities at the individual and collective level in the process of questioning their position in the context of *supra* and in society at large. Analysing ethnographic data, this process is caught in the tension between internalization and exposure of 'traditional' gender divides, between private reproduction and public reappropriation of hospitality practices. The chapter sheds light on everyday conflicts experienced by women between demands from 'tradition' and certain top-down modernization narratives which frame women's empowerment as unquestioned endorsement of Western values and lifestyles.

Research Methods and Fieldwork Experience

The ethnographic material presented in this chapter (which is supported by the analysis of film, media and literary sources, as well as by the discussion of data and insights provided by relevant surveys and academic literature) was collected during my stay in Georgia (mainly in Tbilisi, but also travelling around the country) in 2008–2009 and 2014, as well as in a pilot project conducted with Georgian people living in London from 2012 to 2014. The material has been partially included in my Ph.D. thesis on Georgian hospitality practices as a way to channel reciprocity and solidarity vis-à-vis the social, political and economic disintegration brought about by the post-Rose Revolution modernization project. Using participant observation and semi-structured interviews as main research methods, I spent time with women and men aged 18–80, getting involved in a variety of activities—from feasting to cooking, from shopping to exploring Tbilisi's neighbourhoods—accompanied by more focused discussions on various social and cultural issues which my participants considered to be prominent in their everyday life. Gender relations, particularly when played out in hospitality practices, were a pivotal point of many of my conversations with women, but often with men as well.

Women who helped me with my research belonged to different generations, social and economic backgrounds and educational and professional experiences: among my participants were students, teachers, housewives, psychologists, engineers, university lecturers, political activists, artists, shop assistants, hairdressers and retired people. When our discussions revolved around gender and the relation between men and women in Georgian society, the main topics which emerged regarded motherhood, the role of religion, family life, marriage and divorce, virginity and sex and, more generally, the set of responsibilities and expectations with which the community surrounds the two genders.

Feelings and attitudes towards *supra* and the role which hospitality practices envisage for women were expressed and discussed by my participants within this bigger pictures of norms and role attributed to men and women.

Opinions on such topics differed greatly according to my participants' age, as well as socio-cultural and economic background. While, on a general basis, older generations tended to be more conservative and support the traditional division of gender roles and identities, critical perspectives on the role of women around the table, but also in the family and the larger community, did not miss from the standpoint of women over their 50s. Conversely, several young women seemed to feel comfortable with the role of wives and mothers—quite commonly, since an early age—which society still largely bestows upon their female members. Thus, while generational divides are a significant indicator for analysing women's approaches towards gender dynamics into play at hospitality events and in society at large, different views are to be attributed to the combination of multiple factors, which will be analysed in details throughout the paper.

My relationship with female participants was largely based on deep respect, complicity and intimacy, but in some cases coldness, distrust and even open disapproval were displayed. This was due to the fact that, on most occasions, I did not conduct my research with male and female participants separately. Instead, I was involved in the life of households or neighbourhood communities which were formed by many different men and women. In such cases, my interactions with men and women of different age and cultural, social and economic background interplayed with one another, and gender divides had a double-edged effect on my opportunities to talk about certain topics, meet certain people and enter certain spaces. My male participants did not expect me to behave like a Georgian woman, so, in the framework of hospitality practices, it was not usually problem for me to be involved in activities such as drinking and even toasting with men. Also, I was usually not supposed to help other women with the tiring tasks underpinning the preparation and delivery of a *supra*. Such an ambivalent position as a female foreigner, who arrived as an outsider but then became something more than a short-term guest, was regarded with suspicion by some—mostly elderly—women, who were at odds with what they considered as rather unorthodox behaviour for a female. Nevertheless, I developed ties of affection with most of my female participants, who, even in the case of disagreement, enjoyed an open discussion, and possibly confrontation with me on a variety of topics, including the tension between oppression and security which they perceived as entailed by living in a highly patriarchal society.

Gender Divides at the Georgian Table

Literally meaning 'tablecloth', *supra* is the traditional way of feasting in which hosts and guests gather at a table for many hours, consuming huge quantities of food and drink, delivering elaborated toasts and singing traditional songs. *Supra* is considered a founding national institution, to such an extent that 'whoever wishes to learn about Georgian society, to understand Georgian culture, the supra encapsulates it all' (Altman 2011, p. 2; see also Nodia 2014; Mühlfried 2005, 2006). Defined as a practice 'heavily loaded with political implications', particularly regarding issues such as 'gender, labour and consumption' (Tuite 2005, p. 9), *supra* has a moral, cultural, social, political and economic scope which spreads beyond the boundaries of receiving guests privately within a domestic space. Food and drink consumption in traditional hospitality settings is regulated by norms which have public meaning in assigning people a place within society. *Supra* must be as conspicuous as possible (Altman 2011; Polese 2010). The traditional pattern for this event requires that a large variety of food is put on the table from the beginning of the feast, with piles of small serving dishes which are constantly refilled throughout the banquet. Basic supra food includes fresh bread and cheese, tomatoes, cucumbers, herbs, pickles, *khach'ap'uri* (cheesy bread), aubergines stuffed with walnuts, *pkhali* (beetroot or spinach mixed with walnuts and spices), cold meat and fish, as well as cakes and sweets. In addition, hot dishes, mostly in the form of boiled, stewed and roasted meat and *khink'ali* (big meat dumplings), are served throughout the feast.

Supra has a highly codified structure of toasting and drinking (Douglas 1987), called *tamadoba*, which regulates the conspicuous consumption of alcohol pivotal to big hospitality events. *Tamadoba* is led by a toastmaster, the *tamada*, who is chosen from the males present to deliver toasts (*sadghegrdzelo*).[1] The *tamada* has a key role in the successful outcome of a *supra*, since he is expected to create 'social heat' (Chau 2008, p. 485). Toasts have 'a predictable internal organisation, combined with an apparent freedom of expression'. To some extent, improvisation is allowed 'within a well-defined structure. Repetition, formulaic speech, parallelism, extravagant wording, and other factors of verbal art play an important role' (Kotthoff 1995, p. 354). A good *tamada* has sense of humour and mastery of Georgian history and culture. He brings about matters of shared knowledge, creating a sense of commonality among participants (Mühlfried 2007). He is sensitive to the participants' mood and ensures everyone's involvement while avoiding boredom, awkwardness and cold-heartedness. Scrupulous management of drinking also prevents *supra* from degenerating into chaotic drunkenness (Manning 2003; Chatwin 1997).

A *supra* may start with praise of the host (*maspinzeli*), and his/her family. Drinking to children, women, the dead and ancestors is also customary. Many toasts are dedicated to love and friendship, to Georgia and its history and culture, to the homelands of foreign guests and to friendship between people (guests'co-nationals and Georgians). All toasts are pronounced with the formulaic expression '*gaumarjos!*', '*victory to…*' For example, '(victory) to Georgia!' is '*Sakartvelos gaumarjos!*' Sipping wine is not allowed outside of proposed toasts, when glasses are emptied in one go. In certain toasts, specific items are used as wine containers—namely horns (*q'antsi*) and clay pots of various sizes. On such occasions, the *tamada* drinks first and then passes the container on to the others, who in turn say a few words and drink. Participants are expected to follow the given structure.

When the most solemn toasts are made (including the toast to women), men stand up and women sit. Lasha (28, chef) once told me that this is a sign of respect for women, so that they do not get tired. This explanation sounded absurd to me, given that most demanding tasks at a *supra* are overwhelmingly performed by women without this raising much concern in men. However, Lasha's words expressed the ambivalence underpinning not only men's perspective on women, but also the way women think of themselves and their role in the making of *supra* and in family and society at large.

Georgian tradition is permeated by a cult of women, who are seen as the embodiment of the nation. Women are 'the potential source and bearers of life, it is thought that all essential female characteristics derive from that' (Dragadze 1988, p. 159). Also, 'Georgia itself, as a nation, culture, ethnic entity is invariably symbolized by a woman. Your country is referred to as your *deda-mits'a*, "mother-ground" [...]. The Georgian language is *deda-ena*, "mother-tongue" [...]. The capital of Georgia, Tbilisi, is *deda-kalaki*, "mother-city"' (Dragadze 1988, p. 158). Certain positive qualities, which are considered to be weaker in men, are attributed to women, such as stability, reliability, bashfulness and pragmatism (Lundkvist-Houndoumadi 2010). Far from being regarded as lower beings per se in the society, women are fundamental parts of the historical and cultural imagery of the national community. However, social narratives value women as Georgians—and even as 'proper' human beings (Dragadze 1988)—only to the extent to which they fit what are regarded as their natural roles and identities. As a consequence, womanhood and motherhood are largely considered inseparable issues, while male and female behaviour concerning premarital sex, adultery, divorce and remarriage are judged by different standards (Buckley 2005; Sumbadze and Tarkhan-Mouravi 2003, 2006).

Traditional gender divides are made apparent in the structure of hospitality events. It is misleading to look at hospitality as a practice which forces women to toil against their will for men's enjoyment. Traditional *supra* have a rigid division of roles which supposedly fit men's and women's respective natural attributes. Assigning women to the cleaning and cooking is not necessarily meant to excuse men from tiring tasks. Rather, women are regarded as the revered guardians of housekeeping traditions passed down the female generations (Chatwin 1997). Certain chores in the organization of *supra* are also allocated to men, especially the provision of food and drink in general and meat in particular.

However, the main feeling expressed by most of my female participants was estrangement from *supra*. The way in which hospitality events unfold does not envisage women as autonomous actors in hospitality performances. Although it is unthinkable to display a *supra* without the contribution of women, the female role is that of a passive presence determined by the rules of the male-dominated plot of the event. Women's participation in a *supra* is desirable for everyone, and not only for practical reasons. Yet, women are denied agency over hospitality events, as if hospitality practices belong to a parallel yet unattainable male world. Practices of consumption of food and, especially, wine at a *supra* reinforce bonds of affection and even intimacy between men, while at the same time excluding women by the making and strengthening of these social ties.

The recurring division between public and private as respective male and female worlds (Landes 2003; Slater 1998; Weintraub 1997; Pateman 1987) is relevant here. Even when celebrated in private households, *supra*s are public events which act as a stage to display the host's worldview. The dynamics of a *supra*, including roles and identities attached to men and women, are publicly shared norms which affect the public position of individuals and groups in the community. Since in the national imagery the active producers of public social narratives are male, the stage of hospitality is managed by men. Women are a fundamental part of the plot, but only to the extent to which they fit the narrative ascribed to the event. The only link between the private and the public is represented by thoughts, words and objects—such as food, or toasts, as the example from *In Bloom* indicates—which embody the traditional ideas of womanhood to be made public on the stage.

Modernization narratives brought about by the Rose Revolution targeted *supra* as an authoritarian and backward practice, which upheld stereotypes of masculinity and femininity largely questioned and outdated in liberal Western societies. The next section will analyse the main points underpinning such narratives to outline the framework within which women questions the roles and identities ascribed to them in traditional hospitality practices, which are a useful lens through which gender divides in Georgian society can be investigated.

Past Against Future: The Rose Revolution's Modernization Narratives

The Rose Revolution unfolded in November 2003 as ultimate expression of citizens' anger towards president Eduard Shervardnadze and his government, which, in power since 1992, had plunged the country into a spiral of economic collapse, endemic corruption, organized crime and ethnic conflict. After a series of peaceful protests, Shevardnadze was removed and Mikheil Saak'ashvili, a young lawyer educated in the US, was elected president by a landslide. From the perspective of the new leader and his entourage, this political turn consisted in 'changing everything, and changing everything fast' (Full Speed Westward 2013) through a relentless move from the back to the front, from the 'before' to the 'now' and the 'after'.

The newly elected political leadership's narratives which underpinned the country's transformation rested on dichotomies which divided society into mutually opposed parts. Despite the often strong nationalist rhetoric which accompanied Saak'ashvili's raise to power (Vach'ridze 2012), these narratives classified citizens according to specific clear-cut oppositions. First and foremost, the post-revolutionary government emphasized a deep cleavage separating the 'future' from the 'past' in the development of Georgian society (Gotfredsen 2014; Frederiksen 2013). This opposition delineated people's moral, cultural and social attributes as either compatible or incompatible with the post-revolutionary project of radical renovation not only of political and economic institutions, but also of society and its members as a whole (Frederiksen and Gotfredsen 2017). As a consequence, narratives and practices underpinning the Rose Revolution and its aftermath, while being supposed to unite all citizens under the banner of modernization, transparency and democratization after years of troubles, contributed to the creation and deepening of moral, cultural, social, political and economic cleavages across the population (Curro 2017; Frederiksen and Gotfredsen 2017). Post-revolutionary modernization narratives attempted to justify social and economic inequality brought about by the government's reforms (which included swift privatization and deregulation of the economy,

Rekhviashvili 2015; Gugushvili 2014) on citizens' supposedly different moral and cultural standings.

In this framework, while being preserved in stereotyped images to depict Georgia to outsiders as a rapidly modernizing yet still romantically exotic country, *supra* and its main constituents have been questioned as fundamental expressions of that kind of backwardness and irrationality that the Rose Revolution and the reforms which followed meant to get rid of. *Supra* had been at the centre of a debate between the older Soviet intelligentsia and the post-revolutionary class of intellectuals, academics and third sectors workers even before the events of 2003 (Mühlfried 2005; Shatirishvili 2003; Gotsiridze 2001; Nodia 2000). Yet, following the progressive consolidation of Western neoliberal models brought about by the Rose Revolution among a certain part of the population—in terms of politics and economy, but also of culture and morality—different perspectives on *supra* increasingly became a marker to differentiate between 'new' and 'old' Georgians.

The spending of money and time to organize and deliver *supra*s was deemed to be in contrast with principles of economic rationality and individualism which the neoliberal doctrine pointed out as the key to economic and, therefore, political and social development (Curro 2017; Mühlfried 2014; see also Swader 2013). Many citizens who enthusiastically embraced what post-revolutionary narratives promoted as Western values turned to kinds of socialization and entertainment which radically differed from *supra* both from a quantitative and, most importantly, a qualitative perspective. Quantitatively, people who gained from the reforms implemented after the Rose Revolution seldom employed their increased economic and social capital to perform grandiose hospitality events in the traditional fashion. In the view of several participants in my research who belong to this social group, throwing huge *supra*s with many guests and massive amounts of food and drinks would amount to gross pretentiousness. Instead, many people would spend money to offer (particularly Western) guests' expressions of hospitality which were qualitatively different inasmuch as they were articulated as more refined and therefore 'modern'. When I was invited for dinner at her luxurious flat, my host Nana (38, housewife) explained that, apart from the ubiquitous *khach'ap'uri*, she had prepared only 'European food' (soufflé, roasted vegetables and apple crumble) because she thought it was more appropriate for me. In a similar fashion, other participants from the same milieu praised what they articulated as 'more European' expressions of hospitality. Among these are so-called *alapurshet'i* (*à la fourchette*) standing receptions (Tuite 2005; Manning 2003), which are the opposite of *supra* in both ritual form and symbolic content: there is no clear hierarchy between participants, and people are free to move around, help themselves with food and drinks and engage in conversation with other guests as they please. In contrast with such moderate forms of hospitality, *supra* was seen as an antiquated and authoritarian practice, still enjoyed only by very traditional people who abide by a patriarchal social structure, or by heavy drinkers who have nothing else to do.

It can be hypothesized that, in such a framework, women felt encouraged to rethink and challenge their subordinated position at *supra*, which was to a large extent a mirror of the strong gender divides still prominent across Georgian society. As it will be shown in this chapter, my female participants related in different ways to their exclusion from the male world of hospitality. The competence needed to behave appropriately between the private and the public realms entails women's internalization of ascribed gender identities. However, gender roles in hospitality can also be approached from a detached and sometimes critical perspective, which enables women to challenge the discrimination of which they are the object.

Internalizing Gender Roles or Exposing Exclusion?

Framed across society as timeless tradition, or even as biological attributes, normative ideas of womanhood are hardly questionable. Widely popular institutions, first and foremost the Georgian Orthodox Church, assertively promote traditional gender norms, influencing both public policy and private beliefs and practices (Rekhviashvili 2010). As a result, moral standards of female behaviour appear to be largely internalized by many Georgian women.

3 'Supra Is Not for Women': Hospitality Practices ... 55

To use Bourdieu's concepts, women's internalization of gender roles amounts to symbolic violence, which takes the form of habitus and is expressed through misrecognition (Bourdieu 1977, 1990; Bourdieu and Wacquant 2004). While talking to me about their thoughts and feelings with regard to their condition as women, some of my participants 'misrecognised' gender discrimination, denying that hospitality practices demand a lot from women while actually excluding them. In a conversation with Teona (42, teacher), I pointed out that in one of the families with whom I used to live, *supra*s were very formalized in terms of gender divides. While men feasted in the garden with wine and meat, women (when they were not busy cooking and serving) would sit in the house looking after the children, drinking coffee or sweet liqueurs and eating cake. Teona made clear that this was not 'tradition', but my host family's distortion of norms. She also told me that, when the separation of genders happens, it is not an enforced rule, but women's choice. Teona explained to me that men's conversation topics are of little interest to female tablemates, who prefer to sit next to their female friends and relatives and discuss other things.

However, in many other participants' view, these divisions were neither unusual nor spontaneous. In my own experience, I often witnessed the separation of genders around the table, which, if not enforced upon women, seemed at least passively accepted. Rather than engaging in their own conversations, the female part of the table listened silently to the speech of the *tamada* and the other men without actually being involved. This lack of participation in table talk, rather than expressing women's freedom of choice, was perceived by several women as a clear sign of female exclusion from the active making of *supra*.

A similar downplaying of the 'discriminatory' character of hospitality came from Ia (48, housewife). At a big *supra*, men and women sat at opposite ends of the table. The men followed the hectic pace of toasting and drinking set by the *tamada*, while the women sat quietly, ate moderately and drank no wine. Ia reassured me that these divisions were not compulsory. Of course, in her words, women were free to drink if they wished so. As for the separation at the table, men congregated at the same end simply in order to follow the *tamada*, but it was no problem for men and women to mix. Understanding symbolic violence as 'violence which is exercised upon a social agent with his or her complicity' (Bourdieu and Wacquant 2004, p. 272), in these examples what could seem a blatant expression of women's exclusion from all-male narratives and practices is expressed by women themselves through a discourse of self-empowerment. Gender divisions are framed either as occasional deviations from otherwise 'good' traditions or as a matter of free choice.

Habitus—which Bourdieu defines as 'subjective but not individual system of internalized structures, schemes of perception, conception and action common to all members of the same group or class'—can also take the form of women's passive but also uncomfortable compliance with traditional hospitality norms. In the abovementioned scene from the film *In Bloom*, the two female protagonists feel awkward in the male-dominated public realm of the wedding supra. To recreate a comfortable environment, they shut themselves in the bathroom, which becomes a private sphere where they can behave spontaneously and open up to one another. I observed this shift between public and private when I visited the home village of Tamazi (56, engineer), in the mountains of western Georgia, as a guest of him and his wife Lela (53, social worker). In the first few days, I shared the house just with Lela, her niece and some female in-laws, since the majority of men has stayed in Tbilisi busy working. In this all-female environment, women were not under pressure to cook meals for everyone or keep the house spotless at all times. We prepared and consumed food and wine together, with little distinction between hosts and guests and with no specific attention paid to *supra* conventions, which were often mocked.

However, when Tamazi and other male relatives arrived from Tbilisi for the *ormotsi* (a celebration held forty days after a person's death) of Tamazi's mother, who was a native of the village, the context shifted from private to public. My female hosts' attitudes became awkwardly formal, not only towards the men, but also between one another. The domestic space split along gender lines. Men congregated in 'public' areas, such as the living room and the balcony. Women spent most of their time in the kitchen, cooking all day, both to feed the men and for the forthcoming *supra* organized for Tamazi's late mother. The interaction between public and private spaces was minimized. The women's automatic yet radical change of attitudes is revealing of the habitus of shifting between public and private, embodying behaviours appropriate to each case.

Some of the women I met in my research expressed increasing awareness and criticism of gender discrimination in hospitality. In these women's thoughts, words and actions, symbolic violence was pinpointed, exposed and rejected. The alienation and even hostility experienced by many women at *supra* was efficiently phrased by Lik'a (27, Ph.D. student and activist). We were returning from a village where Lik'a's family had organized a traditional *supra*. During the celebration, Lik'a barely sat at the table, and left soon saying that she wanted to visit some childhood friends in the village. Later, she apologized to me for her absence, explaining that she could hardly tolerate attending a *supra*. I confessed that, after an initial fascination with these events, I had realized that some *supras* are boring for many of the participants. Lik'a was surprised at what for her was an obvious observation: 'Come on!' she exclaimed. 'Of course *supra* is not for women!'

Marina (25, student) had the same opinion. Living between Georgia and London, she told me that when she is abroad she enjoys meeting her co-nationals for food and drink. However, she felt relieved that on these occasions the traditional structures of hospitality are not necessarily followed. 'In Georgia women are not allowed to toast traditionally'—she explained—'They are supposed just to sit and eat and listen'. Women's exclusion from *supra* is also detrimental to the good outcome of hospitality events, which supposedly aim at common enjoyment: 'Since women can only talk to each other'—Marina told me—'what happens is that they do so even when someone is toasting. So it gets really loud and men try to shush women. Women are excluded, you bet they don't respect *supra!*'

In Marina's view, *supra* is not a discriminatory practice per se. It is the crystallization of traditional gender identities into such practices which prevents hospitality from being enjoyed in an inclusive and horizontal way. Similarly, Lik'a maintained that 'traditions' are taken for granted to the extent that people do not question whether they are right or wrong:

> When I was a child I used to help my mum set up the *supra*, serve food and so on. Once my dad had guests, all men, and I said I wanted to sit with them because I wanted to enjoy what I had helped prepare. They were very happy with that, and everyone was nice and flattering to me!

The male-dominated *supra* is accepted and reproduced passively, without reflection on alternative models of hospitality. However, these alternatives can disclose ways in which hospitality is accessible and enjoyable for everyone. Such a possibility is expressed by Ana's (31, academic) account of a *supra* organized by her father, to which her and her friend took part:

> I went back to Georgia for summer. My dad wanted to organise a *supra* at our place to welcome me back. So he invited his friends and I invited mine, plus there were some relatives of ours as well. I never had so much fun at a *supra*, which in fact can be quite boring. But this time both me and my friends acted as *tamada*, and none of the older men at *supra* thought that this was inappropriate. There was this very nice atmosphere in which everyone wanted to have fun with other people, eating, drinking, toasting and singing. And we chatted about different topics, involving everyone in the conversation.

As the thoughts and words of some of my participants indicate, gender norms enacted at *supra* may be internalized by women as a form of symbolic violence. Internalization is expressed in two main ways: first, through the misrecognition of gender discrimination, with women attributing an empowered role to themselves in hospitality practices; and second, through a passive and often unconscious adaptation to gender norms, in the form of a female habitus which entails the shifting of social competence between private and public roles. However, women also criticize the gender divides at *supra*. Opposition to women's alienation creates room to envisage inclusive practices of hospitality. I identify two main ways in which women implement these alternative models, framing hospitality from their own perspectives: the reproduction of traditional hospitality features in the private sphere and the public reappropriation of hospitality practices.

Women's Hospitality: Private vs. Private

Another scene in *In Bloom* features the celebration of Natia's birthday. Since the wedding, the girl has moved in with K'ote's family and is being suffocated by a bully of a husband and an intrusive mother-in-law. Her birthday is an opportunity to escape this everyday reality and, with her best friend Ek'a, enjoy a small *supra* prepared by her grandmother. The girls sit on the balcony of Natia's flat, surrounded by a gloomy landscape of concrete blocks. However, the atmosphere is merry as they enjoy being together and the consumption of food and wine without social pressure, free to eat, talk, drink and joke as they wish. In this relaxed context, the girls reproduce traditional models of hospitality practices. They toast in the *tamadoba* way, to 'all the grandmothers of the world', and then 'to us' (*chven gagvimarjos!*), emptying their glasses in imitation of male behaviour mixed with pride and mockery.

This representation of hospitality contrasts with Natia's wedding supra, where the girls were denied agency (see above). Appropriating traditional hospitality models, from which they are usually excluded, the young women enjoy conviviality without the anxiety entailed in rigid social rules. A similar scene occurs at Ek'a's place, when Ek'a's older sister and her female friends gather with Ek'a and Natia in the living room to drink small glasses of liqueur, smoke cigarettes, play the piano and sing love songs. As soon as they notice that Ek'a's mother is returning home, the girls tidy up hastily and sit quietly around the table pretending to study.

The scenarios reproduced in the film recall experiences from my research. Living in a house with women for a while, as the men worked out of town and only came home at weekends, I observed how my female hosts sometimes did not just want to feed me (and themselves), but meant to improvise a hospitality event which loosely followed the *supra* model. This was usually marked by the preparation of some 'special' food, such as *khink'ali* (dumplings) or *khach'ap'uri* (cheesy bread), and most importantly the consumption of wine. My hosts sometimes asked me, as well as other female friends and relative who occasionally were around, to sit around the table and drink 'a glass each' of home-made wine. Regardless of the improvisation and the small size of the event, toasts were made properly and the glasses (of which we usually drank more than one) emptied and refilled, reproducing the *tamadoba* structure.

These examples show women approaching hospitality by reframing the usually male-dominated traditional models. Echoing Lik'a's and Marina's points (see above), rather than being discriminatory per se, hospitality practices can be recreated in a spontaneous fashion, even following traditional patterns. Yet, in the examples mentioned, recreation takes place in the private realm of the house, within an exclusively female circle. Both in *In Bloom* and with my female hosts, it is challenging for women to translate the sense of relaxation experienced in their privately reproduced hospitality moments into public claims against the way traditional norms work. Women's reproduction of hospitality practices in the private domestic sphere reinforces ties of solidarity and empathy between female relatives, friends and neighbours. However, reproducing home hospitality among female tablemates does not make practices such as *supra* more inclusive. The traditional male-dominated, hierarchical structure of hospitality is hardly challenged, leaving the public stage of hospitality largely inaccessible to women.

During my research, I came across several cases in which women appropriated hospitality traditions in ironic, critical or even subversive ways, exposing gender discrimination to the public. A friend of mine who works at an LGBT rights organization in Tbilisi told me that some activists had reproduced *supra* with the *tamadoba* structure in a feminist fashion. Similarly, in 2014, art galleries in Tbilisi and other Georgian cities hosted an exhibition called 'Supra of her own' ('Sak'utari supra'), organized by a Georgian artist, a Polish anthropologist and a Georgian NGO. The exhibition, drawing upon in-depth interviews with women victims of gender-based violence, was 'about the invisibility of women's painful experiences and about novel ways of making these public' (Chabashvili and Dudrak 2014).

An exhilarating example of the public exposure by women of the male-dominated hospitality tradition is provided by artists Sophia T'abat'adze and Natia Ts'uluk'idze's (2006) work 'Georgian Table Traditions'.[2] In a video called 'Let's Drink to Love', a Georgian man (recalling the large dark-haired *supra* figures in Nik'o Pirosmani's paintings)[3] sits in a barbershop being shaved while holding a glass of wine. The man, covered in shaving foam, begins a toast 'to love'—*Siq'varuls gaumarjos!*—and continues to declaim odes to love for several minutes. When the barber warns 'Careful, I might cut you!' the man solemnly declares: 'What is a knife wound next to love?? Cut me, my brother, cut me!' At the end of the shave, the man terminates his toast and drinks the wine. Text accompanying the video provides excerpts from an 'Introduction' to the Georgian table traditions from a 'tamadaonline' website: 'Do you want to know where the Georgian man reveals himself in his entire splendour? This is the Georgian Table! [...] High-flown and magic words seem to help him (the *tamada*, author's note) to establish contact with Heaven...' At the end of a series of 'unwritten rules' for *tamada*, regarding sense of humour, hierarchy and timing, it is recommended to: 'Never forget the women in the kitchen [...]. Make sure the granny, aunties, moms and sisters are invited into the presence of the guests and toasted. [...] Praise the meal [and conclude the toast with] the traditional saying: "May we never lack your guidance and care" or "May your hands and arms always be healthy"'.

The reproduction of hospitality practices among women often re-enacts traditional patterns, possibly but not necessarily in an ironic way, remaining largely confined to the private domestic sphere within a circle of female relatives or friends. However, criticism and subversion of male-dominated hospitality are also expressed in a public way, as indicated by examples of certain artistic performances. Ties of female hospitality developing in the house can spread to the public realm of art, education and social and political activism, demanding more inclusive practices of hospitality accessible to all members of society. Who are the women who internalize, reproduce or subvert hospitality practices? What are the dividing lines between women along which the passive internalization, private reproduction and public reappropriation of hospitality unfold?

Women of the Past and the Future: Hospitality and Gendered Social Cleavages

Different attitudes to hospitality can be investigated along with divides between women on the basis of age, social class, education and life experience. Generally, among my participants, women with deeply internalized gender roles belong to an older generation with respect to women who have a more critical approach to gender divides. This is a fairly expected feature, since intolerance of tradition and drive for change are usually prominent in younger generations (Sumbadze and Tarkhan-Mouravi 2003, 2006).[4]

The still fairly widespread habit of early marriage (for women earlier than for men) contributes to this generational divide. Many of my participants in their fifties had been wives and mothers for more than thirty years, with limited experience of other sides of womanhood. Although early marriage habits have far from disappeared, people are gradually getting married at a later stage (Roberts et al. 2009). As a consequence, young women are 'dispensed' for a longer time from child-rearing and housekeeping, spending more time with their peers in schools, universities or workplaces, and being less likely to be extensively involved in *supra* mechanism since their teenage or early youth.

Women's marriage age and level of education, which are positively correlated, are in turn linked to class, intended both in its economic and social senses (Roberts and Pollock 2009). Women (and young people in general) with lower socio-economic status tend to follow the dominant sequence of family formation—(early) marriage, becoming parents, remaining married. This pattern is largely due to the impossibility of young people purchasing their own place. Moreover, many households, including those of young adults, are viable only due to multiple incomes (Roberts et al. 2009; Sumbadze and Tarkhan-Mouravi 2003, 2006). Living with older generations is sometimes the only chance for young women to have a job outside the house. The loss of free nurseries and kindergartens after the end of communism, alongside the reluctance of private sector employers to finance maternity leave, makes the help of older women in child-rearing indispensable (Roberts and Pollock 2009). Yet, living at one parents' place also means being largely subject to the rules through which older generations run the household, which often include the expectation that all family members contribute to the making of *supra*s organized in the domestic space according to socially established rules and norms.

The likelihood of attending university is also related to the socio-economic status of one's family. A 2007 survey conducted in the South Caucasus, dividing families into lower, intermediate and higher socio-economic groups according to their parents' degree of education and occupation, showed that young people progressing to higher education made up 21, 40 and 69% of each group, respectively (Roberts and Pollock 2009, p. 586). The majority of my female participants with an openly critical stance towards hospitality traditions were young unmarried women (usually under 30), most likely with experience living abroad, which was usually linked to attendance at higher education institutions.

These divides among women are reflected by a gap separating the private reproduction of hospitality practices in the female domestic sphere from the public reappropriation and criticism of *supra*. I could often observe a lack of connection between women's gatherings which 'domesticate' male-dominated hospitality (Smith and Rochovská 2007) and public expressions which denounce gender discrimination at *supra*. These instances, exemplified by the artistic performances mentioned in the previous section, are fundamental manifestations of rising awareness and changing attitudes among women, which should certainly be cultivated. However, these critical practices need to be connected to women's everyday lives, otherwise they risk becoming locked in an enclosed circle of female artists, activists and intellectuals, losing potential for a wider social and cultural change.

The past/future opposition which pervaded post-Rose Revolution narratives had a large impact on ideas of womanhood. In some of my participants' view, Western models of sophisticated and independent women were epitomised by Sandra Roelofs, Saak'ashvili's Dutch wife, who was also seen by many as a further confirmation that the president was committed to Western values and lifestyle in the public as well as in the private life. Such allegedly 'Western' female characteristics contrast with images of 'traditional' Georgian women, oppressed and dependent on their men, resilient yet physically and psychologically demeaned by everyday life's hardships.

Many of my participants who proudly defined themselves as liberated from this condition—feeling independent of their husbands, with the possibility of travelling, living and working outside Georgia, and possibly in a comfortable economic situation—sympathized with their co-nationals who were still brutalized by a patriarchal system. However, this solidarity was sometimes expressed in a vertical way. For example, Tako (45, profession unknown), who had lived abroad and who openly criticized the patriarchal structure of Georgian society, referred to her fellow countrywomen in the following terms: 'Of course, these women see nothing beyond being a good wife, mother and daughter-in-law, which means cooking, cleaning, rearing children and serve their men the all day! They have never left Georgia, and they have never had a life outside their houses'. This kind of statement reflects the depth of divisions which post-revolutionary modernization narratives contributed to deepen across the population. In these narratives, 'typically Georgian' men and women were often essentialized in opposition to Western models: the former as despotic masters and/or brutal alcoholics, the latter as passive victims of men as well as of their own narrow perspectives. Post-revolutionary narratives depicted the marginalization of women as a product of moral and cultural backwardness associated with the past, rather than as an attachment of social and economic inequality brought by the government's reforms.

Conclusions

Criticism and reappropriation of hospitality practices create divides between women which follow differences in age, class, level of education and so on. The potential of women's hospitality practices to spread beyond the private domestic sphere and generate more inclusive expressions of conviviality and feasting is partially jeopardized by the clear-cut oppositions between 'old'—that is, 'typically Georgian'—and 'new', 'Westernised' women which post-revolutionary narratives emphasized. However, at the same time divides emerging from different approaches to hospitality may foster debate between different groups of women, which not only take the form of conflict but also of enriching exchange. In one of my host families, three different generations of women lived together. In the summer evenings we would sit on the porch having lively discussions, which often focused on the appropriate behaviour for women in the context of hospitality and beyond. In these debates, everyone was open to learning from other people's differences. Women from older generations, aged between 50 and 60, were usually more conservative and reluctant to accept younger women's non-conformist attitudes, emphasizing their own deeper experience of the way certain things work in Georgia. However, mothers and grandmothers were also keen to listen to their daughters, recognizing that this exchange with the younger generations had a significant impact on their own way of seeing the world. Similarly, young women were not dismissive of their older female relatives' lifestyle as a diminishing and oppressed form of womanhood. On the contrary, there was widespread awareness that women's discrimination and empowerment cannot be predicated upon superficial and misleading dichotomies such as 'Georgia'/'West' and 'tradition'/'modernity'.

Women's ambivalent attitudes towards hospitality tradition—as a dimension from which they are excluded and which therefore needs to be challenged, but also as a set of norms and dynamics playing an important role in women's everyday life—may create divisions, but also common ground for the exchange of opinions and experiences. This kind of interaction can bridge the gap between the private reframing of women's identities and roles and the public exposure of gender divides. In this way, hospitality practices, even in their traditional forms, may become a way through which to channel inclusiveness, solidarity and mutual respect across different social groups—men and women, but also women from different socio-economic milieus, with different life experiences and from different generations.

Notes

1. According to some research (Mühlfried 2007; Tuite 2005) and some participants' views, women can also be *tamada*. However, such an event is reportedly and increasingly rare (I have never witnessed such an occasion, unless the event was an all-female one). Moreover, drinking is still widely considered, by both men and women, as a typically male activity, therefore I refer to *tamadoba* and *tamada* in male terms.
2. T'abat'adze, S. and Ts'uluk'idze, N. (2006). *Georgian Table Traditions*. Available at http://khinkalijuice.blogspot.co.uk/.
3. Nik'oloz Pirosmani (1862–1918) was a Georgian painter whose fame, attained posthumously, mainly derives from works depicting Georgian

food and wine culture in general, and convivial consumption at *supra* in particular (Söderlind 2012). Stereotyped images of Georgian men and women, with traditional clothes, headgear and haircuts (and long moustaches in the case of men), depicted in their allotted roles at hospitality events, are a recurrent feature of many of Pirosmani's paintings.

4. The two researchers first published their survey on Georgian youth's transition to adulthood in 2003 in a paper for the Policy Documentation Centre at the Central European University. The survey was republished with additional new data in an edited volume in 2006. I report both versions of the survey throughout the chapter because certain details which appear in the first were omitted from the second and vice versa.

References

Altman, Yochanan. 2011. "The Georgian Feast: Wine and Food as Embodiment of Networks." 6th AWBR International Conference Bordeaux Management School, 9–10, June. Bordeaux Management School, Bordeaux, France.

Bourdieu, Pierre. 1977. *Outline of a Theory of Practice*. Cambridge: Cambridge University Press.

———. 1990. *The Logic of Practice*. Stanford: Stanford University Press.

Bourdieu, Pierre, and Lois Wacquant. 2004. "Symbolic Violence." In *Violence in War and Peace: An Anthology*, edited by Nancy Scheper-Hughes and Phillipe Bourgois, 272–774. Oxford: Blackwell.

Buckley, C. 2005. "Socio-Cultural Correlates of HIV/AIDS in the Southern Caucasus." In *HIV and AIDS in the Caucasus Region: A Socio-Cultural Approach*. Paris: UNESCO Culture and Development Section.

Chabashvili, Tamar, and Agnieszka Dudrak. 2014. *Sak'utari Supra—A Supra of Her Own*. https://supraofherown.wordpress.com.

Chatwin, Mary E. 1997. *Socio-Cultural Transformation and Foodways in the Republic of Georgia*. Commack, NY: Nova Science Publishers.

Chau, Adam Y. 2008. "The Sensorial Production of the Social." *Ethnos* 73 (4): 485–504. https://doi.org/10.1080/00141840802563931.

Curro, Costanza. 2012. "National Gender Norms and Transnational Identities: Migration Experiences of Georgian Women in London". *Slovo* 24 (2): 114–131.

———. 2014. "A 'Gift from God'? Georgian Hospitality Between Tradition and Pragmatism." *Hospitality & Society* 4 (3): 293–310.

———. 2017. *From Tradition to Civility: Georgian Hospitality After the Rose Revolution* (2003–2012). PhD diss., University College London.

Douglas, Mary. 1987. *Constructive Drinking: Perspectives on Drink from Anthropology*. Cambridge: Cambridge University Press.

Dragadze, Tamara. 1988. *Rural Families in Soviet Georgia: A Case Study in Ratcha Province*. London: Routledge.

Dudwick, Nora. 2004. "No Guests at Our Table: Social Fragmentation in Georgia." In *When Things Fall Apart: Qualitative Studies of Poverty in the Former Soviet Union*, edited by Nora Dudwick, Elizabeth Gomart, Aleksandre Marc, and Kathleen Kuehnast, 213–257. Washington, DC: World Bank Publications.

Ekvtimishvili, Nana, and Simon Groß. 2014. *In Bloom (Grdzeli nateli dgheebi)* [Film]. Big World Pictures.

Frederiksen, Martin D. 2013. *Young Men, Time, and Boredom in the Republic of Georgia*. Philadelphia: Temple University Press.

Frederiksen, Martin D., and Katrine B. Gotfredsen 2017. *Georgian Portraits: Essays on the Afterlives of a Revolution*. London and Washington, DC: Zero Books.

Gotfredsen, Katrine B. 2014. "Void Pasts and Marginal Presents: On Nostalgia and Obsolete Futures in the Republic of Georgia." *Slavic Review* 73 (2): 246–264. https://doi.org/10.5612/slavicreview.73.2.246.

Gotsiridze, G. 2001. "Vin ebrdzvis kartul supras"? ("Who Is Fighting Against the Georgian Banquet?"). *Lit'erat'uruli Sakartvelo*: 7.

Gugushvili, Dimitri. 2014. *Do the Benefits of Growth Trickle Down to Georgia's Poor? A Case for a Strong Welfare System*. PhD diss., University of Kent.

Kotthoff, Helga. 1995. "The Social Semiotics of Georgian Toast Performances: Oral Genre as Cultural Activity." *Journal of Pragmatics* 24 (4): 353–380. https://doi.org/10.1016/0378-2166(94)00063-K.

Landes, Joan. 2003. "Further Thoughts on the Public/Private Distinction." *Journal of Women's History* 15 (2): 28–39.

Lundkvist-Houndoumadi, Margharita. 2010. "Treading on the Fine Line Between Self-Sacrifice and Immorality: Narratives of Emigrated Georgian Women." *Transcience Journal* 1 (2): 50–71.

Manning, Paul. 2003. "Socialist *Supra*s and Drinking Democratically: Changing Images of the Georgian Feast and Georgian Society from Socialism to post-Socialism." PhD diss., Trent University.

———. 2009. "The Epoch of Magna: Capitalist Brands and Postsocialist Revolutions in Georgia." *Slavic Review* 68 (4, Winter): 924–945. https://doi.org/10.1017/S003767790002458X.

Mars, Gerald, and Yochanan Altman. 1983. "The Cultural Bases of Soviet Georgia's Second Economy." *Soviet Studies* 35 (4): 546–560. https://doi.org/10.1080/09668138308411503.

———. 1987. "Alternative Mechanism of Distribution in a Soviet Economy." In *Constructive Drinking: Perspectives on Drink from Anthropology*, edited by Mary Douglas, 270–279. Cambridge: Cambridge University Press.

Mühlfried, Florian. 2005. "Banquets, Grant-Eaters and the Red Intelligentsia in Post-Soviet Georgia." *Central Eurasian Studies Review* 4 (1, Winter): 16–18.

———. 2006. *Postsowjetische Feiern: Das Georgische Bankett im Wandel*. Stuttgart: Ibidem Verlag.

———. 2007. "Sharing the Same Blood: Culture and Cuisine in the Republic of Georgia." *Anthropology of Food* 53. https://journals.openedition.org/aof/2342.

———. 2014. "A Taste of Mistrust." *Ab Imperio* 4: 63–68. https://doi.org/10.1353/imp.2014.0120.

Nodia, Ghia, ed. 2000. *Kartuli supra da samokalako sazogadoeba* (The Georgian Banquet and Civic Society). Tbilisi: Caucasian Institute for Peace, Democracy and Development.

———. 2014. "The Values of the Georgian Supra: Nationalist or Nativist?" *Ab Imperio* 4: 69–74. https://doi.org/10.1353/imp.2014.0125.

Pateman, Carole. 1987. "Feminist Critiques of the Public/Private Dichotomy." In *Feminism and Equality*, edited by Anne Phillips, 103–126. Oxford: Blackwell.

Polese, Abel. 2010. "The Guest at the Dining Table: Economic Transitions and the Reshaping of Hospitality—Reflections from Batumi and Odessa." *Anthropology of Eastern Europe Review* 27 (1): 76–88.

Rekhviashvili, A. 2010. *Nationalism and Motherhood in Contemporary Georgia*. Master of Arts, Central European University.

Rekhviashvili, Lela. 2015. "Marketization and the Public-Private Divide." *International Journal of Sociology and Social Policy* 35 (7–8): 478–496.

Roberts, Ken, and Gary Pollock. 2009. "New Class Divisions in the New Market Economies: Evidence from the Careers of Young Adults in Post-Soviet Armenia, Azerbaijan and Georgia." *Journal of Youth Studies* 12 (5): 579–596. https://doi.org/10.1080/13676260903081640.

Roberts, Ken, Gary Pollock, Sabina Rustamova, Zhala Mammadova, and Jochen Tholend. 2009. "Young Adults' Family and Housing Life-Stage Transitions During Post-Communist Transition in the South Caucasus." *Journal of Youth Studies* 12 (2): 151–166. https://doi.org/10.1080/13676260802600854.

Shatirishvili, Zaza. 2003. "'Old' Intelligentsia and 'New' Intellectuals: The Georgian Experience." *Eurozine*, June 26. http://www.eurozine.com/old-intelligentsia-and-new-intellectuals-the-georgian-experience/.

Shelley, Louise, Eric R. Scott, and Anthony Latta, eds. 2007. *Organized Crime and Corruption in Georgia*. New York: Routledge.

Slater, Don. 1998. "Public/Private." In *Core Sociological Dichotomies*, edited by Chris Jenks, 138–150. London: Sage.

Smith, Adrian, and Alena Rochovská. 2007. "Domesticating Neo-Liberalism: Everyday Lives and the Geographies of Post-Socialist Transformations." *Geoforum* 38 (6): 1163–1178. https://doi.org/10.1016/j.geoforum.2007.03.003.

Söderlind, Ulrica. 2012. "Georgia's Food and Drinking Culture in the Eyes of Nik'oloz Pirosmani." *Review of Applied Socio-Economic Research* 3 (1): 170–183.

Sumbadze, Nana, and George Tarkhan-Mouravi. 2003. *Transition to Adulthood in Georgia: Dynamics of Generational and Gender Roles in Post-Totalitarian Society*. Budapest: Policy Documentation Centre, Central European University. http://pdc.ceu.hu/archive/00002563/01/Transition_to_adulthood_in_Georgia.pdf.

———. 2006. "Transition to Adulthood in Georgia: Dynamics of Generational and Gender Roles in Post-Totalitarian Society." In *A New Youth? Young People, Generations, and Family Life*, edited by Carmen Leccardi and Elisabetta Ruspini, 224–252. London: Ashgate.

Swader, Christopher. 2013. *The Capitalist Personality: Face-to-Face Sociality and Economic Change in the Post-Communist World*. London and New York: Routledge.

T'abat'adze, Sophia, and Ts'uluk'idze, Nadia. 2006. Georgian Table Traditions. http://khinkalijuice.blogspot.co.uk/.

Tolz, Stefan. 2013. *Full Speed Westward*. Film Documentary. Germany: Cologne Filmproduktion.

Tsitsishvili, Nino. 2006. "'A Man Can Sing and Play Better Than a Woman': Singing and Patriarchy at the Georgian Supra Feast." *Ethnomusicology* 50 (3, Fall): 452–493. https://www.jstor.org/stable/20174470.

Tuite, K. 2005. "The Autocrat of the Banquet Table: The Political and Social Significance of the Georgian Supra." Conference on Language, History and Cultural Identities in the Caucasus, 9–35, IMER, Malmoe University, Sweden, June 17–19.

Vach'ridze, Zaza. 2012. "Two Faces of Nationalism and Efforts to Establish Georgian Identity." *Identity Studies in the Caucasus and the Black Sea Region* 4: 82–88.

Weintraub, Jeff. 1997. "The Theory and Politics of the Public/Private Distinction." In *Public and Private in Thought and Practice: Perspectives on a Grand Dichotomy*, edited by Jeff Weintraub and Krishan Kumar, 1–40. Chicago: University of Chicago Press.

4

Women Against Authoritarianism: Agency and Political Protest in Armenia

Ulrike Ziemer

In spring 2018, opposition leader Nikol Pashinyan, started a protest march from the central square in Gyumri—Armenia's second biggest city—to Yerevan. Very quickly, Pashinyan's march developed into a full-blown, non-violent, political protest movement (the so-called Velvet Revolution), shaking Armenia to its political foundations. For three long weeks, thousands of people blocked roads and public spaces in a bid to paralyze the transport system and government institutions. This political protest movement addressed many of the grievances and discontents within Armenian society, in particular with the oligarchic and corrupt government which has ruled the country for the past two decades. These street protests drew support from all segments of Armenian society to challenge the regime's hold on power, as well as its legitimacy to govern. Eventually on April 23, 2018, Serzh Sargsyan, Armenia's Prime Minister and former president[1] resigned and his corrupt semi-authoritarian regime disintegrated.[2]

U. Ziemer (✉)
University of Winchester, Winchester, UK
e-mail: Ulrike.Ziemer@winchester.ac.uk

© The Author(s) 2020
U. Ziemer (ed.), *Women's Everyday Lives in War and Peace in the South Caucasus*,
https://doi.org/10.1007/978-3-030-25517-6_4

'*Serzh is not our father – we don't have a father*' (Serje mer papan che, menq papa chunenq) was the chant used by some female protesters during the protests to allude to the rejection of Serzh Sargsyan not only as an authoritarian leader, but also a patriarchal ruler. Yet slogans expressing a clear feminist stance were not the only or even main ones in use. Predominantly, the language of the protests, as seen in the hand-held banners and placards carried by the protestors proclaimed the revolution 'an act of love and tolerance' rather than of hate and revenge. One of the key slogans of these street protests was '#RejectSerzh' (#MerzhirSerzhin), thus, gender equality and broad feminist causes were not explicit aims of the protest movement, but rather the fight against an oligarchic and corrupt government.[3]

On the international stage, most observers were surprised at the speed and success of this political movement in ending the reign of Sargsyan's government, confirming in a broader perspective the unpredictability of social movements. As de Waal (2018) correctly observed, events in Armenia offered a classic illustration of the latent potential of semi-free societies, where the public were simultaneously alienated and angry but with enough freedom to vent their frustrations and protest without fear of mass repression (cited in Eckel 2018). While there is no denying that this protest movement was novel both in terms of outcomes and the values of nationwide inclusivity it promoted; it nevertheless resembled protest movements found in other regions and contexts in terms of the contours of its gendered processes (Kuumba 1990; Sharoni 1995). The gendered nature of protests, however, is never straightforward, but relates to and is dependent on the social construction of gender within wider society.

This chapter takes a feminist perspective to explore women's participation and contributions to the success of the protest movement. In this way, this chapter contributes to the existing and emerging literature on gender in the post-socialist region which retains significant gaps, in particular regarding women's roles and contributions in political protests and protest movements.[4] All kinds of women participated in the mass actions of April 2018, including feminist activists and women with more 'traditional' gender role self-perceptions. However, it was the patriarchy of Armenia's semi-authoritarian regime that presented a shared experience for women protestors. This patriarchy was not only exacerbated by the superficial gender equality promoted by the regime and the suppressive mechanisms that all authoritarian political systems employ (cf. Alvarez 1990; Chuchryk 2018; Mama 1998; Noonan 1995), but also by the particular militarist nature of Armenian authoritarianism, in a country that has resided in a state of war readiness with neighbouring Azerbaijan for the entire duration of its post-Soviet existence (Broers 2018, 2019; de Waal 2013). As such, in a patriarchal society such as Armenia's, women's 'proper role' is confined to being self-sacrificing mothers. Women are praised for their ability to produce future soldiers, while men are expected to be the 'defenders of the nation' against the enemy (Ishkanian 2018).

In terms of approach, taking a feminist perspective means understanding Armenia's Velvet Revolution from the bottom-up, specifically from the point of view of those most marginalized, to enable a fuller understanding of dominant structures and discourses in society. This chapter draws on 25 in-depth interviews with female Armenia-based experts, journalists and representatives of non-governmental organizations (NGOs), as well as female protesters. The interviews were conducted in July 2018. The drawbacks of this research design, in particular the problem of bias (Green and Kohl 2007, p. 159) were mitigated by triangulating statements from research participants with other sources and by conducting a greater number of interviews to allow data to be drawn from a larger sample. This project is part of a larger ongoing ethnographic study exploring gender issues and political transformations in the Nagorny Karabakh region[5] and Armenia (cf. Roberts and Ziemer 2018; Shahnazarian and Ziemer 2012, 2014, 2018; Ziemer 2018). As part of this research project, the author made several fieldwork trips to the region from August 2015.

This chapter proceeds as follows: the first section unpacks the broader gender inequalities that existed prior to the protests in spring 2018. This is important as social movements have the potential to either reproduce or transform existing gender inequalities, structures and social belief systems. The second section reviews current research on women and social movements to highlight the significance of exploring women's agency during the protests. The final empirical section examines women's agency by exploring three facets of women's agency during the demonstrations. Overall, and as argued in this chapter, gender, in inter-related and multifaceted ways was pivotal for the success of the protest movement.

Gender Relations Prior to the Protest Movement

Social movements have the potential to reproduce, as well as to transform gender inequalities, structures and belief systems. Hence, it is salient to unpack the broader gender inequalities that existed prior to the street protests in April 2018. A growing body of feminist research demonstrates that patriarchy and gender inequality are positively associated with national and inter-state conflict (Caprioli 2000, 2005; Hudson 2010; Hudson et al. 2009). In other words, we can expect less violent domestic conflict when women have a strong presence in civil and political society. This section explores the conflicting tendencies and competing tensions between traditional culture strongly prevalent in Armenian society, women's progressive civic activism and militarized state relations.

Armenia is the third most militarized state in the world and the most militarized country in Europe (Mutschler and Bales 2018). This is not a surprising development considering that Armenia and Azerbaijan have endured a stalemate situation over the disputed Nagorny Karabakh territory since the 1994 ceasefire. In this situation, the military as an institution assumes a central role. In a highly militarized state such as Armenia, motherhood often represents for women what soldiering represents for men—an opportunity to serve the nation (Ziemer 2018, p. 8). In the case of Armenia, motherhood is also processed through multiple and distinct historical events, such as surviving genocide attempts, the struggle to preserve 'Armenianness' for the diaspora after their forceful eviction from their historical homeland as well as the more recent war in Nagorny Karabakh (Beukian 2014, pp. 262–263; Shahnazarian and Ziemer 2018; Ziemer 2018). Each of these distinct historical moments is linked to conflict, war and militarism.

Thus, Armenian cultural traditions are based on conflict and military discourse, considering women as the nurturers of the nation; having childbearing responsibilities to keep the nation growing.

Alongside motherhood, the family, as the nucleus of Armenian society has always been a key tenet of Armenian cultural traditions (Ziemer 2011). Against this backdrop women have come to play key roles in maintaining the family and its values and norms, thereby solidifying the image of the 'sacred mother' in Armenian society (Ohanyan 2009). Discourse analysis of Armenian society has also stressed the role of women as being 'inside the wall of the Armenian hearth', while men are occupied with external roles. Moving beyond these symbols women are central in the private sphere of society whereas men have been more dominant in the public sphere. Put differently, women's roles have traditionally been considered central to both the family and child-rearing and in general more inwardly oriented (Ohanyan 2009, p. 231).

Although it may seem that strong patriarchal power relations have always been a key characteristic of Armenian cultural traditions there is evidence that, at the same time Armenian culture also had historical moments characterized by gender equality. For example, in the sixth and seventh centuries it was documented that women and men had equal rights and opportunities with regard to property, divorce and remarriage (Shahnazarian et al. 2016, p. 59) and overall it seems that the equality discourse was relatively strong in Armenian society until the late Middle-Ages. Vardan Hacuni in his book on Armenian women in history wrote that Armenian women lost their rights and freedoms because of the constant fear of assimilation with other nations (ibid.). This indicates that the militarization processes evident in Armenian society have led to paradoxes that, on the one hand strengthened patriarchal relations subordinating women, while producing courageous women able to struggle alone and counter the prevailing norms of society (Ohanyan 2009, p. 213).[6]

During the Soviet era (1922–1991), the tensions between cultural prescriptions and governmental policies were particularly acute, as the official equality of men and women was one of the cornerstones of Soviet ideology and policy. The Communist Party of the Soviet Union (CPSU) introduced legislation that targeted numerous aspects of women's lives, instituting a range of freedoms and rights in education, political participation and social development (Ishkanian 2003, p. 478). It was believed that women were central to socialist state-building with all of these initiatives designed to empower them. However, as a vast amount of literature has demonstrated, instead of empowering women the USSR created a double burden, reinforcing patriarchy in both public and private spheres (Buckley 1989; Corrin 1992; Ohanyan 2009).

The invisibility of gender discrimination is thus an institutional legacy inherited from the Soviet era, and in Armenia this double burden remains strong to this day, in particular as the period following independence in 1991 has been described as a 'slow return to patriarchy' (Kaser 2008 in Khachatryan et al. 2015). A 2012 report from the National Statistical Service of the Republic of Armenia, for example, showed that in 2008 women spent up to 5.24 hours a day on housework compared to 1.59 hours for men (National Statistical Service of the Republic of Armenia2012, p. 139). Despite modest progress in recent years, women in Armenia continue to suffer from major inequalities in political, social and economic life, as evidenced by several international rankings on gender equality and women's empowerment. The World Economic Forum's (WEF) 2017 Global Gender Gap report ranked Armenia 97th out of 144 countries in terms of overall gender equality (Mijatovic 2019, p. 3). In terms of employment, women have been hit far harder than men with unemployment and a host of problems associated with privatization following the collapse of the USSR. In 2018, the average unemployment rate for women in Armenia stood at 17.3% (ibid., p. 17). Thus, according to the latest report of the International Labour Organization (ILO) Armenia has the highest unemployment rate among women in all post-Soviet countries (Mkrtchian 2018).

Soviet legacies of gender segregation have continued to restrict women's ability to play active roles in politics in the post-Soviet era. Men who formed a closed elite dominated the Soviet political system, and the same is true of the post-Soviet period. Likewise, even though women in Armenia, as in Soviet Armenia, tend to be better educated than men they are rarely found in decision-making positions. Still, the Armenian legislative system was in some ways 'gender-sensitive' before the 2018 events, mainly due to a series of amendments made to existing laws. In 2007, for example, a female party-list quota of 15% was introduced to ensure women's engagement in elections (Shahnazarian et al. 2016, p. 62) and in 2011 this quota was increased to 20% (ibid.). Nonetheless, and after 20 years of independence (1991–2011), the number of women in Armenia's legislature increased by only 7% (ibid., p. 64). According to Hasratyan et al. (2012) at the current pace of change at least another 25 years will be needed in order to meet the 20% quota.

Until April 2018, the modest number of women in Armenian politics can in part be accounted for by the widely practised phenomenon of self-withdrawal (Shahnazarian et al. 2016, p. 65). In addition, and in circumstances where elections departed from the norm of 'free and fair' under Sargsyan, women were twice as likely to be disadvantaged (ibid., p. 76). Overall, research has shown that the existing 'dirty' rules of the game played in Armenia's political life were not part of women's political culture (Shahnazarian et al. 2016; Ishkanian 2008; Ohanyan 2009). In 2018, the proportion of female legislators in Armenia's parliament stood at 18%: three quarters of the global average of 24% (World Bank 2018).

Hence, many women found alternative spaces in civil society to express their political activism, away from formal politics. This meant that the majority of NGOs in Armenia were run by women during the 1990s and even today are heavily dominated by women. According to the NGO Resource and Training Centre in Yerevan, by the mid-2000s, 80% of NGO leaders and over 80% of members were women (Ishkanian 2008, p. 59). Although women's activism has enjoyed some notable achievements in Armenia,[7] it has not achieved mass membership, diffusion or approval in post-Soviet political and human rights areas. In fact, women's organizations and activists have been targets of anti-gender/anti-feminist campaigns and corresponding accusations of being 'fifth columnists' intent on destroying traditions (Roberts and Ziemer 2018). This trend, unfortunately, is still evident in the immediate aftermath of the democratic developments of 2018.[8] In other words, while feminist activism is ripe in post-Soviet Armenia, until the protests of April 2018, it remained an activism practised by a minority of women, and mainly in the capital city, Yerevan.

Viewing Political Protests Through a Gender Lens

There is no denying that much of the success of the Armenian protest movement in 2018 can be attributed to its advocacy of new values such as freedom, dignity, tolerance, love, courage and justice, which united all segments of society (Ishkanian 2018). It presented the climax of a decade of peaceful protest centred on human rights, women's rights, environmentalism and labour and employment issues—all explicitly non or minimally political causes (Ohanyan 2018). Yet, although highly active, to date, the specific experience of women during these protests has only been documented in a few online publications (cf. Roach 2018). This contrasts with the position of the protest leader and newly appointed Prime Minister, Nikol Pashinyan, who instead of rendering women invisible, used part of his inaugural speech on May 8, 2018, to acknowledge the unprecedented participation and effort of women in the political life of the country (Manasyan 2018). This does not necessarily mean that women in Armenia are no longer in a subordinate position, but rather indicates the pressing need to uncover the gendered processes of the protest movement and to highlight women's specific experiences and contributions. Such situated knowledge of women's lived experience during the protests allows a more complete understanding of dominant structures and discourses in Armenian society. Hence, it is a way of mapping power practices from a bottom-up perspective (Harding 2011).

Over the past four decades, scholars have made concerted efforts to study the gendered processes of social movements, mainly to reduce the invisibility of women (Deane and Aune 2015; Einwohner et al. 2000; Jaquette 1994; Kuumba 1990; Lorber 2000; Molyneux 1998; Zemlinskaya 2010). This is particularly notable when it comes to the Arab Spring uprisings and the focus on women and their roles during these political transformations, which have received substantial attention in the scholarly literature (Al-Ali 2012; Kadry 2015; Khalil 2016; Mhajne and Whetstone 2018; Moghadam 2017; Sadiqi 2016). Most of these publications highlight the significant roles of women and the way gendered processes have contributed to achieving political aims and outcomes. Yet, some of these publications also highlight counter processes, such as the intimidation of women to prevent or hinder the overall progress of these revolutionary movements (cf. Hafez 2014). In other words, these publications have explored the contradictory experiences of women resulting from an interplay of existing patriarchal gender ideologies and authoritarian state rhetoric.

When it comes to gendered perspectives on social movements and political protests in the post-Soviet space, the literature on women's roles during the so-called 'coloured revolutions' and the impact of these episodes on women's political representation is still growing (Badashvili 2013; Chkheidze 2017; Jakeli 2018; Nikolayenko and DeCasper 2018; Onuch and Martsenuk 2014; Sabedashvili 2007; Schofield et al. 2010). To date, some publications, in particular those focusing on women's participation in Ukraine's Orange Revolution (2004–2005) have documented how gender ideologies are embedded in these political processes (cf. Kostiuchenko et al. 2015). Phillips (2014), for example, shows how women's contributions went largely unnoticed during the Orange Revolution and how men tried to exclude women from more dangerous activities 'for their own protection'[9]: yet were still able to generate some important creative feminist responses that produced impact.

Most studies on women and transitions to democracy in the post-Soviet space have stressed the influence of the Soviet legacy on gender relations in post-socialist societies (cf. Funk and Mueller 1993; Gradskova and Morell 2018). These publications have highlighted how specific patriarchal gender ideologies were formed alongside and as a result of the Communist ideological project of 'state feminism' that attempted to overcome bourgeois patriarchal family relations to empower women. Nonetheless, in many parts of the post-Soviet space these transition processes have led to a reinforcement of patriarchy in opposition to the prior existence of state feminism (Ashwin 2000; Ishkanian 2003; Zhurzhenko 2001). In particular, and in terms of political representation, it has been documented that the persistence of hierarchical patriarchal structures is a key explanation for the relatively low numbers of women engaged in politics in the post-Soviet space (Galligan et al. 2007; Rueschemayer 2016). In Georgia, for example, although women were active in civil society prior to and during the Rose Revolution (2003), this activism did not translate into representation for female legislators in the post-Revolution parliament (Chkeidze 2017).

While the impact of post-communist patriarchal gender ideologies on women's everyday lives has been widely analysed, questions of how and why women come to mobilize against authoritarian regimes in the post-Soviet space have not received explicit attention.[10] Instead, attention has been mostly been afforded to exploring how women find alternative spaces in civil society to display their political activism away from formal politics (Ishkanian 2008; Popkova 2004; Tohidi 2004). The main argument in these publications is that women tend to seek political activism in alternative spaces due to the fact that mechanisms for women's increased political involvement are either absent or that women feel alienated from them by the prevailing political culture.

An exploration of how and why women participate in political protest movements, such as Armenia's Velvet Revolution, requires an examination of women's agency during the protests. Feminist scholars do agree that regardless of the repressive nature of the social system, women act and make choices and decisions that influence their lives (Kabeer 1999). The form of agency they use determines how social change happens. Agency is inseparable to the analysis of power and thinking through broader issues such as the interrelationship between individual freedoms and constraints. Agency denotes a cluster of actions considered to be categorically distinct from the types of unreflective, habitual and institutional behaviours which are held to be quasi automatic responses to external structural forces (McNay 2016, p. 41). Agency needs to be understood as a situated, embodied and relational phenomenon whose substantive content and form of action is unthinkable outside specific cultural and social contexts (ibid.). Thus, one needs to analyse the underlying power structures that create the possibilities for gendered agency.

Women's agency is closely linked to their bodies in discursive ways; the ways in which they are constituted and constitute themselves. Political, social and cultural norms are manifested in body praxis, performance and images. In Foucault's work, power and agency are relational and power for him is constituted by 'a set of actions upon other actions' (Foucault 1982, p. 220). At the same time, bodies are active and acted upon. While Foucault, analysed the body as object, Butler (1990) regards the body as a subject that produces and performs social meaning. In this sense, the body retains its agency although it is a socio-historical and political construction, perceived differently in different historical periods (Foucault 1982). Bordo argues that women's bodies are often vehicles of resistance that re-inscribe the very principles of social control being resisted, providing 'a paradigm of one way in which potential resistance is not merely undercut but utilised in the maintenance and reproduction of existing power relations' (Bordo 2003, p. 168). In doing so, and as bodies appropriate the forms of dominance that oppress them, they normalize the logic of male-centric gender ideologies even as they seek to overcome them. In this regard, the subsequent empirical analysis will show how women use their bodies actively and strategically to resist power structures and to encourage others to join them in the protest.

In Armenia, as in other protest movements, the female body gained symbolic and material importance during the protests. While 'feminine' bodies can be disciplined and regulated through discourses of patriarchy, they can also become sites of dissent and revolution. As shown in the next section, women's bodies became sites of resistance and sites for maintaining peace during the protest's street blockades. Women employed their bodies as visible markers of new socio-political values introduced as part of the protest effort.

The 2018 Protests: Women's Agency and Activism

> I want to address my sisters who stand together hand in hand, and who fought a double fight for the change of power in Armenia and for their equal rights in public. Long live our sisters!

This excerpt is from a speech by Maria Karapetyan[11] in Yerevan's Republic Square on 18th April 2018 (Khudoyan 2019). She was one of the leading female figures during the protests. Her speech clearly indicates the gendered aspect of the protests. Women were being viewed as sisters and voicing their support for one another and their fight for equality (Shahnazarian 2019). Thus, although the protests' primary aim was to peacefully overthrow Serzh Sargsyan and his corrupt regime, for women the events of April 2018 represented more. As Gayane Abrahamyan[12] explains: '*in* [the previous protests of] *2008, there were no women. These protests* [of 2018] *were breaking a taboo that women were not only back stage but they were all on stage*'. For the first time ever, women were occupying political spaces reserved for men and acting as strategists, organizers and active participants in the movement, as well as having discussions about gender roles and equal rights (Shahnazarian 2019).[13]

While Maria Karapetyan's speech clearly addressed the political inequalities women have been experiencing for years, Lena Nazaryan, a former journalist and (from January 2019) one of three Vice Parliamentary Speakers,[14] in contradistinction, takes a different approach, de-emphasizing gender differences. Politics, for her, is not about emphasizing gender differences but simply doing your best as a politician. She wants to be judged only on her achievements rather than on her gender as a woman in politics. In this way, she feels she can empower women as she is living an example of power, one which includes an image of the new nation unconstrained by the old patriarchal structures of an unequal state—echoing a desire shared by many young protesters to break with the old (Ghazaryan 2018).

Both emphasizing and de-emphasizing gender differences are strategies for promoting gender equality. De-emphasizing gender does not mean ignoring differences but rather seeing them as less important than other factors. Both strategies have their advantages and are largely dependent on the specific context in which they are applied (Herrnson et al. 2003). Research has shown that in certain contexts, de-emphasizing gender differences works better as it removes the 'male' connotations from traits and behaviours like assertiveness, competitiveness and risk taking (Martin and Phillips 2017). 'Ungendering' these qualities makes women more likely to recognize them in themselves and to feel more confident (Martin and Phillips 2017; Torres 2018). As the protests were primarily about political change it worked advantageously, inspiring many other women, in particular once Lena Nazaryan assumed centre stage following the one-day detainment by the police of protest leader Nikol Pashinyan. As one female research participant explains:

> We could finally see women in politics. They were now in leading positions. When Nikol [Pashinyan] was arrested for one day, when he could not manage the negotiations with Sargsyan, all our eyes turned to Lena. She was now the one we relied and listening to her was amazing! She was live on TV and you could see how scared she was. She had her baseball cap on, and she told people to protest, to continue organizing in a decentralized manner ... It was a very tense time...people picked up rocks and wanted to hit each other with them, but she was the one who conveyed the message that we should continue with peaceful protests.

While Lena Nazaryan used her agency to downplay her gender, Maria Karapetyan and Zaruhi Batoyan—a disabled feminist activist, who is now the Minister of Labour and Social Affairs—emphasized their female agency to inspire and reach out to women:

> I was calling on women through the whole process to make speeches on stage. Women were always involved in important issues and I was happy when four of them agreed to speak ... because they actually had a say ... Yes, nobody stopped or hindered them, but as we know, not stopping doesn't mean supporting or encouraging. (Khojoyan 2018)

It was also Batoyan's idea to get people creating '15 minutes of noise' starting at 11 p.m. as part of the anti-government protests. In April 2018, Zaruhi Batoyan headed a disability-rights group in Armenia, called Disability Info, presenting the 15 minutes of noise as the 'sound of inclusiveness' in that anyone who could not go onto the streets could still protest and be part of the protests (Synovitz 2018). She also emphasized that gender mattered in these protests, as for many women it was Armenia's patriarchal society that was separating them from the protests: '*Many mothers and wives are expected to stay at home. They are not as free as men to protest*' (Synovitz 2018).

Kitchen utensils, utilized in confrontational actions are common 'instruments of protests' for women (Kramarae and Treichler 1985, p. 350). By creating an arena of noise, women were 'sounding the alarm' to attract public support against oppressive authorities. In the mid-1980s for example, Chilean women banged pots and pans to show their displeasure with the choice of dictator Augusto Pinochet as a sole nominee in a 1988 national referendum (West and Blumberg 1990, p. 27). The fact that everyday items such as pots and pans can become instruments of protests is an example of the way gendered processes, as well as women's and men's institutionalized roles get incorporated into social movement strategies (Kuumba 1990, p. 95). Pots and pans are utensils that are, in many cases, accessible because of (and symbolic of) the domestic gendered division of labour to which women have been relegated. The relationship between women, pots, and pans is part of a larger institutionalized system of gender inequality and separation of roles. While social movements pose challenges to established social structures, as legitimate political processes they also reflect aspects of these social structures. Thus, they are very much structured by and grounded in the concrete social context and subjective interpretations of both the movement and the wider society (Tarrow 1996). In other words, and in this instance, prescribed gender-role behaviour in a patriarchal society has provided strategic opportunities for protest.

While these are all expressions of the way in which gender interacts with social movement strategy, as instruments of protest they also helped reinforce the peaceful nature of the street protests, as Maria Karapetyan explained to the crowds during one rally:

> Women, we need you to reinforce the peaceful nature of the protests … We have been discussing the tools of peaceful disobedience today and Zara Batoyan has suggested this tactic. Tonight, when we get home, everybody take your pots and pans to your windows and ring Serzh Sargsyan's 'last call' at 11 p.m., for 15 minutes only, because we have to sleep peacefully after that. (Synovitz 2018)

Another telling moment, when prescribed gender roles interacted powerfully with social movement strategy was when mothers took to the streets with their prams. In Armenian society, motherly love and the instinctive desire to protect one's child are perceived as an essential cultural characteristic of femininity. Using motherhood as a resource to protest was very powerful. The mythical strength assigned to motherly love seems to legitimize any form of action. In the context of these protests, the power conferred to motherhood and the romanticization of its calling helped camouflaged inequalities and presented women as active citizens. This is particularly true in a society like Armenia's, which glorifies motherhood as a public role to serve national goals. As bearers of children, women are entwined with the biological and social reproduction of the national collective. Essentialist notions of women claim that through centuries of socialization women have become more equipped to resolve conflicts through peaceful means rather than through competition and violence. However, the transfer of maternal practice from the private lives of women to the public sphere of politics represents an empowering moment. Instead of disregarding the gendered construction of mothers' bodies tied to the private sphere, they engaged with their symbolic importance and reworked it in the context of the protests by transferring their support to the streets. This was possible to happen quite naturally, in the final analysis, *because the street was not hierarchic* (Karapetyan 2018 in Khojoyan 2018).

Most importantly, mothers are symbolic to the nation and, to some extent, have immunity in protests. If police would have touched mothers with their children in prams during the protests that would have brought shame on them individually, but also the state apparatus they represent. Noteworthy here is that Armenian socio-cultural relations are defined by concepts such as honour and shame[15]: *pativ* (best transliterated as a fusion of honour and dignity); *amot* (a sense of shame, especially public shame) (Kopalyan 2018). These concepts, inherently, are constructed, shaped and defined by cultural mores, which are superimposed upon the very behaviour of the individual (Kopalyan 2018). In a very masculine militarized culture, such as Armenia's, which is defined by honour and its distinct devotion to the family and extended family, the prospects of shame are unthinkable for 'real men'. Accordingly, one could reason that it would have been 'shame like' not to support the protest movement, as one female protester explained:

The Armenian community is based on shame, a shame-based culture… So shaming people, 'shame on you, you don't participate' worked…*amot* is the word. I think a lot of people were out there because it was shameful not to be out there…a lot of shame was directed against the police…

In short, when mothers walked onto the streets they declared themselves 'mothers' protesting for their children's future. This is an aspect of gendered protesting, taking action in a capacity beyond citizens desiring a better future. They actively and strategically invested their traditional gender identity with huge emotional and symbolic value, so as to encourage others to join them. In this way, they were able to claim a space in the protest movement.

As stressed in the previous section, many female activists believed that woman had played a significant, long-standing, historical role to affect social change in Armenian culture. Yet, from 2008, the main route to formal protest through institutionalized politics had been effectively closed to women. As explained in the previous section, in Armenian politics women have been consistently under-represented. Political life has been a 'man's space' dominated by patriarchal toughness and aggression. Since effective official routes have been closed off to women for so long, they have in their time learnt to use the street to express themselves, as one female activist explains:

For many, the revolution was short … but actually the revolution unfolded over several years… women were active for years on many issues… this time it was decentralized and successful pretty much because of our experience from protests in previous years. When the protests started in April, there were already lots of informal groups established, which were then easy to mobilize – feminist groups, opposition media, even green environmental groups …all of us had some experience in this, which helped us to self-organise and decentralise activities.

A queer feminist activist mentioned that she felt drawn to these protests not because she supported Nikol Pashinyan but because she felt she needed to support others with her years of experience of protesting:

Pashinyan gave his speech saying that tomorrow we start our decentralized movement. We're going to block the streets we're going to march everywhere. We're going to boycott everything ... I listened to this and felt really enthusiastic about it ... But I looked around and people looked tired ... I suddenly felt very sceptical about it ... so I spoke to my activist friends to decide what position we take ... we decided we won't fully support Pashinyan. We would only participate to show the regime that we oppose them and that we don't like the situation in this country ... it's difficult to explain but ... I felt the responsibility that I have to show them what to do as I've some experience. I've at least 10 years' experience [of protesting] and there were 17 year olds who'd never seen the inside of a prison. That's why, I thought I had to be there.

In a similar way, Gayane Abrahamyan, former journalist and founder of the 'Article 3' Club, a hub for public discussions for journalists, youth and NGO representatives, talked about her previous experience, and how she made sure protestors would get advice on what to do, if detained by the police:

…there were hundreds of activists detained and we tried to put them in touch with lawyers. Our main task was to spread the message about the hotline information on Facebook. But then it turned out to be less useful because detained people don't have a phone, it gets taken away from them. We started to spread information sheets on the streets about what to do when they get detained. We distributed them everywhere, just like 'in case you need it'.

In addition to previously acquired protest experience, established networks proved especially helpful for women organizing blockades. In April 2018, women were particularly active in organizing street blockades, as one female activist explained: '*Women were much more active than men…if women were closing-off a street and the police came, men would make themselves scarce, while the women would stay and prove their point*'. The blockades became the moments when women's bodies became sites of resistance. This quick and well organized activism was possible because of the pre-established networks, in particular among online groups. As another female activist mentioned; all she needed to do was post on Facebook (a group called *Aghchiknots* or 'girls' space') and a street blockade could be organized quite effectively.

Interestingly, on the streets women ever so often acted in their militarized prescribed gender roles as peacekeepers, using their bodies to keep violence away from the streets, as another female protester elaborates:

> I saw two men fighting and another group of men about to fight. You know, when Armenian men start to fight, other men gather around and try to understand what's going on. Normally women never intervene. When I saw what was going on, I went up to some women nearby asking 'what's going on'. I said let's stop them. Four or five women joined me. I started to talk to the men, saying what are you doing here, this can be seen as a provocation, that people are against each other, our main thing is that we are all together now. We got in-between the two [fighting], pushed them apart and said maybe it's business between the two of you but it's become business for all of us, so stop! And then they went in different directions. I felt brilliant because we were yelling at them and they were listening – usually women never interfere in this kind of thing.

This excerpt shows that while women appear in their prescribed role as peacekeepers and use their bodies on the streets to keep violence away, at the same time they are managing to rework this traditional role in support of the protest movement by standing up to men. These actions illustrate the fact that the gendered social contexts and the social positioning of women contributed significantly to the success of the protests. In this way, the strategic actions taken by women in support of the movement were clearly compatible with normative gender roles in Armenian society. In other words; the societal gender norms and roles influenced the tactics of women during the protests which they used to confront the larger power structures in Armenia.

Conclusions—What Next?

Through empirical analysis this study has examined how women's agency, together with the larger political context shaped anti-government protests in Armenia. While the primary aim of this protest movement was to topple the government, not to draw attention to gender equality issues gender as a factor in the strategy of the wider Armenian protest movement was none the less evident in interrelated ways. For the first time since the protests of 2008, women entered political spaces that were previously reserved for men. In doing so, some female leaders played the 'female card' by either making use of traditionally gendered 'instruments of protest' or by clearly highlighting existing gender inequalities during their speeches in order to appeal to other women. Others preferred to underplay gender differences so as to remove the 'male' connotations associated with public speaking. Through a bottom-up perspective, the empirical discussion has also shown that women used their respectability as mothers to challenge the government on the streets. This chapter has also stressed the role of female informal networks as mobilizing agents, in particular for organizing street blockades where women used their bodies as sites of resistance.

There are a number of research avenues that present themselves following this analysis. First and foremost, as argued at the beginning of this chapter social movements have the potential to reproduce or transform gender inequalities. How then has this active engagement of women during these street protests impacted the status of women in Armenian society and politics? In the December 2018 snap parliamentary election, women comprised 464 candidates or 32% of the total 1444 candidates nominated in the national lists by the eleven political forces competing in the election—nine parties and two alliances (WomenNet.am). 32 women were elected to the 7th convocation of the National Assembly. This brings the percentage of women MPs in the 132-member parliament to 24% (EVN Report 2019). Out of 20 newly appointed cabinet members (albeit interim), only two are women: Zaruhi Batoyan, Minister of Labour and Social Affairs, and Lilit Makunts, Minister of Culture. In other words, only 10% of the interim cabinet represents half of Armenia's population. This distribution of ministers appears to reinforce a gender-based segregation by excluding women from key positions of power.

A second research avenue relates to comparative analysis of women's activism. While in Ukraine and Georgia, for example, recent political developments have, it seems, negatively impacted on the growth of civil society, in Armenia both civil society and women's activism are still relatively strong. Civil society groups seem to have a greater influence than ever before as they are in constant dialogue with the government. This, however, is not to say that gender inequalities will be solved sooner than later. At the same time, the most recent concerning development is that women activists and human rights defenders have become targets of online and offline threats and attacks. In May 2019, the Sexual Assault Crisis Center (SACC) had to cancel an event for security reasons. This is an interesting post-protest dynamic that deserves more attention, as the nascent case of Armenia appears to show women's activism gaining more publicity in mass media outlets with a government largely comprised of activists in power.

Notes

1. In 2008, a flawed presidential election, followed by a brutal crackdown on protesters, saw Serzh Sargsyan come to power. A 2015 constitutional referendum transferred key powers to the prime minister allowing Sargsyan to remain in power at the end of his constitutionally limited two presidential terms of office by assuming the role of Prime Minister in the spring of 2018.
2. In 2018, Freedom House classified Armenia's political system as a 'semi-consolidated authoritarian' regime with a democracy score of 5.43 out of 7—with 7 being the least democratic (Freedom House 2018).
3. Transparency International (2018) ranks Armenia 105 out of 180 countries in terms of perceived corruption. Today, per official statistics, over one-third of Armenians live in poverty, while the country's population has dipped below three million due to a combination of emigration and declining birth rates (Statistical Committee of the Republic of Armenia 2019).
4. The literature on women and their importance for the Orange Revolution is growing (cf. Hrycak 2007, 2010; Nikolayenko and DeCasper 2018; Phillips 2014). In terms of the South Caucasus and the Georgian Rose Revolution, for example, the literature is still very sparse. Analysis has predominantly focused on women's activism and

political representation rather than the contribution of women to protest movements themselves.

5. As explained in the introduction to this edited volume (Note 2), following a constitutional referendum in February 2017, the unrecognized Nagorny Karabakh Republic was renamed the Republic of Artsakh. This chapter also uses the more common 'Nagorny Karabakh'.

6. Noteworthy here is that the First Armenian Republic of 1918–1920 was one of the first republics to give women the right to vote (Aslanyan 2010).

7. See, for example, the issue of domestic violence discussed in the Introduction to this edited volume, specifically Note 7.

8. The founder and Director of the Women's Resource Centre, Lara Aharonian, for example, has received numerous death threats, even after the 2018 protests.

9. When the protests became violent, women were turned away from the barricades by men 'for their own protection' (Phillips 2014, p. 416). Nonetheless, some women resisted and took part in the clashes with the police. Away from the barricades, women served in roles which were dangerous too, such as on-site doctors and nurses, volunteer medics, couriers of emergency medical supplies, on-the-scene journalists, advocates of wounded protesters in city hospitals and lawyers for arrested protesters (ibid.).

10. To date, there are only a few publications dealing with this subject, cf. Nikolayenko and DeCasper (2018).

11. Between 2011 and 2018, she was Development Director and coordinator of regional projects contributing to the establishment of professional networks at the Imagine Center for Conflict Transformation. During the protests she joined the Reject Serzh Movement. As a result of the December 2018 election, she became an elected member of the National Assembly from the national electoral list of the 'My Step' alliance of parties (Official Website of the National Assembly of the Republic of Armenia 2019).

12. Former journalist and founder of the 'Article 3' Club: a platform based on the principles of human rights, equality and equity and other democratic values. It is a hub for public discussions for journalists, youth and NGO representatives. Now Gayane Abrahamyan is a member of the National Assembly and the My Step Faction (EVN Report 2019).

13. Ashot Khurshudyan, an economist expert at Yerevan's International Centre of Human Development said that it was important to note

92   U. Ziemer

that although the public speeches were dominated by men, the extent of female participation in the protests was unprecedented: 'Women are the most neglected part of our society and these demonstrations are a signal not only to the system of governance but to the entire society which is alienated' (Khojoyan 2018).

14. Prior to the political protests of 2018, she worked as a journalist for *Hetq* and as the coordinator for election programmes at the Armenian branch of Transparency International. As a board member of the Civil Contract Party, she ran under the Way Out Alliance (Yelk) during the 2017 parliamentary election and was elected off the Yelk national list. Since January 15, 2019, she is one of the three serving Vice Parliamentary Speakers (along with Alen Simonyan and Vahe Enfiajyan) and a member of the Civil Contract Party (Official Website of the National Assembly of the Republic of Armenia 2019).

15. There are more than just the two concepts that define Armenian socio-cultural relations. Kopalyan (2018) usefully narrowed down the many cultural concepts to four, so to allow parsimony in his analysis of corruption and political culture in Armenia. His analysis not only includes *pativ* and *amot*, but also; *xatr* (an obligatory favour stipulated in familial and close social relations), and *hargank* (respect).

References

Al-Ali, Nadje. 2012. "Gendering the Arab Spring." *Middle East Journal of Culture and Communication* 5 (1): 26–31. https://doi.org/10.1163/187398612X624346.

Alvarez, Sonia E. 1990. *Engendering Democracy in Brazil: Women's Movements in Transition Politics*. Princeton, NJ: Princeton University Press.

Ashwin, Sarah. ed. 2000. *Gender, State, and Society in Soviet and Post-Soviet Russia*. London: Routledge.

Aslanyan, Svetlana A. 2010. "Women's Rights in Armenia." *Social Watch: Poverty Eradication and Gender Justice*. http://www.socialwatch.org/node/11600.

Badashvili, Medea. 2013. "Transformation to Democracy: The Struggles of Georgian Women." In *Postcommunism from Within: Social Justice, Mobilization, and Hegemony*, edited by Jan Kubik and Amy Linch, 211–228. New York: New York University Press.

Beukian, Sevan. 2014. "Motherhood as Armenianness: Expressions of Femininity in the Making of Armenian National Identity." *Studies in Ethnicity and Nationalism* 14 (2) (October): 247–269. https://doi.org/10.1111/sena.12092.

Bordo, Susan. [1993] 2003. *Unbearable Weight: Feminism, Western Culture, and the Body*. Berkeley, CA: University of California Press.

Broers, Laurence. 2018. "The South Caucasus: Fracture Without End?" In *Russia Abroad: Driving Regional Fracture in Post-Communist Eurasia and Beyond*, edited by Anna Ohanian, 81–102. Washington, DC: Georgetown University Press.

———. 2019. *Armenia and Azerbaijan: Anatomy of a Rivalry*. Edinburgh: Edinburgh University Press.

Buckley, Mary. 1989. *Women and Ideology in the Soviet Union*. Ann Arbor, MI: University of Michigan Press.

Butler, Judith. 1990. *Gender Trouble: Feminism and the Subversion of Identity*. New York: Routledge.

Caprioli, Mary. 2000. "Gendered Conflict." *Journal of Peace Research* 37 (1) (January): 51–68. https://doi.org/10.1177/0022343300037001003.

———. 2005. "Primed for Violence: The Role of Gender Inequality in Predicting Internal Conflict." *International Studies Quarterly* 49 (2) (June): 161–178.

Chkheidze, Ketevan. 2017. "Women's Political Representation in Post-Soviet Georgia." In *Gender in Georgia: Feminist Perspectives on Culture, Nation, and History in the South Caucasus*, edited by Maia Barkaia and Alison Waterston, 78–94. New York and Oxford: Berghahn Books.

Chuchryk, Patricia M. 2018. "From Dictatorship to Democracy: The Women's Movement in Chile." In *The Women's Movement in Latin America*, edited by Jane Jaquette, 65–107. London: Routledge.

Corrin, Chris. 1992. *Superwomen and the Double Burden: Women's Experience of Change in Central and Eastern Europe and the Former Soviet Union*. New York: Scarlet Press.

Dean, Jonathan, and Kristin Aune. 2015. "Feminism Resurgent? Mapping Contemporary Feminist Activisms in Europe." *Social Movement Studies* 14 (4) (November): 375–395. https://doi.org/10.1080/14742837.2015.1077112.

de Waal, Thomas. 2013. *Black Garden: Armenia and Azerbaijan Through Peace and War, 10th Year Anniversary Edition*. New York: New York University Press.

Eckel, Mike. 2018. "A 'Color Revolution' in Armenia? Mass Protests Echo Previous Post-Soviet Upheavals." *Radio Free Europe/Radio Liberty.* April 24. https://www.rferl.org/a/armenia-mass-protests-echo-previous-post-soviet-upheavals-colored-revolutions/29189559.html.

Einwohner, Rachel L., Jocelyn A. Hollander, and Tosko Olson. 2000. "Engendering Social Movements: Cultural Images and Movement Dynamics." *Gender & Society* 14 (5) (October): 679–699. https://doi.org/10.1177/089124300014005006.

EVN Report. 2019. *New Armenia's Parliamentarians.* January 13. https://www.evnreport.com/politics/new-armenia-s-parliamentarians.

Foucault, Michel. 1982. "Afterword: The Subject and Power." In *Michel Foucault: Beyond Structuralism and Hermeneutics*, edited by Hubert L. Dreyfus and Paul Rainbow, 208–226. London: The Harvester Press.

Funk, Nanette, and Magda Mueller, eds. 1993. *Gender Politics and Post-Communism: Reflections from Eastern Europe and the Former Soviet Union.* London: Routledge.

Galligan, Yvonne, Sara Clavero, and Marina Calloni, eds. 2007. *Gender Politics and Democracy in Post-socialist Europe.* Leverkusen, Opladen: Barbara Budrich Publisher.

Ghazaryan, Karine. 2018. "Lena Nazaryan: Living Examples of Power Are the Shortest Way Towards Equality." *Regional Post Caucasus #2.*

Gradskova, Yulia, and Ildikó A. Morell, eds. 2018. *Gendering Postsocialism: Old Legacies and New Hierarchies.* London: Routledge.

Green, Andrew T., and Richard D. Kohl. 2007. "Challenges of Evaluating Democracy Assistance: Perspectives from the Donor Side." *Democratization* 14 (1) (May): 151–165. https://doi.org/10.1080/13510340601024363.

Hafez, Sherine. 2014. "The Revolution Shall Not Pass Through Women's Bodies: Egypt, Uprising and Gender Politics." *The Journal of North African Studies* 19 (2) (March): 172–185. https://doi.org/10.1080/13629387.2013.879710.

Harding, Sandra. 2011. "Feminist Standpoints." In *Handbook of Feminist Research: Theory and Praxis*, edited by Sharlene Nagy Hesse-Biber, 46–64. London: Sage.

Hasratyan, Jemma, Lilit Zakaryan, Tamara Hovnatanyan, and Gayane Armaghanova. 2012. Women's Political Participation in Parliamentary Elections in 2012. Association of Women with University Education and OSCE Office, Yerevan. https://www.osce.org/yerevan/116089.

Herrnson, Paul S., J. Celeste Lay, and Atiya Kai Stokes. 2003. "Women Running 'as Women': Candidate Gender, Campaign Issues, and Voter-Targeting Strategies." *The Journal of Politics* 65 (1) (February): 244–255. https://doi.org/10.1111/1468-2508.t01-1-00013.

Hrycak, Alexandra. 2007. "Gender and the Orange Revolution." *Journal of Communist Studies and Transition Politics* 23 (1) (March): 152–179. https://doi.org/10.1080/13523270701194987.

———. 2010. "Orange Harvest? Women's Activism and Civil Society in Ukraine, Belarus and Russia Since 2004." *Canadian-American Slavic Studies* 44 (1–2) (January): 151–177. https://doi.org/10.1163/2210023910X512840.

Hudson, Valerie M. 2010. "Sex, War, and Peace: Rank, and Winter on Rank." *Political Psychology* 31 (1) (February): 33–39. https://www.jstor.org/stable/25655443.

Hudson, Valerie M., Mary Caprioli, Bonnie Ballif-Spanvill, Rose McDermott, and Chad F. Emmett. 2009. "The Heart of the Matter: The Security of Women and the Security of States." *International Security* 33 (3) (May): 7–45. https://doi.org/10.1162/isec.2009.33.3.7.

Ishkanian, Armine. 2003. "Importing Civil Society? The Emergence of Armenia's NGO Sector and the Impact of Western Aid on Its Development." *Armenian Forum: A Journal of Contemporary Affairs* 3 (1): 7–36.

———. 2008. *Democracy Building and Civil Society in Post-Soviet Armenia*. London: Routledge.

———. 2018. "Armenia's Unfinished Revolution." *Current History* 117 (801): 271–276. http://www.currenthistory.com/Article.php?ID=1518.

Jakeli, Tamar. 2018. "Beyond 'Co-Opted NGOs' and 'Radical Grassroots Movements': Women's Mobilization in Georgia." *Women's Studies International Forum* 69 (July–August): 85–91. https://doi.org/10.1016/j.wsif.2018.05.009.

Jaquette, Jane S. 1994. *The Women's Movement in Latin America: Participation and Democracy*. New York: Routledge.

Kabeer, Naila. 1999. "Resources, Agency, Achievements: Reflections on the Measurement of Women's Empowerment." *Development and Change* 30 (3) (December): 435–464. https://doi.org/10.1111/1467-7660.00125.

Kadry, Ahmed. 2015. Gender and Tahrir Square: Contesting the State and Imagining a New Nation. *Journal for Cultural Research* 19 (2): 199–206. https://doi.org/10.1080/14797585.2014.982922.

Khachatryan, Karen, Anna Dreber, Emma von Essen, and Eva Ranehill. 2015. "Gender and Preferences at a Young Age: Evidence from Armenia." *Journal of Economic Behavior and Organization* 118 (October): 318–332.

Khalil, Andrea (ed.). 2016. *Gender, Women and the Arab Spring*. London: Routledge.

Khojoyan, Sara. 2018. "Where Are the Women in Armenia's Revolution? Global Caucasus Voices." *Global Voice Caucasus*, May 17. https://iwpr.net/global-voices/where-are-women-armenias-revolution.

Khudoyan, Knar. 2019. "To Change the System from Within or Without—The Dilemma for Feminists in 'New Armenia'." *OC Media*, January 23. https://medium.com/@oc.media.social/to-change-the-system-from-within-or-without-the-dilemma-for-feminists-in-new-armenia-8e2e4d74629c.

Kopalyan, Nerses. 2018. "Between Honor and Shame: Understanding Corruption in Armenia's Political Culture." *EVN Report*, March 9. https://www.evnreport.com/raw-unfiltered/between-honor-and-shame-understanding-corruption-in-armenia-s-political-culture.

Kostiuchenko, Tetiana, Tamara Martsenyuk, and Svitlana Oksamytna. 2015. "Women Politicians and Parliamentary Elections in Ukraine and Georgia in 2012." *East/West: Journal of Ukrainian Studies* 2 (2): 83–110. http://dx.doi.org/10.21226/T2X30R.

Kramarae, Cheris, and Paula A. Treichler. 1985. *A Feminist Dictionary*. New York: Pandora.

Kuumba, Bahati M. 1990. *Gender and Social Movements*. Oxford: Rowman Altamira.

Lorber, Judith. 2000. "Using Gender to Undo Gender: A Feminist Degendering Movement." *Feminist Theory* 1 (1): 79–95. https://doi.org/10.1177/14647000022229074.

Mama, Amina. 1998. "Khaki in the Family: Gender Discourses and Militarism in Nigeria." *African Studies Review* 41 (2) (September): 1–18. https://doi.org/10.2307/524824.

Manasyan, Nvard. 2018. "A Story About Armenian Emancipation: The Long Way to the Dawning." *Heinrich Boell Stiftung*. http://feminism-boell.org/en/2018/12/27/story-about-armenian-emancipation-long-way-dawning?fbclid=IwAR07dyFGUSsN3fHWC0jAC-Ql7NIEZnLTyhO9EVBKmWDw-JE26CRZuDrFbSMU.

Martin, Ashley E., and Katherine W. Phillips. 2017. "What 'Blindness' to Gender Differences Helps Women See and Do: Implications for Confidence, Agency, and Action in Male-Dominated Environments." *Organizational Behavior and Human Decision Processes* 142 (September): 28–44. https://doi.org/10.1016/j.obhdp.2017.07.004.

McNay, Lois. 2016. "Agency." In *The Oxford Handbook of Feminist Theory*, edited by Lisa Disch and Mary Hawkesworth, 39–60. Oxford: Oxford University Press.

Mhajne, Anwar, and Crystal Whetstone. 2018. "The Use of Political Motherhood in Egypt's Arab Spring Uprising and Aftermath." *International Feminist Journal of Politics* 20 (1): 54–68. https://doi.org/10.1080/1461674 2.2017.1371624.

Mijatovic, Dunja. 2019. "Report on Armenia." *The Commissioner of Human Rights of the Council of Europe.* https://www.coe.int/en/web/commissioner/-/report-on-armenia-recommends-measures-to-improve-women-s-rights-protection-of-disadvantaged-or-vulnerable-groups-and-establishing-accountability-for-p.

Mkrtchian, Anush. 2018. "Armenia Has Highest Female Unemployment Rate among Post-Soviet Countries." *Radio Free Liberty/Radio Liberty.* https://www.azatutyun.am/a/29089151.html.

Moghadam, Valentine M. 2017. "Explaining Divergent Outcomes of the Arab Spring: The Significance of Gender and Women's Mobilizations." *Politics, Groups, and Identities* 6 (4): 666–681. https://doi.org/10.1080/21565503.2 016.1256824.

Molyneux, Maxine. 1998. "Analysing Women's Movements." *Development and Change* 29 (2) (April): 219–245. https://doi.org/10.1111/1467-7660. 00077.

Mutschler, Max M., and Marius Bales. 2018. "Global Militarization Index 2018." *BICC, Bonn International Center for Conversion.* https://www.bicc. de/publications/publicationpage/publication/global-militarization-index-2018-833/.

National Statistical Service of the Republic of Armenia. 2012. *Women and Men in Armenia: A Statistical Booklet.* https://www.armstat.am/file/article/gender_2012.pdf.

Nikolayenko, Olena, and Maria DeCasper. 2018. "Why Women Protest: Insights from Ukraine's EuroMaidan." *Slavic Review* 77 (3) (Fall): 726–751. https://doi.org/10.1017/slr.2018.207.

Noonan, Rita K. 1995. "Women Against the State: Political Opportunities and Collective Action Frames in Chile's Transition to Democracy." *Sociological Forum* 10 (1) (March): 81–111.

Official Website of the National Assembly of Republic of Armenia. 2019. http://www.parliament.am/deputies.php?sel=details&ID=1280&lang=eng.

Ohanyan, Anna. 2009. "State-Society Nexus and Gender: Armenian Women in Postcommunist Context." In *Women and Politics Around the World: A Comparative History and Survey*, vol. 2, edited by Joyce Gelb and Marian Lief Palley, 231–245. Oxford: ABC CLIO.

Ohanyan, Anna. 2018. Armenia's Democratic Dreams. *Foreign Policy*, November 7. https://foreignpolicy.com/2018/11/07/armenias-democratic-dreams/?fbclid=IwAR3mpn1tOwdCfDLNdAtWwXCuUm7uECuz7PwcfV0BNzdW36_4fSiNLuAF4FY.

Onuch, Olga, and Tamara Martsenyuk. 2014. "Mothers and Daughters of the Maidan: Gender, Repertoires of Violence, and the Division of Labour in Ukrainian Protests." *Social, Health, and Communication Studies Journal* 1 (1): 105–126.

Phillips, Sarah D. 2014. "The Women's Squad in Ukraine's Protests: Feminism, Nationalism, and Militarism on the Maidan." *American Ethnologist* 41 (3) (August): 414–426. https://doi.org/10.1111/amet.12093.

Popkova, Ludmila. 2004. "Women's Political Activism in Russia: The Case of Samara." In *Post-Soviet Women Encountering Transition: Nation Building, Economic Survival and Civic Activism*, edited by Kathleen Kuehnast and Carol Nechemias, 172–194. London: The Johns Hopkins University Press.

Roach, Anna B. 2018. "Heard but Not Seen: How Women Became the Unrecognised Architects of the Velvet Revolution." *OC Media.* https://oc-media.org/analysis-heard-but-not-seen-how-women-became-the-unrecognised-architects-of-the-velvet-revolution/.

Roberts, Sean, and Ulrike Ziemer. 2018. "Explaining the Pattern of Russian Authoritarian Diffusion in Armenia." *East European Politics* 34 (2): 152–172. https://doi.org/10.1080/21599165.2018.1457525.

Rueschemeyer, Marilyn. 2016. *Women in the Politics of Postcommunist Eastern Europe*. London: Routledge.

Sabedashvili, Tamuna. 2007. "Gender and Democratization: The Case of Georgia." *Heinrich Boell Stiftung.* http://bssupgrade.oceaninfo.ru/library/files/41271.pdf.

Sadiqi, Fatima, ed. 2016. *Women's Movements in Post-"Arab Spring" North Africa*. London: Springer.

Schofield, Juliet, Steven Schoofs, and Hema Kotecha. 2010. "Building Inclusive Governance: Women's Political Participation in Conflict-Affected Georgia." *IFP Gender Cluster: Country Case Study: Georgia—Initiative for Peace Building, International Alert.* https://s3.amazonaws.com/academia.edu.documents/46802727/Women_Participation_in_Georgia_Nov_2010.pdf?AWSAccessKeyId=AKIAIWOWYYG-Z2Y53UL3A&Expires=1556464576&Signature=zLm3i3siwe4%2F-242hSiuEV4LgyfY%3D&response-content-disposition=inline%3B%20filename%3DBuilding_Inclusive_Governance_Womens_Pol.pdf.

Shahnazarian, Gohar. 2019. "Shahnazaryan Illuminated Women's Role in Velvet Revolution and Aftermath in Glendale Talk." *The Armenian Mirror-Spectator,* April 18. https://mirrorspectator.com/2019/04/18/shahnazaryan-illuminated-womens-role-in-velvet-revolution-and-aftermath-in-glendale-talk/?fbclid=IwAR0d2rYJcPzFSNHha-BJjR1HNyBTKwh3wu-JNVdeWcTZ4ct0B3tgnlzHVfOs.

Shahnazarian, Gohar, Zaruhi Aznauryn, and Lusine Saghumyan. 2016. *Representation and Participation of Women in the Political Parties and Political Initiatives in Armenia: Gender Analyses.* Yerevan: Women's Resource Centre.

Shahnazarian, Nona, and Ulrike Ziemer. 2012. "Young Soldiers' Tales of War in Nagorno Karabakh." *Europe-Asia Studies* 64 (9): 1667–1683. https://doi.org/10.1080/09668136.2012.718423.

———. 2014. "Emotions, Loss and Change: Armenian Women and Post-socialist Transformations in Nagorny Karabakh." *Caucasus Survey* 2(1–2): 27–40. https://doi.org/10.1080/23761199.2014.11417298.

———. 2018. "Women Confronting Death: War Widows' Experiences in the South Caucasus." *Journal of International Women's Studies* 19(2): 29–43. http://vc.bridgew.edu/jiws/vol19/iss2/3.

Sharoni, Simona. 1995. *Gender and the Israeli-Palestinian Conflict: The Politics of Women's Resistance.* New York: Syracuse University Press.

Statistical Committee of the Republic of Armenia. 2019. "Socio-Economic Situation of RA, January–February 2019." https://www.armstat.am/en/.

Synovitz, Ron. 2018. "Armenian Women Raise a Glamor for Sarkisian's 'Last Call'." *Radio Free Europe/Radio Liberty,* April 23. https://www.rferl.org/a/armenia-women-raise-clamor-for-sarkisians-last-call-/29187558.html.

Tarrow, Sidney. 1996. "States and Opportunities: The Political Structuring of Social Movements." In *Comparative Perspectives on Social Movements: Political Opportunities, Mobilizing Structures, and Cultural Framings,* edited by Doug McAdam, John D. McCarthy, and Mayer N. Zald, 41–61. New York: Cambridge University Press.

Tohidi, Nayereh. 2004. "Women, Civil Society, and NGOs in Post-Soviet Azerbaijan." *International Journal Not-for-Profit Law* 7 (1) (November): 36–41.

Torres, Nicole. 2018. "Women Benefit When They Downplay Gender." *Harvard Business Review*, July–August. https://hbr.org/2018/07/women-benefit-when-they-downplay-gender.

Transparency International. 2018. "Armenia." https://www.transparency.org/country/ARM.

West, Guida, and Rhoda L. Blumberg. 1990. *Women and Social Protest.* Oxford: Oxford University Press.

World Bank. 2018. "Proportion Seats Held of Women in National Parliaments." https://data.worldbank.org/indicator/SG.GEN.PARL.ZS.

Zemlinskaya, Yulia. 2010. "Social Movements Through the Gender Lens." *Sociology Compass* 4 (8) (August): 628–641. https://doi.org/10.1111/j.1751-9020.2010.00301.x.

Zhurzhenko, Tatiana. 2001. "Free Market Ideology and New Women's Identities in Post-socialist Ukraine." *European Journal of Women's Studies* 8 (1): 29–49. https://doi.org/10.1177/135050680100800103.

Ziemer, Ulrike. 2011. *Ethnic Belonging, Gender, and Cultural Practices: Youth Identities in Contemporary Russia.* Stuttgart: ibidem-Verlag.

———. 2018. "'The Waiting and Not Knowing Can Be Agonizing': Tracing the Power of Emotions in a Prolonged Conflict in the South Caucasus." *International Feminist Journal of Politics* 20 (3): 331–349. https://doi.org/10.1080/14616742.2018.1480900.

Part II
Experiencing War and Displacement

5

Between Love, Pain and Identity: Armenian Women After World War I

Anna Aleksanyan

In April 1920, a women's magazine in the USA, *The American Woman,* published an article 'Salvaging the Womanhood of Armenia' (Miller 1920, pp. 16–17). Miller's article was unique at the time since it addressed the emotions and feelings of Armenian women who had been abducted and forced to marry a Turkish husband as part of the genocidal campaigns in 1915–1920, but were eventually discovered by international rescue organizations. This article gives a rare glimpse into the emotional accounts of young Armenian women who told rescue workers about their experiences.

> They laid me down to kill me with a knife, and I fainted. When I recovered, I was surrounded by Turkish officers who had been trying to wake me up. I was naked. The officers dressed me in officers' clothes. They told me that I had been found on the ice and that half my body had been in the water. I had been almost frozen.

A. Aleksanyan (✉)
Clark University, Worcester, MA, USA

© The Author(s) 2020

U. Ziemer (ed.), *Women's Everyday Lives in War and Peace in the South Caucasus,*
https://doi.org/10.1007/978-3-030-25517-6_5

During the deportation from Bitlis in 1915, this Armenian woman was separated from her mother. She was taken to Diarbekir, where a pasha kept her in his house for eight days, then she was forcibly married to a sub-governor. She continued: *'For four years, I was his wife. I had a child. He is now two years of age'*. But the most tragic part of her narrative was that she confessed to one of the matrons of the rescue house. *'There is now a great wound in my heart. I see that I love my boy more than I had expected. I miss him very much. But I'll bear it because any Armenian woman loves her nation more than a son born of Turkish blood'*.[1] After the confession, the matron put her arms around her and held her until she had cried herself to sleep (Miller 1920, p. 16).

There are no exact totals for the women and children kidnapped by Muslim families. Some sources estimate approximately 200,000 (Akçam 2006, p. 199). After, and even during, the genocide, the Armenian community acknowledged the specificity of the experiences of these Armenian women (Derderian 2005, p. 5). Therefore, the rescue and reintegration of these women became a very important part of the national rebuilding process. Yet the emotions and feelings of the Armenian women who had been rescued were mostly ignored and only a very few Armenian women activists and writers spoke about the consequent feelings and emotions (Yesayan 1919; Galemkerian 1952).

Four years after Miller's article was published, an American doctor, Dr. Mabel E. Elliott, who went to Istanbul in 1920 as a representative of Near East Relief and worked at the Rescue Home in Scutari where Miller had worked, published a book in 1924, commenting on four years of her travels and work in the Near East. According to Elliott, before her arrival none of the rescued girls and women had ever discussed their experiences during the war. She was the person in the house to whom the girls confessed and shared their stories for the first time, and she interviewed them because it was necessary for the Near East Relief recordings (Elliott 1924, p. 21). Like Miller in his article, Elliott (1924) documents stories of pain, suffering and torn feelings. Some women were suffering because they had had children by Muslim men and had left them when they escaped or were rescued; some were suffering because they had been pregnant when they were rescued and did not want to have the child, as Elliot (1924, pp. 24–25) writes:

Her manner was bold, almost callous, and one could not wonder at it, remembering that she had been only twelve years old when the Kurds took her. For a year she had lived through a phantasmagoria of adventure, always captured, always escaping. She had been wounded, beaten, hunted through hills and underbrush. In the end, the Vali, the governor of the province, took her. He and his family had been kind to her. I told her that in a few months she would be a mother. With a laugh like a snarl, she said that she would send it to its father. 'The Vali's wife loved me like a mother, and he loved me like a lover ... and I love nobody. What did they leave me to love when they killed the last of my family?'

This part of Armenian history focusing on women's emotional journeys and often contradictory feelings has long been generally ignored in Armenian historiography, mainly because traditional historians did not focus on a gendered analysis of the genocide. This shortcoming was first addressed by Sanasarian (1989) and Derderian (2005), who were among the first scholars to see the genocide through a gender lens. During the last decade, the literature on gender-specific aspects of the Armenian genocide has been growing (Sarafian 2001; Tachjian 2009, 2014; Bjørnlund 2009; Watenpaugh 2010; Üngör 2012; Ekmekçioğlu 2013, 2016; Holslag 2015; Akçam 2016; Jinks 2018). But there is still a pressing need to research and explore women's emotions and contradictory feelings after their rescue from Muslim marriages. Therefore, the aim of this chapter is to analyse the complex choices of the women who were forcibly married as part of the genocide campaigns.

The Fate of Women and Girls During the Genocide

The Armenian genocide had a clear gender dimension. Men were mostly killed, whereas women were often abducted. During 1915–1916, there was a widespread and systematic abduction of Armenian women to serve as slaves, concubines and wives of Muslim men of the Empire and in some cases beyond (Kévorkian and Tachjian 2006, p. 89). Most of these women became concubines of their Muslim owners.

These women were used not only for sexual purposes, but forced to perform hard physical work and household duties, take care of family and work for and instead of everyone else. They would often become the victims of both their owners and his wives, who would periodically abuse, humiliate and torture them.

Forced marriages were organized and ordered by the central government (Akçam 2012, pp. 287–339) and were part of the genocide programme, serving two main purposes: first, to assimilate Armenian women into Turkish culture; and, second, to obtain more property. After taking an Armenian bride, a Muslim man would become the legal owner of her father's or husband's property (Akçam 2016, p. 240). Thus, Turkish officers and officials were compelling girls and women from wealthy and prominent Armenian families to marry them (Bryce and Toynbee 2000, p. 63), while less wealthy men would try at least to get a healthy and beautiful Armenian wife 'for free'. According to Muslim religious law, a groom normally has to pay a sum of money to his prospective bride's father. The Danish missionary, M. Jacobsen, who was in the town of Mush during the genocide, wrote in her memoirs:

> Yesterday [June 1915] Vardapetyan's beautiful 12-year-old daughter Rebecca came to the hospital. She had been captured by a Turk, who came with her to demand back from the doctor all that her father had given him. How terrible it is to think of the poor young girl with a crude man, who has killed her father, and whom she must accompany back and live with in her parent's beautiful building. (Jacobsen 1979, p. 82)

After a forced marriage, women were coerced into denouncing Christianity and, on becoming Muslims, were given new names. They no longer had the right to speak Armenian, and in any case had no one to talk to in the language, having mostly been taken far from their birthplace. After the marriage, they normally could not leave the house without an escort. These women had to forget everything that would remind them of their Armenian past. Some had with them children from their pre-genocide marriages. Daughters could stay with their mother, share her fate (hence, growing up as a Muslim) and take a new, Turkish name. Upon maturity, she would marry someone chosen by her new 'father'. For males, the scenario was generally different; mothers could not persuade their Muslim husbands to keep the boys; these children were either murdered or deported, or given to a Turkish orphanage. Nonetheless, some of these girls or women found husbands who had fallen in love with them and treated them with respect. These men gave them all the comfort and conditions of normal life, except for their Armenianness.

The Rescue of Armenian Women in Urfa

At the end of World War I, many Armenian and international organizations, foreign missions and individuals focused on helping these women, searching for survivors, saving them from servitude or slavery and restoring their Armenian identity. The rescue efforts became known as the 'Mission of Salvation' or 'Liberation Mission'. But it was not easy to save Armenian women who had been adopted by or married to Muslim men (Turks, Kurds, Arabs, Circassians, etc.) and had converted to Islam. They were dispersed across the entire Ottoman Empire and each region had its own difficulties and challenges which, conditioned by both political and interethnic relations in the region, were different every day. For example, after the allied troops occupied Istanbul in late 1918, Armenian representatives, with the help of British authorities and the police, were able to negotiate with Turkish families the release and return of Armenian women or girls whom they were hiding in their households.

In the Syrian region where many Armenians had been deported, however, the situation was different. In the country's desert regions most of the Armenian women and orphaned girls had been taken in by Arab families or Bedouin tribes. There, they were not always seen as slaves or free labour; some of them became beloved daughters or wives in these families. Moreover, after the war when rescue organizations started their negotiations, the 'patrons' 'fathers' or 'husbands' of these women or girls often did not want to return them. Thus, they hid the identity and existence of the women and orphans from the Armenian rescuers, erasing all traces of them within the tribes of Mesopotamian and moving them from one place to another. Therefore, for rescue organizations without any precise records, searches of this kind could sometimes take months or years, often without any result (Tcholakian 2001, p. 53).

It should be noted that these Armenian rescue groups were formed in the spring of 1918, well before the end of the First World War. The first group, called the 'Armenian Expeditionary Rescue Group' was led by Levon Yotnakhparian, an Armenian soldier originally from Urfa who had served in the Fourth Ottoman Army in Damascus. It enjoyed the support of the famous Arab leader Emir Faysal (who had struggled for the liberation of Syria from the Turks) and the British General Staff (Parian and Jinbashian 2012, pp. 49–55). Most of the soldiers of this Rescue Group were originally from Urfa (Kévorkian 2011, p. 758). The Young Turk leaders; flight to Turkey on November 1, 1918, gave a new start to the rescue activities. In November 1918, the members of the Egyptian-Armenian National Relief Committee of AGBU, the Armenian National Union and the United Orphan-caring Union formed a special committee. All its members were volunteers who considered it a duty to the Armenian nation. The rescue operations were not easy and were even more complicated when it came to women who had married Muslim men. '*The Turks were not in a hurry to give up the Armenians in their houses. Only if they were sick and ailing were they sent out on to the street*', wrote Jakob Künzler,[2] the Deutsche Orient-Mission's doctor in Urfa (Künzler 2007, p. 89), who stayed in the city with his family during the war and witnessed the genocidal events and their aftermath.

It should be mentioned that Urfa is a special case for studying the situation of Armenian women both during the genocide and in its aftermath. This city was one of the rare places where Armenian women in 1915 had actively taken part in armed resistance (Sahakian 1954, pp. 916–928). This ancient city, also known as Edessa, was located between Mesopotamia and Asia Minor, and was inhabited by a very diverse population. The Armenians had arrived in the region in the eleventh century and, according to Turkish official sources, on the eve of the First World War approximately 30,000 Armenians were living in Urfa and its surroundings. The Armenian quarter was in the northern part of the city, most of which rose up the slopes of Mount Telfedor. Armenians were affluent in the city because they dominated its commercial activity (Kévorkian 2011, p. 613).

During the genocide, the city and its surroundings became a transit point through which Armenian deportees from different areas had to pass (Kévorkian 2011, p. 308). Before receiving their own deportation orders, the Armenians of Urfa witnessed the miserable conditions of their compatriots, who were exhausted, hungry, beaten, robbed and raped (Kévorkian 2011, p. 614). Although by the end of August most of the Armenian nobles in the city had already been arrested and killed, those who remained organized a defensive rising in September–October of 1915. Women were very active during this resistance, because they knew what awaited them; hence, they preferred to fight next to their men and die with honour (Donoyan 1991, pp. 93–105). One of them was Yeghizabet Yotneghbarian, the wife of the resistance leader.[3] With the women fighters, she fought until she was captured by Turkish soldiers after the fall of the defence.

When the Armenian resistance was defeated, and the Armenian quarter was demolished, those who were not killed were faced with immediate deportation. Rather than be deported, women preferred to commit suicide or stay and hide in the city as the wives, concubines, maids or just slaves of Muslims (Künzler 2007, pp. 50–59). Almost immediately, some Armenian women and children asked for domestic shelter with Doctor Künzler and Karen Jeppe, the Danish missionary, who was also working for the German Orient Mission. Both of them accepted more than 50 women and children, telling the Turkish government that they needed their assistance. However, the Turkish government did not agree, but forced these women and children to join the deportees. From all of them, Jeppe could save only one Armenian woman, Lucia Nartanian.[4]

After the armistice in 1918, when the news of rescue operations reached Urfa, these Armenian women began to run away from their Muslim husbands and masters and asked Künzler and his wife for shelter and protection. At the time, Jeppe had already left the city, and Künzler's family was the only option open to them:

A woman fled to us, leaving behind her infant with the Turks. Then the father came with the children and asked that we see to it that the runaway mother continued to nurse the child. The mother would resist because she knew that the child would ultimately belong to the Turks. (Künzler 2007, p. 89)

According to records by the Armenian patriarchate, 394 Armenian survivors had managed to return to their homes in Urfa early by 1919 (Kévorkian 2011, p. 748), a number which grew to about 6000 following the arrival of survivors from other regions (Minasian 2015, p. 721). The Armenian National Union was formed in Urfa, which immediately started on a mission to rescue women and girls. It was not easy to provide appropriate supplies for the rescued orphans and women, given the financial difficulties of the returned Armenians at first. Turkish families were afraid to show resistance to the return of Armenian women and therefore tried to hide them from outside observation and keep them isolated from any information. Nonetheless, those Armenian women who openly had avoided deportation and lived in other parts of Urfa were able to provide information about Turkish households hiding Armenian women and thus helped to rescue them. Among these women was Lucia Yessayan (Ketendjian) who worked closely with the Armenian rescue group and supported the rescue mission (Sahakian 1954, p. 954).

In March 1919, the American mission also returned to Urfa; it had been in the city since 1890 but had had to leave it because of the war (*The New Near East*, p. 13). Upon arrival, Mary Caroline Holmes (1923, p. 29), the American representative of Near East Relief in Urfa, wrote the following in her diary:

Immediately it was known that American relief workers were in Urfa, women and girls from [Turkish] homes, as well as those who had been camping in ruined houses, began to descend upon us. And the women and girls from Turkish, Arab and Kurdish harems we received and cared for, many with children who had to be left with their Muslim fathers.

5 Between Love, Pain and Identity ...   111

After the armistice people knew that the war was over, and the Party of Union and Progress had lost its power, but there were no Allied forces around to keep peace in the city and prevent ethnic clashes. Armenians were the most vulnerable in this situation because the Armenian quarter after the deportation was inhabited by Turkish and Kurdish refugees who did not want the Armenians back. As they began to return, the risk of clashes started to rise. The other source of conflict was the work of the rescue groups who were trying to find Armenian women and orphans in Muslim households and rehabilitate them. The rescue work was very dangerous both for Armenians and foreigners. The Turks planned to assassinate Doctor Künzler and Karekin Turekian a member of the Armenian National Union, who helped to shelter the rescued. According to the latter, Turks had planned these assassinations because they did not want to give up their Armenian wives (Künzler 2007, p. 99).

In the first months, the rescued women and orphans in Urfa all stayed together in the building which belonged to the American Mission, but in due course the need arose to separate the women and girls from the children. Most of these women and girls needed special medical care as a result of the severe psychological trauma they had sustained from physical and sexual abuse. With the help of the Armenian General Benevolent Union (AGBU), 250 rescued women were moved to St. Sargis Armenian church[5] for special medical treatment. A representative of AGBU, Doctor Hreshtakian, took care of the financial and administrative work of the shelter until July 1919. At this point, the representative of the Armenian National Relief Organization (*Hay Azgayin Khnamatarutyun*) came to replace Doctor Hreshtakian. Until the end of 1919, 50 women remained in this shelter. With the help of Hreshtakian and representatives of *Azgayin Khnamatarutyun,* most of them had found a relative and had left the shelter. At the end of 1919, approximately 220 women from Karin (Erzurum), Severek and Sebastia (Sivas) had found a place in another shelter known as '*Azgayin pandok*', while another 50 women from Karin and Malatya were being sheltered in the big house of Nshan Der-Bedrosian's family, an Armenian from Urfa whose son and daughter had also had been rescued and returned to their family (Sahakian 1954, p. 1198). Overall, the British authorities, the American Near East Relief and Armenian organizations were supporting and taking care of the rescued women as they drew nearer to recovery. Over time, many of these women through their work managed to help themselves and gain some financial independence. Approximately, 200 women were working at the rug factory, and more than 400 were working for the tissue factory established by American Relief (Kévorkian and Tachjian 2006, pp. 116–117).[6]

Nonetheless, the women knew that the shelter was temporary, and they could not stay there forever. These women had to figure out their future. In those difficult days, there were two main options for them: to find and join relatives who had also survived or to marry an Armenian man and make a new family. Both options presented some additional dangers, especially to young girls. There is some evidence that random Armenian men, who were seeking an easy path to financial independence and a better place to stay, sometimes asserted that a girl or woman was their only surviving relative and claimed custody of them (Holmes 1923, p. 48). They could sometimes even provide documents, but these were not conclusive, for white slave traders who tried to exploit the vulnerable situation of these women were also in operation at the time. The conditions in the shelter were not perfect. These women did not know what the future had in store for them and were trying to secure their lives as quickly as possible. Some men would come to a shelter and promise a girl a better life if she escaped and worked for them. Most of these girls were very young and naive, and some fell into this trap (Holmes 1923, pp. 48–50).

In addition to these dangers, women with Turkish husbands would find every opportunity and method being used to persuade them to return to the marital home. They were sometimes accused of theft (Holmes 1923, p. 58) because the husbands hoped that such an accusation would lead to the put these women in their power once more, as Künzler writes in his memoirs (2007, p. 99):

> In reality, the women were no thieves. Armenian loyalty is proverbial in the Orient. Just because of that fact they were coveted, and the Turks tried everything to get them back again.

5 Between Love, Pain and Identity ... 113

Other men also claimed legal ownership over these women. A coachman Elias, an Albanian Muslim, who was well known to Künzler, was one of those who claimed that his Armenian wife legally belonged to him and was taken to court. Before the deportations, he had married an Armenian woman, who told him that her husband had been killed and she was thus a widow. A bachelor, Elias decided to marry her and take in her two children. He had his marriage legalized by the *kadı*[7] and *'lived very happily with the Armenian woman'* (Künzler 2007, p. 78). But in 1918, her Armenian husband suddenly appeared. He had been a prisoner of war, and after his release had come to find his family. He approached Elias peaceably, asking him to give his family back, and, when refused, brought the matter to the *kadı*. The case would have been more straightforward if the marriage had been conducted illegally, like many others. The judge invited them all to attend the court and there declared that, while legally she belonged to Elias, he should at the same time recall the terms of their marriage and the desperate situation of the woman, who had had to choose between this marriage and not surviving. The judge advised Elias to return the woman to her first husband, and he acquiesced (Künzler 2007, p. 79).

Another interesting case was reported by Künzler when the British army came to Urfa and he was about to leave the country. Two Turks from the city who had Armenian wives came to ask him if the British would protect them from the Turkish government if they became Christians. They did not want to lose their wives and thought it would be possible to keep them if they converted to Christianity. Afterwards, Künzler (2007, pp. 108–109) wrote in his memoirs what these two men had told him about their Armenian wives:

> These women taught us a family life that we never knew before ... and you should know that we are not alone in this view and this situation. There are about fifty other men who sent us here, who are ready to become Christians in order to hold on to their new lives with Christian women.

While Künzler was very excited about this incident, many Armenians perceived such stories negatively. The Armenian Patriarch, Zaven

Yéghiayan, was also upset about such stories as he records in his memoirs (Der Yéghiayan 1947) written in Iraq after escaping from Istanbul in 1922. One of the Armenian rescuers sent by the Armenian Patriarchate told him that when he was working in Urfa, an American missionary criticized him for rescuing Armenian women from Turkish households and suggested that they should be left there so that their husbands would eventually be encouraged to convert to Christianity. The rescuer completely disagreed with such a suggestion and responded angrily that the American missionaries should try themselves to turn Turks into Christians by going and living in their harems (Der Yéghiayan 1947, p. 297).

Nonetheless, some Armenian women decided to return to their Muslim husbands after staying a while at the shelter, mainly because of the conditions they found themselves in, as Künzler (2007, p. 90) notes:

> Many of them did not have a bad situation in the Muslim homes, where they had a generous amount of food, good clothing, and beds. When the Armenians were picked up, their best clothing was taken from them.

Although the life in a women's shelter was harsh, it was not the only reason why some Armenian women chose to return to their Muslim husbands. Miss Holmes, the director of an American orphanage in Urfa, wrote in her memoirs:

> A small number of the rescued women voluntarily returned to their Muslim husbands, usually because of their little children they had been obliged to leave. It is only fair to say that one and all had tales of kindness and real affection for their Muslim men ... and a number came to us who were expecting little ones and who had to have special care and consideration. None of these – all girls – had any desire to return to their harem homes. (Holmes 1923, pp. 30–31)

Thanks to the efforts of the Armenian Patriarchate, the Ottoman government in Istanbul[8] eventually decreed that converted and forcibly married women had the right to choose what was best for them. On November 28, 1918, an order to the provinces maintained that 'the constitution commands freedom of conscience' and that married women over twenty had the right to choose whether to return to their previous Armenian life or to stay with their Muslim husbands. If they chose to reintegrate into Armenian life, their previous conversion to Islam and their Muslim marriage would be annulled. If they wished to return to their original religion but not divorce their Muslim husbands, they had to apply to the courts (Ekmekçioğlu 2013, p. 538). Married women under twenty, even though their conversion to Islam was considered invalid, would not be forced to reintegrate into Armenian life or to divorce their Muslim husbands. The Ottoman government decided that their cases would be resolved in court, in the presence of members of their birth family (if they had any), church authorities, Christian missionaries (or other Westerners) and Ottoman officials (Ekmekçioğlu 2013, p. 538).

The news about this new order came to Urfa a little later; it was always regarded as a peripheral place. Even in Istanbul, it took time for Muslims to admit the new situation and obey the new law. The women and girls who had been in Muslim homes in Urfa were sooner or later released upon these new government orders from Constantinople (nowadays Istanbul). But these new orders did not come without trouble. Miss Holmes, for example, reported that one Armenian girl who was taken from her Muslim husband and sent to Miss Holmes' orphanage, cried and declared she could not live without her husband. When she persuaded them to let her go, she left happily but returned within ten minutes saying that her husband was afraid to have her back without a written statement from the administrative commander that this was her wish. He feared that in view of the orders from Constantinople the police might object to a Christian woman living with him. After a few years of marriages, this couple still had no children. Even though she had received the requisite papers to return to her husband, her husband eventually ceased to want her since she did not seem able to conceive. This time, there were no tears when she returned to the rescue home and some time afterwards she married a well-to-do Armenian.

In the autumn of 1919, the British forces abandoned the city of Urfa, replaced by the French in November. The latter were constantly fighting, sometimes with the Muslim population of the town and at other

116   A. Aleksanyan

times against the Nationalists. Armenians took a neutral position, merely defending the Armenian quarter. But they had to leave Urfa again in 1923 when the French left, and the Kemalists no longer tolerated anyone else besides Turks (Tachjian 2006). The Armenians who stayed had to hide their identity.

Regulations of Marriage Law and the Condemnation of *'Azgurats'*[9]

In the Armenian language the word *worb* means 'an orphan', and the word *ayri* means 'a widow', but there is another word, *worbevayri,* the combination of the previous two words, which was largely circulated during and after the Armenian genocide. Before the genocide, the word *'worbevayri'* as an adjective was used for both women and men, whose husband/wife had been killed, or had abandoned/divorced her/him (Aucher 1868, p. 799; Minassian 1902, p. 373; Gabamatchian 1910, p. 1082; Kouyoumdjian 1950, p. 627; Aghaian 1976, p. 114). Interestingly, during and after the Armenian genocide, the word *'worbevayri'* changed its meaning. It became only a female adjective, describing a woman of any age whose husband and whole family had been killed or were missing, someone who had become both an orphan and a widow (Ekmekçioğlu 2016, p. 28). This linguistic change did not happen by chance, and it tells us about society's perception of these women, and what it saw as the rightful place of these *'worbevayri'*. They were treated as orphans, for whom *azgy* (the nation) was responsible; the *azgy* were taken care of and decisions were being made on their behalf.

After rescuing women and giving them temporary shelter, the solution most welcomed for both women and relief workers was marriage. But this brought up another problem: many of these women had been married before the genocide and many of the candidates also had wives in their pre-genocide lives. The question of divorce and the question of the right to remarry was a pressing issue. According to traditional Armenian marriage law, which was regulated by the Armenian Church

Statute, a marriage could be recognized as annulled when: (1) it was not confirmed by the parents; (2) it was the third marriage; (3) one of the spouses did not wait for his/her missing spouse to appear for the period fixed by law (5–7 years) and married somebody else; and (4) the couple had been married in the course of a kidnapping. The divorce was satisfactory when (1) there was proof of adultery/unfaithfulness; (2) in cases of infertility; and (3) one of the spouses was missing for a period fixed by law (5–7 years). According to the same law, when a husband was divorcing his wife for no reason or because of her bodily defects, he was obliged to share not only the children but all his property (land, house, profit) with her (Ghltchian 1904, pp. 79–81).

On December 14, 1918, not long after the war, the Armenian Judicial Commission of the National Assembly[10] was re-organized in the Armenian Patriarchate of Istanbul. There was a special announcement in the Armenian newspapers about it, especially emphasizing, that all those who wanted to resolve their marital problems were invited to apply to the Patriarchate and proceed legally.[11] This haste had a serious basis. During the Armenian genocide, families were intentionally broken up and sent away in different directions (Sarafian 2001). As a result, many had no idea of the fate of their previous spouses in the aftermath of the genocide, but were trying to rebuild their lives, remarry and recover from it all. Some even married in concentration camps if it felt essential for their survival to do so. During the genocide, these marriages mostly took place in conditions where traditional marriage laws had been neglected. Even with a great desire to follow the law, it was very difficult, almost impossible, to do so because every day might be one's last. There were not enough priests even for the burials, let alone for blessing and recording the marriages. Moreover, there were not enough staff to check if both partners were unmarried at the time, or if a previous husband and/or wife were still alive. The only source of information for deportees in those days was rumour. In these conditions, keeping the rules was of the least concern for them. Even after the war, the situation did not change much. As in many other towns, in Urfa, for example, there were no priests for the marriage ceremonies in 1919; instead, a teacher from Armash Grigor Gappendchian took on the role of priest in wedding ceremonies (Sahakian 1954, p. 954). Even so he seldom had the required information to bless the new marriage.

Although everyone was happy at first with such practices to get people married, it became complicated when Armenian refugees returned. The chance of finding information about a missing family member increased, but still it sometimes took years to find. In this way, Armenian women's situation was much more complicated, since even if after being rescued they found that their Armenian husbands were still alive, they could not be sure of returning to their husband since under these marriage practices, he might already have remarried. Similarly, if Armenian men wanted to find their displaced wives or find information about their marital status, they needed financial resources and relevant connections. For many of them, the only source of information for many years was the columns of '*Ku pndrvi*' (looking for) published in Armenian newspapers around the world, where people published the names of those who had survived and those who were looking for survivors.

Thus, it became clear that the age-old Armenian marriage laws did not quite cover the new situation. After the war, this issue set off a huge debate among Armenian intellectuals because many lives and individual decisions and the fate of many rescued women depended on it. In December 1918, the Armenian daily '*Jamanag*' wrote that a representative of the Patriarchate, Father Yervand, who had worked before the war as a judge in marital problems, considered that the new situation required a new marriage law. He therefore prepared a document containing 100 articles. It was presented for approval at the hearings of a special committee of clergymen. The final approval was to be conferred by the National Assembly.[12] In October 1919, a year after, the same daily announced that a new law project had been drafted, this time concerning divorce issues.[13] But, according to the author, irrespective of the changes in martial law to be introduced by Constantinople (Istanbul), even if the relevant national institutions approved it, the final decision should have been made in Etchmiadzin by the Armenian Catholics because these laws were essential and should apply to all Armenians. Years were passing, but these committees could not make a final decision on the amendment. Moreover, this court did not always make objective decisions, but showed evidence of an anti-feminist discrimination. For example, the verdict on a woman who had refused to come back to the community and remained with her Muslim husband was *azgurats*.[14] That meant that she was effectively dead as far as the Armenian Church and community were concerned, whereas a man who converted to Islam during the genocide and had married a Muslim woman, and then refused to leave her, received no such verdict.[15] The unjust decisions of the court were also highlighted by Armenian women writers of the time.[16] They even offered to transform The Armenian Judicial Commission and engage women to serve on it, but this offer was refused (Ekmekçioğlu 2016, pp. 68–69).

Between 1918 and 1924 the Judicial Commission of the National Assembly examined about 250 cases of divorce and remarriage. All records of marriage trials after the war remained in the collections of the Armenian Church. Most of the applicants were men, and only some of them were women. There are 12 cases in the records in which the Armenian husbands of women who had married or were in a relationship with a Muslim man as a result of the genocide, applied for a divorce from the court and permission to marry another Armenian woman. Karapet Shahapian from Urfa was one of them. He was married to Haykanush Dertsakian before the war. Haykanush's parents testified in the court that she was in an illegal relationship with Pursali Zade Ahmed from Antioch and had run away with him. The court decided to give Karapet a divorce and permission to marry someone else; it expelled Haykanush from the Armenian Church and pronounced her *azgurats*.[17]

Some of these women came to the court and confessed that they had married a Muslims. The wife of Hakob Poz-Oghlanian from Zeitun, Haykanush made such a confession in the court, declaring that she was with a Turkish man called Khulus during the genocide and now lived with him. In the records, her confession was marked as 'anpatkar' (impudent), and the court identified her as *azgurats*, because she refused to go back to Hakob.[18] It should be mentioned that in all nine cases Armenian husbands first had to try to find and bring back their wives, and went to the court only if they could not do this. They needed to present proof of their search and recorded the results so that the court could make a decision in favour of the divorce and could approve their new marriage.

There are nine cases in the records of women who had abandoned their Muslim husbands after the war and had returned to their first/ legal Armenian husbands, but then left them and went back to their Muslim families. Their Armenian husbands applied for a divorce and got permission to marry other women. The reasons for these women's decisions were quite diverse. Ruben Papazian from the Dörtyol region was married to Yeprakse Nalbandian from the same village. They lost each other during the genocide. After the armistice, relief workers found her in an Arab household and returned her to Ruben, but a few days later she escaped and returned to the Arab household and declared that she had converted to Islam and would not go back. Another case concerned Hovhannes Akikian from Aintab. He married Nazlu, who had been living in Sivas with her Turkish husband before being rescued by Armenian soldiers from Adana. Nazlu did not tell Hovhannes about her previous marriage, but married him, then after a few days left and joined her Muslim husband. Hovhannes came to the court to ask it to annul his marriage with Nazlu, which it did. Nazlu was designated *asgurats*.[19] We should keep in mind that both men and women were traumatized and stigmatized and it was almost impossible to go back to their pre-genocide life. They were all changed as a result of their traumatic experiences.

The life of these women was very complicated. We can see from the Court records that they were forced to make difficult choices. Nshan Gevorgian's wife Siranush, for example, had during the genocide married a Circassian under duress, then was rescued and returned to her husband, then again went back to the Circassian man with whom she moved to Aleppo, where she left him as well and went to work in a brothel.[20] A woman who was happy and was feeling protected would never have left her home for work in a brothel. These cases demonstrate how complicated everything was.

There were cases where women were refused by their Armenian husbands when they had chosen to abandon their Muslim husbands. This happened with Yeghisabet, who had been married to Harutiun Avanian from the village of Mkhal (Zeitun province). When the Zeytuntsi

Armenians escaped to Djermuk, she did not follow her husband but escaped with several other women to Peheseni. There she was forced to marry a Turkish man. She was rescued after the war, but her husband refused to take her back.[21] She ended up in the shelter. Ruben Barseghian's wife Gulik from the village of Araz (Mush province) was forced to marry a Turk in Diarbekir. Ruben had thought that she had been killed and married Mariam Nalbandian in Izmir. After the war, Gulik was rescued and wanted to be reunited with her husband, but Ruben refused because he felt closer to his second wife after such a long time.[22] The court sent her to the shelter. These stories come to demonstrate that no matter what decisions these women had made, their life did not always lie in their own hands and no matter where they remained, or what they decided, all of them went through sacrifices which brought them pain and suffering.

Conclusions

As part of the genocidal programme many women were converted and integrated into Muslim households for the purpose of forced assimilation. To be able to save women, girls or children from being killed or abducted during and after the genocide, Armenian and other international organizations started to work side by side and together. The important part of this work was first to rescue, then to restore Armenian women and reintegrate them back into Armenian society. This work was not only full of danger but also very hard psychologically and emotionally, both for the rescuers and those rescued. In some cases, the perpetrator and survivors had to live in the same city, side by side, which made things even more complicated. Such a place was the city of Urfa, where many crimes against Armenians were committed during the genocide and where Armenian survivors returned after the war and tried to rebuild their lives. Part of this rebuilding process was to return those women, who had sometimes under compulsion and sometimes 'voluntarily' married Muslims before the deportation. The lives of these women were very diverse, depending on the attitude of their Muslim husband and his family. Some of them were treated as slaves, some as concubines, some were regularly tortured, beaten and raped, but some were treated with love and respect. The rescued women found shelter in the temporary rescue houses. Often their Muslim husbands would try every method to persuade their Armenian wives to go back to them. Some women would finally go back because they had had children together and they could not face the prospect of never seeing their children again. After being rescued and safe, the next problem they faced was the uncertainty of life beyond the shelter. If they left their safe houses and their children, what vision of the future could they contemplate? The luckiest ones could find a suitable Armenian and marry, while others tried to find a surviving relative, and some even managed to find their first husband. But what if none of these options worked? Apart from the pain of abandoning their children, some were frightened by this uncertainty. These women had to face a dilemma: to go back to their community and try to start a new life overcoming difficulties and ignoring their own feelings, or to stay with their Muslim families, forget their Armenian origin and become a part of the society which had committed the genocide against their nation.

Notes

1. In the end, the son remained with the father because it was safer for his mother not to take him with her. The system of jurisprudence that operated in the Ottoman Empire was the Hanafi School of Islamic law (*madhhab*). According to this School, non-Muslim women had a restricted right of custody to their children; mothers could keep them until the so-called age of discernment (seven years). The law stated that an apostate mother would be disqualified from having custody until she converted to Islam (cf. Gallala-Arndt 2015).
2. Jakob Künzler was a Swiss of German origin who had worked for the Deutsche Orient-Mission in Urfa since 1899. During World War I, Künzler continued to direct the mission hospital and secretly helped Armenians who remained in the city. In 1920, he organized and carried out the evacuation of more than 8000 Armenian orphans from Urfa to safety in Syria.

3. Yeghizabet Yotneghbarian was released from prison after the war and wrote her memoirs in Paris in February 1919, which were published by Aram Sahakian (1954). After Paris, she joined her brother in New York, but, unfortunately, was not able to recover from her trauma and passed away in one of the mental hospitals of New York.

4. She also managed to hide and protect five young men, among them her adopted son and her husband Misak Melkonian (Sahakian 1954, pp. 959–976). After the war, when Jeppe was appointed in Aleppo as Director of the League of Nations' Commission for the Protection of Women and Children in the Near East, Melkonian became one of the leading rescuers of Armenian women and children (Tcholakian 2001, pp. 51–64).

5. After demolishing the Armenian quarter and deporting the rest, many Armenian orphans left in the streets of Urfa without a shelter and food to die. The orphans were assembled and settled in the St. Sargis Armenian church, which turned into an orphanage. Armenian orphans were given Turkish names and converted to Islam. The orphanage conditions were so cruel that most of the orphans died before the war was over.

6. Urfa Armenian women were very famous for their carpet-making skills and needlework (Tcholakian 2001, pp. 43–48).

7. A *kadı* was an official in the Ottoman Empire, who presided over matters to do with Islamic law.

8. On October 8, 1918 Talat Pasha's government resigned and was replaced by a cabinet led by Ahmet İzzet Pasha, a general who was not a member of the Committee of Union and Progress. The new Ottoman government, which is known as the Istanbul government, changed many times and was replaced by the Ankara government in 1923.

9. '*Azgurats*' is the word for one who denies his origin and nation.

10. The Armenian Judicial Commission of the National Assembly had 22 members who were Armenian attorneys and judges responsible for civic matters, including marriage and divorce.

11. Ariamart, no. 18 (1833), 1918.

12. Jamanak, no. 3713, 1918.

13. Jamanak, no. 3672, 1919.

14. See *Pashtonakan Amusnalutsutyunk ev Veramusnutyunk* (1919–1924) (Beirut: A. Tachjian, 1925).

15. Ibid. (case no. 90), 31.

16. Haykanush Mark, "Amusnalutsumnery," *Hay Kin*, 2, no. 11 (April 1921).
17. *Pashtonakan Amusnalutsutyunk ev Veramusnutyunk* (case no. 10), 5.
18. Ibid. (case no. 21), 9.
19. Ibid. (case no. 27), 10.
20. Ibid. (case no. 34), 12.
21. Ibid. (case no. 17), 7.
22. Ibid. (case no. 229), 77.

References

Aghaian, E. B. 1976. *Modern Armenian Explanatory Dictionary*. Yerevan: Hayastan Publication.

Akçam, Taner. 2006. *A Shameful Act: The Armenian Genocide and the Question of Turkish Responsibility*. New York: Metropolitan Books.

———. 2012. *The Young Turks' Crime Against Humanity: The Armenian Genocide and Ethnic Cleansing in the Ottoman Empire*. Princeton, NJ: Princeton University Press.

———. 2016. *Forced Islamization of Armenians: Silence, Denial and Assimilation*. Yerevan: Tigran Mets.

Ariamart, no. 18 (1833) (Constantinople: December 1918).

Aucher, Pascal. 1868. *Dictionary English and Armenian*. Venice: The Armenian Academy of S. Lazarus.

Bjørnlund, Matthias. 2009. "'A Fate Worse Than Dying': Sexual Violence During the Armenian Genocide." In *Brutality and Desire: War and Sexuality in Europe's Twentieth Century*, edited by Dagmar Herzog, 16–58. New York: Palgrave Macmillan.

Bryce, James, and Arnold Toynbee. 2000. *The Treatment of Armenians in the Ottoman Empire, 1915–1916*. Edited by Ara Sarafian. Uncensored ed. Princeton, NJ: Princeton University Press.

Derderian, Katharine. 2005. "Common Fate, Different Experience: Gender-Specific Aspects of the Armenian Genocide, 1915–1917." *Holocaust and Genocide Studies* XIX (1, Spring): 1–25. https://doi.org/10.1093/hgs/dci001.

Der Yéghiayan, Zaven. 1947. *Patriarqagan Hushers: Vaveragrer ev Vkayutyunner*. Cairo: Nor Astgh.

Donoyan, Armen. 1991. *Armenian Heroic Battles in the Name of Justice*. Glendale, CA: Navasart Publishing House.

Ekmekçioğlu, Lerna. 2013. "A Climate for Abduction, a Climate for Redemption: The Politics of Inclusion During and After the Armenian Genocide." *Comparative Studies in Society and History* 55 (3): 522–553. https://doi.org/10.1017/S0010417513000236.

———. 2016. *Recovering Armenia: The Limits of Belonging in Post-genocide Turkey.* Stanford, CA: Stanford University Press.

Elliott, Mabel E. 1924. *Beginning Again at Ararat.* New York: Fleming H. Revell.

Gabamatchian. 1910. *New Wordbook for the Armenian Language.* Constantinople: R. Sagaian Publication.

Galemkerian, Zarhi. 1904. *Kyanqis Tchampen.* Antilias: Tparan Katoghikopsutyan Kilikioy, 1952. Ghltchian, Arsen. *Amusnutyun, Amusnalutsutyun Tsnoghneri, Vordots, ev Amusinneri Qaghaqats Iravunqneri Masin Petakan Orenqner. Hayots Ekeghetsu Kanonner, Amusnalutsakan Datavarutyun.* Aleksandrapol: Tparan Hakob Gasapiants.

Gallala-Arndt, Imen. 2015. The Impact of Religion in Interreligious Custody Disputes: Middle Eastern and Asian Approaches. *The American Journal of Comparative Law* 63 (4): 829–858. https://doi.org/10.5131/AJCL.2015.0025.

Haykanush Mark. 1921. "Amusnalutsumnery." *Hay Kin* 2 (11).

Holmes, Mary Caroline. 1923. *Between the Lines in Asia Minor.* New York: Fleming H. Revell.

Holslag, Anthonie. 2015. "Exposed Bodies: A Conceptual Approach to Sexual Violence During the Armenian Genocide." In *Genocide and Gender in the Twentieth Century: A Comparative Survey,* edited by Amy E. Randall, 87–106. London: Bloomsbury.

Jacobsen, Maria. 1979. *Oragrutyun 1907–1919: Kharberd.* Antelias: Tparan Katoghikopsutyan Kilikioy.

Jamanak, no. 3713 (Constantinople: December 1918).

Jamanak, no. 3672 (Constantinople: October 1919).

Jinks, Rebecca. 2018. "'Marks Hard to Erase': The Troubled Reclamation of 'Absorbed' Armenian Women, 1919–1927." *The American Historical Review* 123 (1): 86–123. https://doi.org/10.1093/ahr/123.1.86.

Kévorkian, Raymond. 2011. *The Armenian Genocide: A Complete History.* New York: I.B. Tauris.

Kévorkian, Raymond, and Vahé Tachjian. 2006. *Dar my Patmutyun Hay Baregortsakan Undhanur Miutean (1906–1940).* Vol. I. Cairo, Paris, and New York: AGBU.

Kouyoumdjian, Mesrob. 1950. *A Comprehensive Dictionary Armenian-English.* Cairo: Sahag-Mesrob Press.

Künzler, Jakob. 2007. *In the Land of Blood and Tears: Experiences in Mesopotamia During the World War (1914–1918).* Arlington, MA: Armenian Cultural Foundation.

Miller, Hugh S. 1920. "Salvaging the Womanhood of Armenia." *The American Woman* (April).

Minasian, Mihran. 2015. "Aram Andonian's Notes on the Massacres of Deyr Zor." *Haygazian Armenological Review* 35: 685–724.

Minassian, M. K. 1902. *A Hand Dictionary Armenian-English.* Constantinople: H. Matteosian Printer.

National Archives of Armenia, Heryan's Folder 420, List 65.

Nubarian Library, National Delegation Archives, Zabel Yesayan, "La liberation des Femmes et Enfants Nonmusulmans en Turquie." The March 1919 Report: 1–15, Correspondence February–March 1919.

Parian, Levon, and Ishkhan Jinashian, eds. 2012. *Crows of the Desert: The Memoirs of Levon Yotnakhparian.* Tujunga: Parian Photographic Design.

Sahakian, Aram. 1954. *Dyutsaznakan Urfan ev ir Hayvordinery. Hushapatum.* Antelias: Tparan Katoghikopsutyan Kilikioy.

Sanasarian, Eliz. 1989. "Gender Distinction in the Genocidal Process: A Preliminary Study of the Armenian Case." *Holocaust and Genocide Studies* 4 (4): 449–461. https://doi.org/10.1093/hgs/4.4.449.

Sarafian, Ara. 2001. "The Absorption of Armenian Women and Children into Muslim Households as a Structural Component of the Armenian Genocide." In *In God's Name: Genocide and Religion in the Twentieth Century,* edited by Omer Bartov and Phyllis Mack, 209–221. New York: Berghahn.

Tachjian, A. 1925. *Pashtonakan Amusnalutsutyunk ev Veramusnutyunk (1919–1924).* Beirut.

Tachjian, Vahé. 2006. "Expulsion of the Armenian Survivors of Diarbekir and Urfa, 1923–1930." In *Armenian Tigranakert/Diarbekir and Edessa/Urfa,* edited by Richard G. Hovannisian. Costa Mesa, CA: Mazda Publishers.

———. 2009. "Gender, Nationalism, Exclusion: The Reintegration Process of Female Survivors of the Armenian Genocide." *Nations and Nationalism* 15 (1): 60–80. https://doi.org/10.1111/j.1469-8129.2009.00366.x.

———. 2014. "Mixed Marriage, Prostitution, Survival: Reintegrating Armenian Women into Post-Ottoman Cities." In *Women and the City, Women in the City: A Gendered Perspective on Ottoman Urban History,* edited by Nazan Maksudyan, 86–106. New York: Berghahn.

Tcholakian, Hagop. 2001. *Karen Jeppe: Hay Koghkot'ayin yev Veradzununtin hed.* Aleppo: Arevelk.

The New Near East, no. 6 (New York: May 1923).

Üngör, Ugur Ümit. 2012. "Converts and Prostitutes: Social Consequences of War and Persecution in the Ottoman Empire 1914–1923." *War in History* 19 (2): 173–192. https://doi.org/10.1177/0968344511430579.

Watenpaugh, Keith David. 2010. "'The League of Nations' Rescue of Armenian Genocide Survivors and the Making of Modern Humanitarianism, 1920–1927." *American Historical Review* 115 (5): 1315–1339. https://doi.org/10.1086/ahr.115.5.1315.

6

'We Are Strangers Among Our Own People': Displaced Armenian Women

Shushanik Ghazaryan

The forced displacement of thousands of people is a key legacy of the conflict between Armenia and Azerbaijan over the Nagorny Karabakh region. But forced displacement has always been a significant issue for Armenians throughout their history. Notably, in 1915, more than 90,000 Armenians were forced to flee the Ottoman Empire to the territory that comprises modern-day Armenia (Danielyan 2002, p. 115). In 1919, an additional 400,000 refugees and orphans fled to Armenia (Sargsyan 1995, p. 59) while one and a half million were massacred. Research on this experience of displacement has shown that the process of refugee integration has its peculiarities and difficulties in every period, especially when it comes to Armenians reintegrating in their so-called homeland (Kharatyan 2008). The reintegration of displaced people is a difficult task not only because great numbers of people are displaced at the same time but also because refugees should be guaranteed access to housing accommodation, medical assistance,

---

S. Ghazaryan (✉)
Institute of Archaeology and Ethnography, National Academy of Sciences, Yerevan, Armenia

© The Author(s) 2020
U. Ziemer (ed.), *Women's Everyday Lives in War and Peace in the South Caucasus*,
https://doi.org/10.1007/978-3-030-25517-6_6

food, education and professional and language training (Ghazaryan 2000, p. 3).

This chapter explores the challenges of reintegration using oral history interviews with displaced Armenian women. The discussion is based on 40 in-depth interviews with women above 55 years old. All the interview participants were displaced from Baku and still live in either Artzakh or Shirak, two temporary dormitories in Yerevan. The interviews focused on the participants' personal narratives and were analysed to illustrate the most significant changes in their social lives (Eastmond 2007). This chapter examines how displaced women were able to overcome integration issues and become part of Armenian society, adopting ethnic identity features. It was assumed by Armenians who used to live in Soviet Azerbaijan that they would easily be able to integrate into Armenian society, but surprisingly, even now they continue to have integration issues and are considered 'strangers' by local Armenians.

The displacement of Armenians from Azerbaijan to Armenia as a result of the conflict over Nagorny Karabakh occurred in several stages. The first group of around 20,000 refugees was forced to leave after the pogroms in the Baku suburb of Sumgait in February 1988, when over 20 local Armenian residents were murdered and hundreds injured. The second and biggest wave of refugees began in the second half of 1988 and lasted until the end of 1989, involving around 215,000 refugees. The third wave, of around 45,000 people, started in 1990 after the violence in central Baku (Poghosyan and Avagyan 1996, pp. 5–7; Ayunts 2011, p. 23). In 1991, by the last stage of the military operation *Ring*[1] the remaining population in the territories populated by Armenians adjacent to the Nagorny Karabakh Autonomous Oblast (NKAO), Shaumyan region (around 12,000 people) and Getashen sub-region, including the villages of Getashen and Martunashen (around 5100) were forced to leave (Poghosyan and Avagyan 1996, p. 12; Ayunts 2011, p. 23). In addition to these divergent processes of displacement, approximately 70,000 IDPs in Armenia were evacuated during the war in 1992–1994 from the villages adjoining the border with Azerbaijan (Greene 1998, p. 271; Ayunts 2011, p. 23).[2]

At the outbreak of this war, the Soviet government was not prepared to accept a large-scale influx of refugees fleeing to Soviet Armenia between 1988 and 1992. In the 1990s, there was no official institution for the assistance and rehabilitation of refugees and the existing Soviet Committee (the Governmental Committee for Organizing the Acceptance of Armenians from abroad)[3] responsible for reintegrating Armenians from abroad did not have sufficient experience and knowledge to handle these large-scale influxes of Armenians from Azerbaijan.[4] When the refugees began to arrive in 1988, new institutions were set up to help them in resettlement. These institutions included the Refugee Committee attached to the Council of Ministers of the Republic of Armenia, formed in December 1990, on the basis of the State Committee for the Admission and Accommodation of the Armenians returning to the Armenian SSR and the State Agency for Refugee Affairs of the RA, established in February 1992.[5]

It is worth mentioning that, alongside the influx of refugees from Azerbaijan, these state agencies had to cope with the near total economic blockade resulting from the war with Azerbaijan; this crippled the economy and infrastructure of the newly independent Republic of Armenia. In addition, Armenia was hit by a devastating earthquake in 1988.[6] These conditions narrowed even further the possibilities for supporting Armenian refugees from Azerbaijan since the country already faced problems with housing and supporting nearly 500,000 citizens made homeless by the natural disaster (Avagyan 1996). In this situation, the refugees who had barely escaped violence[7] would face even greater difficulties than simple reintegration. They had lost everything they owned, abandoning their communities and all that was familiar. They had to begin a new life in a new environment. Because of the chaotic situation, many of these refugees to this day face socio-economic hardships, struggle with unemployment and live in temporary shelters. This chapter examines how displaced Armenian women from Azerbaijan attempted to integrate into Armenian society without any institutional support. Specifically, the chapter considers how they tried to overcome the social difficulties to look like and blend with local people and how they tried to eliminate all the elements that made them feel different from local Armenians, particularly language,[8] behaviour, style/dressing, way of thinking, etc.

Armenians in Soviet Baku

Baku, the capital city of Azerbaijan, went from a provincial city to an industrial centre of the Caucasus region due to the development of the oil industry in the late nineteenth and early twentieth centuries. By 1913, Baku was producing almost 95% of all Russian oil and 55% of the total world's oil (Valiev 2013, p. 626). In response to the demand for labour, masses of peasants throughout the region migrated there. At the time, an estimated 45,000 Armenians were living in Baku, one of the predominant ethnic groups beside Russians. In the 1930s–1950s, there were 80 Armenian secondary schools, a college of education and Armenian language faculties in the University of Baku and Pedagogical Institute. The last Armenian school in Baku was closed in 1983. To sum up, the Armenian community was well-established and Baku was a multi-ethnic city (Grant 2010). Baku's development during the Soviet period was no different from many other cities of the Soviet Union (Valiev 2013, p. 626). According to Grant, Baku was a place where many different nationalities gathered.

> You'd get together at someone's birthday ... there would be all different kinds of people. Someone would have just arrived from Dagestan, Armenia, the Russians would be there – you didn't even think about who was who. Someone made rice this way, rather than that way. You wouldn't even think that it was international; it was just the way it was. You know who came from what background and there was a physical factor, some people looked a little different. Of course. But it didn't lead to conflict. It just wasn't in question. (Grant 2010, pp. 127–128)

Similarly, the participants in the present research remember Baku as a very cosmopolitan city:

> All my neighbours were from different nations, Jewish, German, Azeri, Russians and if someone had to celebrate something we shared food, happiness, had discussions, we respected each other, knew each other's customs, traditions. (Svetlana, 77 years old, in Grant 2010, p. 131)

Although the city was cosmopolitan and provided equality and multicultural tolerance for many different nations, there was nevertheless an ethnic hierarchy, hierarchic diversion, which was not officially acknowledged but had some impact on its inhabitants, who knew it and lived accordingly (Grant 2010, p. 131).

> We Armenians were respected and always had good positions in Azerbaijan, but Armenians never were allowed to be directors or the chiefs of something. The main engineer, main specialist was Armenian, but the director was always an Azerbaijani one. (Emma, 76 years old)

Patriarchal Gender Ideology in Armenia

In Armenian society women are expected to follow religious and cultural traditions. The main role of women is seen to be in the private sphere, in the home, where women are expected to fully devote themselves to the upbringing and education of their children. According to Armenian tradition, women are expected not to engage in activities in the public sphere. Thus, women in politics, for example, are considered an exception or often even negatively perceived by society, which tends to marginalize them (Poghosyan 2010, p. 162; Shahnazaryan et al. 2016). As many publications have documented, marriage and motherhood have huge symbolic meaning in Armenian society (Beukian 2014; Shahnazarian and Ziemer 2018; Ziemer 2011, 2018). Marriage marks a stage of transition from being controlled by the father and male relatives to being controlled by the husband and his relatives. One could argue that the persistence of these patriarchal gender roles can be derived from a popular understanding that Armenian women have to be subservient to their husbands (Ziemer 2011; Nahapetyan 2009, p. 1). The idea of women being subservient to Armenian men is conveyed, for example, during Armenian wedding ceremonies, where the groom says to the priest 'I speak for her' (*ter em*), while the bride says 'I am submissive' (*hnazand em*) (Ziemer 2011, p. 136).

While these norms are traditional and are thus subject to change over time, their basic tenets are accepted in Armenian society. Even today, Armenian society is very patriarchal and a woman's state of health and status depends largely on the way that she corresponds to the image of a traditional and 'perfect' woman. According to Armenian gender traditions, the feminine 'image' in public consciousness is characterized by delicacy, obedience, decency, a willingness to concede, loyalty, etc. Because of strong patriarchal gender relations in Armenian society, women even nowadays have an unequal status in society. Traditional stereotypes related to women are still active; this is why most women refuse political, social and economic activities because of their fear of not matching up to the existing conception of femininity (Poghosyan 2010, p. 164).

During the Soviet period, state feminism and the promotion from above of an ideology of gender equality also had a big impact on Armenian society. The Soviet government adopted policies calling for equality between men and women and enforced mechanisms for the legislation of the ideology (Shahnazaryan et al. 2016). Thus, women in general became increasingly engaged in social life and labour, becoming in particular more represented in the ranks of the Communist party (Usha 2005). Noteworthy here is that both Azerbaijan and Armenia were part of the Soviet Union and therefore it is assumed that they had similar experiences of Soviet state feminism. Consequently, Armenian women fleeing from Baku in the early 1990s assumed that there were few differences between the two republics and they would not face any issues in integrating. However, these assumptions were not borne out. Once Armenia declared independence in 1991, a reverse trend took place—women increasingly withdrew from the male-dominated public sphere, politics above all, turning instead towards family life (Shahnazaryan et al. 2016, pp. 24–26). According to a survey of perceptions of gender equality in society, 80% of the respondents agreed that women should earn less money than men, otherwise conflict within the family was inevitable (Oxygen 2016).

Despite all these difficulties coming from the patriarchal gender order that they faced, most of the research participants were able to overcome their everyday problems by themselves, even when so many of them had no husband. One research participant, for example, was a widow who had lost her husband after moving to Yerevan. Another woman separated from her husband in Yerevan, because he could not find a job in Armenia and had left for Russia to find work and never returned.

Despite the hardships of being a woman alone and thus the sole provider for the family, their appearance and being feminine meant a good deal to them. It is not accidental that some of the refugee women said with regret that they had become what Armenian society calls a 'man-woman (*tghamard-kin*)', that is, a woman who has no husband, or one who is disabled and cannot work so that she has to provide for her family by herself. Although, as these women themselves admit, they are not like traditional women in their appearance, the meaning of this term nonetheless indicates a strong sense of morality, a strong character and devotion. Nevertheless, for these women it had a much more negative meaning; they felt hurt because it meant that they had lost their femininity. Moreover, using this term would signal to everyone that they were alone, without a man and had to make decisions, for the whole family, sometimes doing hard and heavy work that they would never have done before. Even though these women were very strong, they took no pleasure from being both man and woman for their family, according to patriarchal thinking, both as 'breadwinners' and its 'carers'.

Generally speaking, because these newcomers often did not match the traditional women's portrait drawn by Armenian society, they were often considered by local Armenian women to be 'dangerous' to 'traditional' Armenian families, potential threats who could 'steal' their husbands. These displaced women from Azerbaijan had appeared in this new society and had to fight for their lives without help: they had a range of jobs and some of them even found a new relationship in their new land. Thus, the local women who had a traditional image of Armenian femininity perceived their behaviour as threatening. Indeed, it was not only local women who harboured a negative image of these displaced women; local men also had some prejudice against them. They feared that, with their different and 'emancipated' behaviour, they could have a negative impact on their wives and daughters:

> Women from Baku are famous for their dyed blonde hair and 'amoral' behaviour.[9] Most of them don't have families and are lonely women. They're able to do any kind of job, there is no one to be responsible for them or to be subservient to. They can be bad examples for our women. (Andranik, 64 years, local Armenian man)

A local woman, Alvard (72 years old) described what local women thought of these displaced women and the way they dressed:

> The economic situation became worse after the blockade. People didn't have the basic conditions needed to live. They had to fight for everyday life. It wasn't the time for thinking about reforms, about construction in disaster areas, or about refugees. While we were fighting for a piece of bread, they were trying to steal our husbands. It seemed they didn't think about anything else but themselves. They were always well turned out, with blonde hair, colourful dresses. They had no heart. How could they wear such vivid colours? There was only one reason – they couldn't find a way to survive, so they tried to find a husband who would keep them.

Refugees, Belonging, Housing

The research participants had to overcome many difficulties to be accepted in Armenian society. Generally, when speaking about their experiences, they divided their life into two periods: when they lived in fairyland (the life in Azerbaijan) before their lives were disrupted by the conflict and when they were forced to flee, struggling to live in Armenian society and to prove that they deserved a place there. Even today they still do not have the feeling of belonging to any new place in Yerevan that one could call home, though they have lived there for more than 20 years. They are always thinking about overcoming social difficulties and recreating a home, but it seems the process of doing so can never be completed, since they still live in dormitories and do not have their own accommodation. Generally speaking, home can refer to a building, a village, a town or a region. Yet for a place to be called home one has to consider social relations on several different spatial scales, implying different levels of property rights and variations in an individual's sense of belonging (Black 2002, p. 127). One of the interviewees fondly remembered the time when she lived in a place called home. In our interview, she began her story with details about her family, in particular her father, who moved from Armenia to Azerbaijan in the 1920s. She described her childhood as filled with happy memories of having a family and home.

We used to live in Kirov's avenue; I saw only love and a carefree life in my father's home. I remember every detail, every moment from that part of my life. I remember our wonderful neighbours. We were the only Armenian family among them: there were Russians, Jewish, Azerbaijani neighbours, I even remember a German girl who was married and lived in the same building. I remember there were different ministries on one side of our building and the sea on the other side. (Jenia, 87 years)

Despite living in such a multi-ethnic city as Baku, she also spoke about her longing for her homeland, Armenia. For her, Armenian *lavash*[10] and cheese have a uniquely wonderful smell and taste. She relayed these details as if she had been living in a fairy tale. Accompanying her nostalgia was pride in her father who had migrated from Armenia and built a new, prosperous life in Baku where he was able to provide his family with everything.

Throughout their lives in Armenia, these displaced women from Azerbaijan would have identified such factors influencing their transition as income, job, language and emotional connections, as shown in the interview excerpt below. Most importantly, like Jenia (mentioned above), many refugees believed that a 'refugee' could 'become a local' through the private ownership of a house or a flat (Baghdasaryan 2009, p. 7). Jenia (87 years old) escaped from violence in Baku and moved to Yerevan in 1989.

I was working at a publishing house and I have a university degree. My husband was an engineer. When we first arrived here (Yerevan), we lived with our relatives. But I knew that I had to do something to find a place to live. I even went back to Azerbaijan in 1990 to try to sell my apartment, but I couldn't, unfortunately. When I returned (to Yerevan), I spent all my days running from one place to another trying to get a place in the dormitory. My husband was very shy to go and ask for support from the government. I was not ashamed and did whatever I needed to do. I had a daughter, a family. Should we live on the street? With all these worries my husband became sick, he had a heart problem. At last, the government gave us a room on the 9th floor of a dormitory. During that time, the elevator generally didn't work, so I had to solve a lot of house issues by myself. Don't look at me now – I used to be good looking and well-turned out, but no one would give me a job. Finally, I got work as a cleaner in a dental clinic. Because of our poor social situation, my relatives little by little lost contact with us.

In this woman's account are certain features that have become the main issues in integration. First of all, she had a housing problem and, as we have seen, solving this is one of the important indicators of being 'local'. Second, she began entering spaces that were supposed to be only for men: she started going into government offices to seek help for her housing problem, sometimes offering bribes, meeting unknown men and so on (Ghazaryan 2000). Third, she had to accept work as a cleaner, even though she had a university degree; she did so despite the social difficulties it entailed. Unfortunately, as she said, she began losing touch with her relatives and the chance to be accepted by the local society.

> I also couldn't make friends among the local people because no one wanted to be friends with a cleaner, a refugee who 'steals' their material assistance. I had to be very strong; it seemed they avoided me, because I didn't look like them. I guess, they didn't like my behaviour, my accent, my language (Russian). I felt like a stranger among my own people. I've never made friends among the local people, least of all the women.

It was no accident that local people rejected these newcomers even though they too were ethnically Armenian. On the one hand, following the collapse of the Soviet Union, the Armenian government adopted a special linguistic policy privileging the Armenian language as a sign of independence from Russia. Unfortunately, this worked against refugees who had been expelled in the late 1980s from Azerbaijan and thus could only speak an Armenian dialect at best (Abrahamyan 1998). On the other hand, refugees were perceived as competitors in difficult economic times when there was little work for anyone. Thus, these displaced women slowly began to realize how little they could restore of what they had lost (apartments, jobs, savings, status, etc.) At the same time, local citizens criticized the aid given to refugees from Azerbaijan because it was seen as a drain on already limited resources. For all these reasons, the individual and social desire to help refugees dwindled (Kharatyan 1999, pp. 58–59).

6 'We Are Strangers Among Our Own People' ...   139

Another refugee from Baku described her experiences of integration, highlighting the difficulty of language, employment and everyday struggle. Her narrative also shows the despair that refugees felt after leaving their homes in Azerbaijan and trying to resettle in Armenia. Her words confirm once again that 'home' is constituted by much more than a physical place in which someone lives (or lived); it also represents 'the accumulation of many relationships and much history' (Black 2002).

> I still miss my neighbours, all of them. We had neighbours, in a mixed marriage – the husband was Azerbaijani and the wife was Armenian. They helped me so much and in the end, they had to leave the country as well. It was difficult for mixed marriage couples; there were cases when a husband took the children and left his Armenian wife. Who'd have thought that one day my family would live in a dormitory? That so many families would be destroyed? I'm 81 years old now, but I look good. Because I used to have a nice life; I had a wonderful husband and family. I divide my life into two parts: before 1990 and after 1990 ... I'm very sad for only one reason: my husband didn't manage to see his dream. He died without having his own place. I hope my grandson has an opportunity to live in his own home. My life has finished. Before my neighbours called me Elyanora Khanum.[11] Now you can call me whatever you wish, I've lost myself ... (Elyanora, 86 years old)

As Elyanora's interview excerpt shows, forced migration introduces a different kind of time. This is often accompanied by a period—months, years, decades—of radical cognitive and affective uncertainty about where and how life is to be lived, with the possibility of a return to an earlier home, in tension with the need to make life more sustainable in the here-and-now, by livelihood activities, homemaking, the education of children and the reconstruction of community (Loizos 2007, p. 193).

> After 1990, it felt like I couldn't go on living. Every moment was a fight simply for life. Though 26 years have passed, I'm still living there in the past. Every day I remember my relatives, my neighbours, and my home. I miss my life in Baku. I wish there was peace everywhere – conflict destroys people's lives. There are no bad nations, only dirty – corrupt – politics.

140 S. Ghazaryan

As with most refugees, these women's struggles did not end with their escape from violence in Baku. The collapse of the Soviet Union and the independence of Armenia in 1991 led to the rise of nationalistic values. In protest against the Soviet legacy, people formed policies to revive the Armenian national values that had been buried and forbidden topics during the Soviet era. For example, Russian schools were closed and people expected everyone to speak Armenian. Though these displaced women were Armenians and, like other Armenians outside Armenia, used to live together in one place, they were all Soviet people now they were back in their so-called homeland, which was always imagined as a place of happiness and desire while they were living in Baku (Stepanyan 2010).

Yet the desire to return came quite unexpectedly and they were unprepared for conditions so different from what they had imagined in Baku. The meanings of 'home' largely depend on the ways that individuals and groups construct them and the attributes they associate with them in a given context. In this sense, home must not be taken for granted as a predefined and changeless notion. Furthermore, home and belonging have pragmatic and emotional/cultural attributes that are constantly being changed and reinterpreted (Dam and Eyles 2012, p. 5). They even had language issues, knew very little Armenian and most were too shy to speak with an accent which revealed where they came from. At the time it was also difficult to find a job in Armenia, a country which had already serious economic issues in the early 1990s as noted above.[12] There seemed no prospect for them to feel a sense of 'belonging' and 'home'.

'Strangers Among Us'

To understand why some refugees felt such despair and difficulty in integrating into Armenian society, we should consider how they were viewed by local residents. This is a problem that has also been experienced by refugees in other parts of the world (Avagyan 1996; Platts-Fowler and Robinson 2015; Wrench et al. 2016). The following interview excerpt shows how refugees often felt rejected by local people.

6 'We Are Strangers Among Our Own People' ...   141

I felt myself very uncomfortable here, especially during the first period of my arrival. I couldn't make friends among local Armenians. They ignored me or insulted me. For example, when I spoke Russian on the bus or when I was standing in line for bread, they called me 'Turk'[13] and said I was talking 'dog language' (Russian).[14] That was one of the reasons I refused to go on trying to make friends with the local people.

Powerlessness against the increasingly aggressive mood of local people towards the authorities made refugees vulnerable as targets of blame and discontent. Everything related to them seemed wrong and unacceptable to local residents. They spoke Russian, were comparatively open-minded, had foreign accents, were poor and proud, etc. As a response to the reaction of local residents, the refugees continued with pride to advertise their cultural values and thus try to subvert traditional Armenian norms (Kharatyan 1999, p. 59). This is why even very small things could become a reason for the constant rejection of refugees by locals. Though almost all local Armenian resident knew Russian perfectly, they refused to talk to the refugees in Russian. It was a form of self-protection and social protest, showing that they had other more pressing things to think about than the refugees. If 'homeland' is no longer regarded as a natural and unproblematic category, homecoming can no longer be treated as a straightforward process, whether as the logical end to displacement or an antidote to the perceived ills of diasporic existence (Laycock 2012, p. 105).

I had a lot of neighbours in Azerbaijan, men, women, no difference. Generally, we gathered together and had a good time in the evenings. Here I tried to make friends, but men misunderstood me. They saw my offer as an invitation for another kind of relationship. Imagine what their wives would have had to say! I used to have blonde hair and I've always liked to have clothes with a bit of colour. Though I am 84 now, I still care about my nails, my clothes. Always I heard people whisper after me, 'Look at her! She is a widow but the way she looks …'

After these words, 84-year-old Alvina remained silent for a while, then went on very sadly.

I loved my husband, but I also wanted to live. Even if I wore nothing but black or never went out, it wouldn't bring him back. I'm also a human being. Yes, perhaps I did want to get married again. Sometimes I felt very lonely. I have a son, but he has his family and lives in Russia. My neighbours always complained that I acted like a young woman. What should I do? If I really feel younger, then I am. Is this a sin? Who made those social rules – how to dress, how to behave. It was really hard for me at the beginning. Now I don't pay much attention, but I'm alone.

In almost all the interviews, the women complained about constantly being watched and under the social control of their neighbours.

There are always neighbours who sit at the window and keep track of others. They know best who comes to your place, what time you go out and come back. In Baku, we all knew about each other, but never discussed or gossiped with others. We shared our birthdays, happy or sad events, but we all had our personal life. Here people live with and for the community.

Misunderstanding and emotional rejection intervened between local women and refugees, not only in the domestic sphere and that of gender, but also in the different perception of concepts beyond these. Generally speaking, displaced women were perceived as enjoying more free contact with men, parents, children, etc. Such perceptions grew to justify the distance between the locals and them. It was based on the following characteristics: you are 'different', although you are called 'one of us'; 'you use foreign languages, Azerbaijani and Russian, instead of our native tongue (Armenian)'. Refugees everywhere were called 'inverted Armenians' (*shurtvatz hayer, perevernutye armyane*). Locals perceived them as irritating because of their 'excessive' loyalty to everything Russian and Azerbaijani. The different manners of the displaced women became a reason even to call them 'prostitutes' (Shahnazarian 2008, p. 104), as Leongina, a refugee woman, discusses in the following interview excerpt:

Sometimes it seems that we are the reason that Armenia was going through a difficult period. We used to live in Baku. The weather was generally warm and we used to wear shorts, skirts, colourful things, high heels. When the situation became tense, I brought with me what

I had and once I got to Armenia, I had no chance to shop – I wore what I had. Here it was hard to find colourful things in the shops. In the 1990s, the fashion in Armenia was to wear black. Maybe because of the difficult times, earthquake, war … but I always like to brighten the place up. I'm a woman and should look properly dressed. The fact that I'm divorced, I've never kept a secret. I know a lot of women, they haven't lived with their husband for almost 20 years, but they're too shy to say they're divorced. When I said to my neighbours that I'm an independent woman, they began to think that I was going to steal their husbands. You know, we think differently, the mentality is different. That's why, I have only got one close friend and she is from Baku too.

During my fieldwork, it appeared that local residents were often ready to find fault with their refugee neighbours. Nearly all the complaints were about the same main subject, social dissatisfaction, as the following interview excerpt shows:

We are neighbours at the dormitory.[15] We are the same age, live in the same poor conditions, but she gets aid from different international organizations, because she is a refugee. Must I go and die of starvation, because I'm not a refugee? It's not right. We are all human beings and we all need assistance.

On the one hand, humanitarian assistance was necessary if the refuges were to survive; it also sometimes gave them an opportunity to feel supported. But on the other, it became one of the reasons why local people were not very welcoming. The irregular/unorganized assistance left the refugees completely unable to predict what would happen next, what resources would be available, or how they might begin to plan for the future. In such an unpredictable environment, rumours of backroom deals and covert political connections began to swirl (Dunn 2014).

It is known, however, that for refugees, state assistance is very important especially in the first stage of resettlement. Only after they have a permanent or semi-permanent shelter can these people realize their situation and ask themselves if they can bear it or not (Avagyan 1996, p. 17). Unfortunately, many of the responses by the government and international organizations to the refugee crisis of the 1990s focused on granting material assistance (Ghazaryan 2000). However, that is only one aspect of solving the refugee problem. A more challenging issue is the socio-economic and psychological integration of refugees and naturalized former refugees into the wider society (Crisp 2004). Although these ethnic Armenians had returned to their homeland, rebuilding their lives in the way they used to live in Baku was not possible because of the cultural differences that they encountered. One of the interviewees, Elyanora, remembered how everything began and how their life unexpectedly changed; they are still 'waiting' to live the way they used to:

> Our life changed since the beginning of the 1980s. My husband began having problems at his workplace (in Baku). There was a lot of surveillance, security checks and discrimination. One day he came home and decided to quit his job. Our friends from Azerbaijan were worried about us and advised us to leave Baku as soon as possible. It was clear that ethnic discrimination was rising day by day. We understood that the situation had become tense, but we couldn't ever imagine that Soviet policy could destroy the world that we had built, with my husband. After the Sumgait pogroms,[16] we realized that our lives were in danger. But we couldn't change our whole life all at once. We had to think how to leave, how to organize everything. We also couldn't bring ourselves to believe that massacres would be organized in cosmopolitan place like Baku. First, we sent our only daughter to Armenia, then I organized my husband's movement to Yerevan and I stayed in Baku to try to sell our apartment.

Although I wanted to ask her during the interview how a woman who had had a carefree life could decide to remain in such dangerous circumstances instead of her husband, I could not manage to. She began to explain why she had to be so strong. While her husband was on his way back to Baku from Armenia, he was caught and beaten up by a frenzied crowd of Azerbaijanis. Since then he had not been able to talk because of an incurable trauma[17] and Elyanora became the head of the family.

> We had always made our important decisions together, but now I had to do it alone. I want to mention that at that time I wasn't scared. I only thought about my family's future life and I knew that I was strong enough to overcome the fear. In those days, it was very dangerous to walk in the street in Baku, especially for Armenian women, but I went to the station and arranged for my husband's travel to Yerevan.

Unfortunately, she was not able to sell their apartment in Baku and hardly managed to escape from Baku herself, going first to Georgia, then finally to Yerevan, where she, her husband and her daughter stayed with relatives.

> First, we began living together with my relatives in Yerevan. Twelve people in one apartment! Though it was very difficult, we managed because we loved each other and we shared all the difficulties. But little by little the situation became more difficult and it wasn't possible to live with our relatives anymore because they couldn't live like that either. I felt like a burden to them. To escape conflict, I began looking for a place to live. I was able to find a room in a dormitory in Yerevan and we moved there and still live here. This period seems like an endless hell to me. For 25 years now the family has lived in only one room.

The government was informed and was aware of disputes between the newcomers and the local people, but unfortunately state organizations were unable to create a bridge between them. Although this paper presents only a few accounts by women of their struggles for life, there were thousands of people who, like them, faced wars and violence. Life continues as normal, but they remain in the past with their memories, as some of the interviewed women do.

Conclusions

Most Armenian refugees from Azerbaijan were not welcome in Armenia because of the absence of an elementary integration policy and the chaotic situation of the nation-state at the time. Even though Baku was one of the big industrial centres in the Soviet Union and Armenians accordingly had specialized skills, by the 1990s all the factories and industrial centres in Armenia were closed, further limiting employment opportunities. Additionally, one of the main industrial cities—Gyumri—was almost completely destroyed by an earthquake in 1988 which killed approximately 25,000 people and destroyed the homes of more than 500,000 people (Hadjian 1992). As a result of these socio-economic difficulties, the Armenian state could not assist the displaced people during the first stage of adaptation and integration into Armenian society (Avagyan 1991). Further complications included language barriers and an unexpected backlash against refugees due to cultural differences from local Armenians.

Generally, refugees resolved most issues either on their own or with the help of their kin and social networks. Some refugees were settled in public buildings (e.g. hotels, hospitals, schools) which had been abandoned. These buildings often were in a miserable condition. Others live in what is termed private accommodation, which can range from a home that they own to an apartment they rent, or even a room that is given them by their family or friends to stay in temporarily. Although the flight of refugees from Azerbaijan took place in the late 1980s and early 1990s, a yet unknown number of refugees have still not been provided with adequate housing and employment opportunities and consequently are in a vulnerable position.

This situation is perplexing because one might not have expected Armenian refugees returning to their homeland to have experienced so many issues with reintegration. This situation raises questions about the meanings of 'home' and 'homeland that challenges causal assumptions about belonging and reintegration. Because Armenians fleeing Baku were resettled in their 'homeland', it seemed as if they would easily be able to settle in their 'homeland again. However, they were in fact displaced refugees who had suffered considerable loss and left behind a rich life. Consequently, for these refugees, home is situated in the past as constructed and reproduced through nostalgia and memory. When home is situated in the past, it becomes associated with normality, security, familiarity, wealth and comfort. One's current losses and hardships are defined against the normality of the past (Kabachnik 2010, p. 323) and a new place becomes a kind of neutral grid on which cultural difference, historical memory and social organization are inscribed (Gupta and Ferguson 1992, p. 7).

For women refugees, the experience of the loss of their homes in Baku was further exacerbated by local Armenian values and practices that questioned the refugees' morality, work ethic and values. Women refugees in Armenia experienced discrimination and harassment from locals who used language, appearance and other cultural differences to exclude them. Refugee women's experiences of discrimination and harassment suggest that there was a triple or even quadruple burden on women during their efforts to reintegrate. Not only were they responsible for managing their own daily needs and the needs of their families during a terrible crisis, they were also expected to learn and adapt to the customs expected of local Armenian women. Their bodies (in terms of style, clothing and appearance) and their homes—two sites at which local women are evaluated according to local, patriarchal customs—were subject to surveillance and scrutiny. More importantly, however, women's ability to live up to local expectations of gender roles served to further justify the lack of support for these refugees from local people. In response to these patterns of discrimination, refugee women stopped their efforts to show locals that they were moral and hard-working; instead they decided to show their own independence and status. In other words, their efforts to reintegrate ended and they embraced their status as outsiders. Now at the beginning of the twenty-first century, as after 1915–1923 and 1988–1992, Armenia is facing similar issues related to those for Syrian Armenian refugees arriving from war-torn areas of Syria. As a result of previous experiences, the Armenian government has managed to put much more effective integration policies in place, yet the question remains whether these new integration policies will have a much more positive effect on the interactions between locals and newcomers.

This research presented here is part of a larger research project for my doctoral studies.

Notes

1. A military operation aimed at forcing Armenians to leave their homes in the northern parts of Nagorny Karabakh (Ayunts 2011, p. 3).
2. During the war and even shortly after the ceasefire, border villages in the northeast of Armenia were subjected to intermittent rocket and artillery shelling by Azerbaijani forces. However, most of the IDP population returned to their homes in the years after the ceasefire, and the main body of IDPs comes from the Armenian territories currently

occupied by Azerbaijan, such as Artsvashen village (3000 people) (Ayunts 2011, p. 23).

3. The official acceptance of immigrants, then called repatriation, was organized several times in Soviet Armenia. The first official body responsible for immigrants, the Main Department of Immigrants (Գաղթականական գործերի գլխավոր վարչություն) was established in the USSR in 1921. It was renamed the 'Committee of Immigration' in September 1925 (Ayvazyan 1976–83, p. 142). A Governmental Committee for Organizing the Acceptance of Armenians from abroad was established in 1958 (Meliqsetyan 1983).

4. Following the Sumgait pogroms in February 1988, 200,000 Armenians were deported. Then in 1989–1991, 350,000 Armenians were deported against their will from Soviet Azerbaijan and 280,000 of them were moved into Soviet Armenia. The rest went to Moscow and other Soviet Union cities (Avagyan 1991, pp. 115–116).

5. This information was obtained from the official website of the Ministry of Territorial Administration and Development of the Republic of Armenia Migration Service at.

6. According to official estimates: 25,000 people died, 50,000 were injured and 500,000 became homeless (Hadjian 1992).

7. Those who could, escaped the massacres in Baku. Gangs broke into houses where Armenians lived, took everything and often injured or killed Armenians. Sometimes Armenians were attacked on the streets and killed (Mosesova and Hovnanyan 1992, pp. 205–271).

8. Armenians in Azerbaijan spoke mainly Russian and less Armenian; hence they encountered language problems in Armenian because they were less fluent in the language.

9. Amoral behaviour, in this case, means, for example, that refugee women could be seen in government offices, among men, trying to solve their housing or other problems. In addition, divorced refugees never concealed the fact that they were divorced and wanted to get married again; some of them had relationships with married men, and etc.

10. Lavash bread is a traditional thin bread that forms an integral part of Armenian cuisine.

11. By 'Elyanora Khanum', she meant that she had a good name: she was treated with respect, because she had status, was well-turned out, always looked good and lived in ideal conditions.

12. Economic activities declined from 81.4 to 52.3% between 1991 and 2009.
13. Historically Turkey is Armenia's enemy: calling someone a Turk is a way of hurting refugees. In colloquial Armenian, all Azerbaijanis are 'Turks'.
14. Again, this was a way of insulting these refugee women. It meant that they were strangers and talking in a 'foreign' language, not Armenian.
15. This local woman told me that during the 1990s her family had financial problems and they had to sell their apartment and temporarily move into this dormitory; they have remained there ever since.
16. The Sumgait pogrom (Armenian: Սումգայիթի ջարդեր, Sumgayit'i jarder lit. 'Sumgait massacres') was a pogrom that targeted the Armenian population of the seaside town of Sumgait in Soviet Azerbaijan in late February 1988.
17. Elyanor's husband was caught on the train in Baku. He was travelling to Armenia, but instead about 20 Armenian men were picked out on this train and beaten up. Elyanora said that it was a miracle that her husband stayed alive. After this incident, her husband had to undergo long months of treatment, but could never talk again. Thus, Elyanora become the head of the family and had to change from being a well-groomed housewife in charge of 'symbolic' domestic work into a man-woman (*tghamard-kin*).

References

Abrahamyan, Levon. 1998. "Mother Tongue: Linguistic Nationalism and the Cult of Translation in Post-communist Armenia." *Berkeley Program in Soviet and Post-Soviet Studies.* Berkeley: University of California.

Avagyan, Gevorg. 1991. "Нагорный Карабах: Ответ фальсификатором." [Nagorny Karabakh: The Answer to Falsifiers]. RA NAS "Գիտություն" Yerevan: Publishing House.

———. 1996. "Փախստականների սոցիալական ադապտացիան Հայաստանում." [Social Adaptation of Refugees in Armenia]. RA NAS "Գիտություն" Yerevan: Publishing House.

Ayunts, Artak. 2011. "Return and its Alternatives, Perspectives from Armenia." In *Forced Displacement in the Nagorno Karabakh Conflict: Return and its Alternatives. Concilliation Resources,* 23–31. London. http://www.epnk. org/sites/default/files/downloads/Forced%20Displacement%20in%20 Nagorny%20Karabakh%20Conflict_201108_ENG.pdf.

Ayvazyan, H. 1976–1983. *Armenian Soviet Encyclopedia.* Vol. 2. RA NAS "Գիտություն" Yerevan: Publishing House.

Baghdasaryan, Milena. 2009. "The Hardships of Becoming 'Locals': Refugees Before and After the State, Housing Program in Armenia." *Caucasus Analytical Digest* 4 (9): 7–11.

Beukian, Sevan. 2014. "Motherhood as Armenianness: Expressions of Femininity in the Making of Armenian National Identity." *Studies in Ethnicity and Nationalism* 14 (2): 247–269. https://onlinelibrary.wiley.com/doi/pdf/10.1111/sena.12092.

Black, Richard. 2002. "Conceptions of 'Home' and the Political Geography of Refugee Repatriation: Between Assumption and Contested Reality in Bosnia-Herzegovina." *Applied Geography* 22 (2): 123–138. https://doi.org/10.1016/S0143-6228(02)00003-6.

Crisp, Jeff. 2004. "The Local Integration and Local Settlement of Refugees: A Conceptual and Historical Analysis." UNHCR, Evaluation and Policy Analysis Unit, No. 102. https://www.unhcr.org.

Dam, Huyen, and John Eyles. 2012. "'Home Tonight? What? Where?' An Exploratory Study of the Meanings of House, Home and Family Among the Former Vietnamese Refugees in a Canadian City." *Forum: Qualitative Social Research Sozialforschung* 13 (2): Art. 19. http://dx.doi.org/10.17169/fqs-13.2.1696.

Danielyan, Eduard. G. 2002. "Անդրկովկասում պատմանած արևմտահայ գաղթականության թվաքանակի հարցի շուրջ (1914–1917թթ.)." [The Issue of the Number of Western Armenian Immigrants in Transcaucasia]. *Herald of the Social Sciences / Լրաբեր Հասարակական Գիտությունների* 2: 12–119.

Dunn, Elizabeth C. 2014. "Humanitarianism, Displacement and the Politics of Nothing in Postwar Georgia." *Slavic Review* 73 (2, Summer): 287–306. https://doi.org/10.5612/slavicreview.73.2.287.

Eastmond, Marita. 2007. "Stories as Lived Experience: Narratives in Forced Migration Research." *Journal of Refugee Studies* 20 (2): 248–264. https://doi.org/10.1093/jrs/fem007.

Ghazaryan, Yulia. 2000. *Obstacles to the Integration and Naturalization of Refugees: A Case Study of Ethnic Armenian Refugees in Armenia.* Center for Policy Analysis, American University of Armenia. http://unpan1.un.org/intradoc/groups/public/documents/nispacee/unpan005595.pdf.

Grant, Bruce. 2010. "Cosmopolitan Baku." *Ethnos* 75 (2): 123–147. https://doi.org/10.1080/00141841003753222.

Greene, Thomas. 1998. "Internal Displacement in the North Caucasus, Azerbaijan, Armenia and Georgia." In *The Forsaken People: Case Studies of the Internally Displaced*, edited by Roberta Cohen and Francis Deng, 213–310. Washington, DC: The Brookings Institution.

Gupta, Akhil, and James Ferguson. 1992. "Beyond 'Culture': Space, Identity, and the Politics of Difference." *Cultural Anthropology* 7 (1): 6–23.

Hadjian, A. H. 1992. "The Spitak Armenian Earthquake, Why So Much Destruction." Earthquake Engineering Tenth World Conference. Rotterdam. http://www.iitk.ac.in/nicee/wcee/article/10_vol1_5.pdf.

Kabachnik, Peter. 2010. "Where and When Is Home? The Double Displacement of Georgian IDPs from Abkhazia." *Journal of Refugee Studies* 23 (3): 315–336. https://doi.org/10.1093/jrs/feq023.

Kharatyan, Hranush. 1999. "Մենք ու նրանք, թե՞ օտարները յուրայինների մեջ (փախստականներ և ինաբնակներ)." [We and They, or Strangers Among Us, Refugees and Local Inhabitants]. Հայ-Ֆրանս իական պատմամշակութային առնչություններ. VI միջազգային գիտաժողովի նյութեր. . Armenian-French Cultural-Historic Relationship, Materials of the 4th International Conference, 56–80. Yerevan.

Kharatyan, Lusine. 2008. "Разгадать Южный Кавказ. Общества и среда обитания." (Figuring Out the South Caucasus: Societies and Environment) *Сборник статей*. Tbilisi.

Laycock, Jo. 2012. "Armenian Homelands and Homecoming, 1945–9: The Repatriation of Diaspora Armenians to the Soviet Union." *Culture and Social History* 9 (1): 103–123. https://doi.org/10.2752/1478004 12X13191165983079.

Loizos, Peter. 2007. "Generations' in Forced Migration: Towards Greater Clarity." *Journal of Refugee Studies* 20 (2): 193–209. https://doi.org/10.1093/jrs/fem012.

Meliqsetyan, H. 1983. "Սփյուռքահայերի հայրենադարձությունը. Լրաբեր Հասարակական Գիտությունների." [Repatriation Armenians from Diaspora] 7: 3–13. Yerevan.

Ministry of Territorial Administration and Development of the Republic of Armenia Migration Service. 2015. *Migration Newsletter*. March. No. 8. http://www.smsmta.am.

Mosesova, I., and Hovnanyan, A. 1992. *Բաքվի ջարդեր* [Genocide in Baku]. Yerevan: Yerevan State University.

Nahapetyan, Rafik. 2009. "Կինը հայոց ավանդական ընտանիքում (Ըստ սասունցիների ազգագրական սովորույթների)." [Traditional Armenian Woman in the Family According to Ethnographic Traditions of Sasunci]. *Historical-Philological Journal* 1: 71–87.

Oxygen and Oxfam. 2016. "Կանանց և տղամարդկանց տնտեսական գործունեությունը Հայաստանում (փաստաթղթերի վերլվերլուծության եւ փորձագիտական հարցման արդյունքների հաշվետվություն)." [Economic Activity of Women and Men in Armenia, Analysis of Document and Report Survey]. Yerevan.

Platts-Fowler, Deborah, and David Robinson. 2015. "A Place for Integration: Refugee Experiences in Two English Cities." *Population, Space and Place* 21 (5): 476–491. https://doi.org/10.1002/psp.1928.

Poghosyan, Svetlana. 2010. "Հայ կնոջ դերը ինքնության պահպանության գործընթացում. հայ կին և օտար տղամարդ ամուսնությունների միտումներ." [The Role of Armenian Woman in the Protection of Identity: Marriage Tendencies Between Armenian Women and Foreigners, Preservation of the Features of Armenian Identity in Mixed Marriages]. *Collection of Workshop Papers*, 162–170.

Sargsyan, Hamlet. 1995. Հայոց ցեղասպանությունը, պատճառներ ու դասեր.[The Armenian Genocide, Reasons and Lessons]. Yerevan: Yerevan State University.

Shahnazarian, Nona. 2008. "'And Where Can We Become Ours?' The Flight of Armenians from Azerbaijan and their Ensuing Migration. *Vestnik Evrazii, Nevazimyi Nauchnyi Zhurnal* 2 (40).

Shahnazarian, Nona, and Ulrike Ziemer. 2014. "Emotions, Loss and Change: Armenian Women and Post-socialist Transformations in Nagorny Karabakh." *Caucasus Survey* 2 (1–2): 27–40. https://doi.org/10.1080/2376 1199.2014.11417298.

Shahnazaryan, Gohar, Zaruhi Aznauryan, and Lusine Saghumyan. 2016. *Representation and Participation of Women in the Political Parties and Political Initiatives in Armenia: Gender Analyses*. Yerevan: Yerevan State University.

Stepanyan, Armenuhi. 2010. XX դարի հայրենադարձությունը հայոց ինքնության համակարգում. [20th Century Repatriation in the Armenian Identity System]. Yerevan: RA National Academy of Sciences "Gitutyun" Publisher.

Usha, K.B. 2005. "Political Empowerment of Women in the Soviet Union and Russia: Ideology and Implementation." *International Studies* 42 (2): 141–165.

Valiev, Anar. 2013. "Baku." *Cities* 31 (April): 625–640. https://doi.org/10.1016/j.cities.2012.11.004.

Wrench, John, Andrea Rea, and Nouria Ouali, eds. 2016. *Migrants, Ethnic Minorities and the Labour Market: Integration and Exclusion in Europe.* London: Macmillan Press.

Ziemer, Ulrike. 2011. *Ethnic Belonging, Gender and Cultural Practices: Youth Identities in Contemporary Russia.* Stuttgart: ibidem Verlag.

———. 2018. "'The Waiting and Not Knowing Can Be Agonizing:' Tracing the Power of Emotions in a Prolonged Conflict in the South Caucasus." *International Feminist Journal of Politics* 20 (3): 331–349. https://doi.org/10.1080/14616742.2018.1480900.

7

Vulnerability and Resilience: Women's Narratives of Forced Displacement from Abkhazia

Nargiza Arjevanidze

Since gaining its independence in 1991, Georgia has experienced dramatic transformations, several waves of armed conflict and forced displacement. As a result of armed conflicts in South Ossetia and Abkhazia, thousands of ethnic Georgians were forced to flee their homes and relocate within the territory of Georgia. The women interviewed for this chapter had to flee from Abkhazia, which, like South Ossetia, is a former Soviet Autonomous Republic in Georgia. Abkhazia, with an area of 8700 square kilometers, lies between the Black Sea and the Caucasus Mountains and comprises an eighth of Georgia's territory, including nearly half of its coastline. In Soviet times it used to be a popular tourist destination; thousands of Soviet tourists visited its resorts on the Black Sea coast. According to the 1989 census, the ethnic Abkhaz population of Abkhazia before the outbreak of the armed conflict was 17.8% of the total population of 525,061, while the ethnic Georgian population took up 45.7% of

N. Arjevanidze (✉)
Tbilisi State University, Tbilisi, Georgia

© The Author(s) 2020
U. Ziemer (ed.), *Women's Everyday Lives in War and Peace in the South Caucasus*,
https://doi.org/10.1007/978-3-030-25517-6_7

155

the total. Armenians and Russians were the two other most numerous ethnic groups living in the Soviet Autonomous Republic of Abkhazia (Human Rights Watch 2011).

By the time Georgia declared independence from the Soviet Union in 1991, ethnic tension had become part of the political discourse. There were three related wars in Georgia between 1989 and 1993: 'the first, over the breakaway region of South Ossetia, began in November 1989, [...] the second war was fought between rival Georgian groups bidding for political power; it began in December 1991 and ended in November 1993 and was triggered by the violent overthrow of President Zviad Gamsakhurdia by a coalition of opposition politicians and warlords. The third war was over the breakaway Autonomous Republic of Abkhazia; it began in August 1992 and ended in September 1993 with the defeat of [the] Georgian troops' (Zürcher 2007, p. 116). Both conflicts over South Ossetia and Abkhazia have so far remained formally unresolved. Both conflicts have cost thousands of lives and resulted in ethnic cleansing when 'Abkhazian forces "cleansed" more than 200,000 mostly ethnic Georgians from the breakaway republic' (ibid.: p. 116). Still, 'the Abkhaz authorities have allowed some to return to the Gali district, but not to other parts of Abkhazia' (Human Rights Watch 2011).

Violence against civilians in these ethnic wars was generally widespread. Thousands of civilians were killed during the fighting, while looting, torture and pillaging on both sides were documented (Buck et al. 2000). According to the International Committee of the Red Cross (ICRC) report the country's casualties numbered 10,000–15,000 dead and at least 8000 wounded (ICRC 1999). The Human Rights Watch report, based on the data provided by the Georgian Government's Committee on Human Rights and Interethnic Relations (1995) notes that 4000 individuals from the Georgian side, both civilians and combatants, were killed, 10,000 were wounded, and 1000 were reported missing. The same report notes that according to the Abkhazian Committee for Human Rights 4040 were killed (2220 combatants and 1820 civilians); approximately 8000 were wounded; 122 were missing in action in the period from August 14, 1992, through

September 30, 1993. Regarding the numbers of IDPs, some estimates put the total of forced displacements at more than 370,000 people (IDMC/NRC 2012). According to more recent figures, there are now approximately 289,000 conflict-induced IDPs in Georgia (IDMC 2018).

In 2008, the conflict between Georgia and the de facto independent South Ossetia resurfaced and grew into what has become known as 'the Georgian-Russian war' (Rekhviashvili 2015, p. 4). Once again it produced a large number of IDPs[1] whom Georgia's political discourse now refers to as 'new' IDPs in, whereas the forcefully uprooted persons from Abkhazia are 'commonly referred to as the "old" IDPs and continue to live in a situation of protracted displacement' (Rekhviashvili 2015, p. 4). After the brief Russian-Georgian war in August 2008, the Russian Federation recognized the independence of Abkhazia and South Ossetia. Nevertheless, even though other states have also recognized Abkhazia, the territory is internationally recognized as part of Georgia (Human Rights Watch 2011). Abkhazia is not recognized under international law as an independent state, the conflict remains unresolved and generally ethnic Georgian IDPs are not allowed to return (except for the Gali district). Thus, IDPs from Abkhazia have been trapped in a waiting that never ends, in the meantime condemned to living for an indefinite term in so-called 'temporary' accommodation. Emotional distress and memories of the war and its aftermath coupled with economic instability and harsh living conditions render the lives of most IDPs in Georgia particularly vulnerable.

This chapter is part of a larger research project[2] and is based on the narratives of internally displaced women who were forced to flee from Abkhazia at the beginning of the 1990s. It focuses on women's experiences of forced displacement and its aftermath. The main aim of the research project is to explore how displaced women reflect on their lives before and during the armed conflict; how they experienced, remember and describe the violent events of the war, now almost 27 years in the past; how they reflect on the tactics for survival that they have developed in the aftermath; and how they reflect on their lives in this protracted displacement.

Methodological Approach: Intimate Ethnography and Storytelling

Social scientists—ethnographers and feminist researchers—have developed a wide array of innovative approaches to help from their own perspectives to incorporate personal, specific experiences in their research into, exploration of and writings about women's lives. The life-story approach has been extensively used by feminist scholars as a successful medium for collecting women's words, 'for reaching a social "group" that does not often speak on the social stage, or, more precisely, whose discourse has not, until recently been perceived as legitimate' (Chanfrault-Duchet 1991, p. 77). These stories have increasingly focused on women's lives and the numerous mundane tasks they daily perform, which are examples of women's specific experiences (Brooks 2007).

This analysis of collected data is based on *intimate ethnography* and life stories. Anthropologists Alisse Waterston and Barbara Rylko-Bauer (2006, p. 405) developed *intimate ethnography* to 'enter a deeply private and interior place as ethnographers'. Their approach resembles autoethnography in that they create an intimate connection between themselves and their subjects, but also attempt to go beyond the reflexive 'I' in order to accentuate the distance between these related methods and their perspective (Waterston and Rylko-Bauer 2006, p. 405). Thus, intimate ethnography is key to this project since it enabled me to learn about respondents' lives from their own perspectives and deepened my deeper understanding of the way that they make sense of their lives and what they deem important (Arjevanidze 2017a). Like Waterston and Rylko-Bauer, who had intimate connections with their informants—Waterston's father and Rylko-Bauer's mother—I was initially inspired to undertake this research by my own mother's experience of being an internally displaced person from Abkhazia.

My informants are people with whom I have very close relations, insofar as I belong to the group that I research—I am also an ethnic Georgian displaced within the territory of Georgia as a result of the armed conflict at the beginning of the 1990s. In 2015, I began by conducting several interviews with my mother, during the fieldwork for my project. Then I interviewed other women—my relatives, family friends and former neighbours from Abkhazia; thus the research that began with my mother's interview later developed into a bigger 'intimate' project[3] (Arjevanidze 2017a).

It is important to consider what the process of sharing signifies for these women. While reflecting on their lives in and after forced displacement, the displaced women in my study were sharing their stories or, in the words of the anthropologist Jackson, were engaged in storytelling. In his work *The Politics of Storytelling*, he explores the links between violence and telling stories, and focuses on the process of sharing stories that are told by individuals who have been forcefully displaced, are in flight, or in crisis. He asserts that when the events are reconstructed in a story, we no longer live those events in passivity; instead, through dialogue with others or with our imagination; through the sharing, we actively engage in reworking not only the stories we tell, but also the situation we are placed in, which then becomes more bearable (Jackson 2002). Jackson explores the ways in which stories help people cope with the consequences of violence. He does not simply suggest that stories have power; 'rather … by enabling dialogues that encompass different points of view the act of sharing stories helps us create a world that is more than the sum of its individual parts' (Jackson 2002, p. 43).

Most interesting for the present research project is Jackson's insight into the act of sharing stories on violence. He asserts that the process of sharing can be experienced as a 're-empowerment', or likened in some ways to the process of confession. The experience of re-empowerment while sharing intimate stories with the researcher applies to some of the interview participants, especially to women such as Teo who, despite the late interview hours, expressed her willingness to talk and even insisted that I talk to her after I had finished another interview with her friend, also one of the interlocutors in this study. Her insistence on sharing was unexpected, since the memories that she revisited were quite painful. In Jackson's words, the process of sharing for her might have worked as a 're-empowerment' and has had a healing effect—not the case for other participants.

Between 2015 and 2017, I conducted in-depth interviews and had follow-up conversations (in the second fieldwork phase) with 17 women overall. All were ethnically Georgian, and all had been displaced from

160 N. Arjevanidze

Abkhazia in 1992–1993 as a result of the armed conflict. The women ranged in age from fifty-five to seventy years old. I met the research participants for interviews and follow-up conversations either in their own apartments, or in former kindergartens and former student dormitories, called collective centres, which the state had transformed into living spaces after the war (Buck et al. 2000). In this chapter, every research participant is given a pseudonym.

The Uncertainty of Protracted Displacement

Both refugees and Internally Displaced Persons (IDPs) are forced to leave their homes, unexpectedly and in large numbers, but, unlike refugees, IDPs do not cross international borders, but stay within their home country and remain under the protection of their own government. Both refugees and IDPs 'begin from a position of loss, including the loss of assets, family and community, and often emotional and physical health' (Jacobsen 2014); the key difference lies in the fact that IDPs are citizens, while refugees are 'foreigners' in a hosting society. Nevertheless, research on IDPs in the Georgian context has shown that, despite living in their own country, IDPs have undergone isolation, stigma, social alienation and marginalization and have felt like outsiders in their own society (Mitchnek et al. 2009; Rekhviashvili 2015; Toria 2015). These experiences are described by the women in this study.

Although IDPs remain within their own country, they are not in the 'right' place; they 'both belong and do not belong; they are simultaneously *insiders* and *outsiders*' (Lundgren 2016, p. 19). Turner's conceptualization of *liminality* and *transitional beings* may also be used to describe the condition of limbo in which IDPs from Abkhazia in Georgia have been trapped for over two decades. In Turner's words 'transitional beings, or liminal personae [...] are neither here nor there, or maybe even nowhere and are at the very least "betwixt and between" all the recognized fixed points in the space-time or cultural classification' (Turner 1967, p. 236). In the circumstances of prolonged displacement, the conflict itself ends or has prospects of doing so; but what is unclear for forcefully uprooted persons is when the *aftermath* ends. In such situations, IDPs feel caught up between their lost homes, present 'temporary' homes and imagined future homes (Kabachnik et al. 2010; Lundgren 2016).

Living in the open-endedness of prolonged displacement has become a chronic condition for most displaced persons in Georgia; it can be characterized as an experience of continuous uncertainty. This is why the concept of *crisis* as an experiential domain, conceptualized by Vigh (2008) not as a moment but as a chronicity is useful for exploring respondents' stories. Drawing on Benjamin's (1999)[4] writing on the 'state of emergency', Vigh conceptualizes a kind of crisis that is social, political or existential, a chronic and constant condition of the lives of increasingly many people in the world. He suggests that we try to understand *crisis* not as a temporary experience of abnormality and rupture caused by a wide array of traumatic events at a specific period of time, but rather as a constant state of affairs and situation of abnormality in which 'the chronically ill, the structurally violated, socially marginalized and poor' continue to live and try to manage their lives (Vigh 2008, p. 7). *Crisis*, in the case of protracted displacement can be understood as abnormality and the open-ended rupture of the everyday, in contrast to the normality of past times.

I also argue that *crisis* in the continuation of protracted displacement acquires multiple forms and is experienced differently as time passes. It does not cease to exist but persists at various levels and dynamics and may have a transformative power, depending on the experience of the war and its aftermath by war-affected communities. In the following discussion, women's narratives are explored in chronological order, starting from their wartime experiences, followed by the experiences of the aftermath, which, for most of the interlocutors in this study has lasted up to the present.

Recollecting the Past: Living with 'Poisonous Knowledge'

The women in this study do not belong to a single, undifferentiated group. They have different connections to the war, hence, different wartime experiences—the circumstances in which they had to flee, the availability of resources to leave when their safety was threatened by the overall duration of the war. For example, some were caught in the midst of cross-fire, others, leaving their husbands behind, had to hide or flee with their small children in search of a safe place, while some of these women escaped relatively unscathed and had access to more resources than others.

Nino recollects the days when she, her mother and her siblings left their house and walked for a few days through mountain passes in Svaneti to reach the point where they could stay overnight:

> The roads were mined and it was not safe any longer to stay in Kodori gorge, the bombing in Tkvarcheli was so close. We left … in the beginning a big truck took us all. With all of us and our belongings on the truck, it took us two days to reach a place where we could spend a night in tents. We left our bags there and rode on horses that someone gave us. We needed them for the three of us, my mother and her 6-year old son took turns to ride on the horse. But this road seemed to have no end. We walked, some people barefoot, in the mud, in the rain. We saw dead people who could not make it and had died on this road. At the top of the mountain it started snowing … and this road went on and on, as if there was no end.

Lamara used to work as a nurse in the hospital; she stayed there for fifty days after her family and neighbours left. She considered she had a responsibility to stay until no patients left in the hospital. The only ones left were wounded soldiers:

> The town was empty, I was in the hospital for days and nights, I didn't sleep at all and I didn't want to … some of us stayed there until the shooting reached the hospital building as well … We had to leave some wounded men. There was no other way as there wasn't enough trans-portation to take all of them with us; the order was that we shouldn't leave anyone, but we couldn't; ships, helicopters, buses, cars - we used everything but still we left many wounded men in the hospital. I didn't want to leave. I assisted the doctor in surgeries up to the last minute … I had to, how could a doctor work without an assistant? … As I left I could see our houses burning. I saw your house burning as well [refer-ring to my house] I wept and wept. I had spent 20 years in the house that we built, and everything I had earned with my hard work was burning in front of my eyes …

These experiences and connections with the war greatly shape their experiences and positions in the aftermath (Meintjes et al. 2002). Furthermore, these 'experiences and connections' can determine the ways in which memories about the war are inscribed within them, the ways in which, having witnessed violent events they have tried to come to terms with the pain caused by war, heal their wounds and move forward (Rydström 2007).

Contributors to the volume *The Aftermath—Women in Post-conflict Transformation* emphasize that the challenge of rebuilding lives in wartorn societies is 'much more complex and difficult than the task of putting an end to fighting' (Meintjes et al. 2002, p. 3). The book brings together activists and academics who bring out the role of women in post-conflict settings and their potential role in the process of transformation. The key aspect analysed in the book is the diverse understanding of the aftermath of armed conflict, or even the possibility that there may be no aftermath at all, insofar as violence and distress continue for women after a ceasefire as well. The authors also single out the importance of women's survival strategies that have 'kept families alive and communities together', which is an often overlooked subject since in a war the 'public rewards go to those who died'. In this volume, they illustrate that 'there is no one aftermath because the scenarios following the war are as various as the conflicts themselves' (Meintjes et al. 2002, p. 17).

Furthermore, the conflict and its aftermath are experienced and remembered in different ways by men and women. The growing body of literature in feminist memory studies has emphasized 'the ways in which the past shapes the present, and all of "us" in the present, in multiple and deeply gendered ways' (Altinay and Pető 2016, p. 5). Similarly, the displaced women in this study do not represent a homogenous group. Their responses to their forced displacement differ; nevertheless, there are certain similarities in their experiences of living in exile. For example, memories of their lost homes and recollections of their lives in pre-war, peaceful Abkhazia take up enormous space in the stories they share. As the following interview excerpt highlights, many women remember nostalgically the frequent gatherings with neighbours and relatives back in Abkhazia, which they recall as a 'family-like environment'.

> Our parents were hard-working people. They didn't have to think about how to provide for their children like I do now. We had a very good life. We worked together. We spent leisure time together. We were happy to help our parents to take care of the cattle, or the yard and garden ... then, there were no beggars on the streets or in their neighborhoods. None of our acquaintances went around asking for food. Nobody was hungry then. (Arjevanidze 2017a, p. 133)

These memories are all positive and evoke nostalgia, consistent with similar research that emphasizes the positive remembrance of the past. Nostalgia as a present emotional experience in post-socialist, post-conflict countries such as Georgia, is very closely linked to the loss of social trust, as well as the present social insecurity, which together strengthen the feeling of longing for the past (Light and Young 2015; Palmberger 2008; Kabachnik et al. 2013; Dunn 2014; Arjevanidze 2017a). At the same time, it can also be read as an expression of criticism of the present conditions. In post-conflict settings, the normalcy, safety and security of the past as recollected by IDPs, whose feeling of belonging to the lost home and the land is strong, is defined against the present situation, constructed in relation to the current harsh circumstances and continuous uncertainty (Toria 2015; Kabachnik et al. 2013; Lundgren 2016; Dunn 2014). Decades later—at a distance from the violent event, rather than in proximity—the women in this study share their recollections of the armed conflict. But these memories are always experienced as a kind of embodied 'poisonous knowledge', that cannot easily be erased (Rydström 2007).

Anthropologist Veena Das's exploration of what it means to witness violent events is useful in understanding the long-term effects of witnessing traumatic events on women, even when the experience is indirect. Das elaborates on the way in which the traumatic past becomes intertwined with the present:

> Even when it appears that some women were relatively lucky because they escaped direct bodily harm, the bodily memory of being-with-others makes that past encircle the present as atmosphere. This is what I mean by the importance of finding ways to speak about the experience of

7 Vulnerability and Resilience: Women's Narratives ... 165

witnessing: that if one's way of being-with-others was brutally injured, then the past enters the present not necessarily as traumatic memory but as a poisonous knowledge. (Das 2000, p. 221)

The stories of two sisters, Salome and Keti,[5] may help to illustrate what it means to be caught in the midst of warfare; witness acts of violence or 'being-with-others', then become reconciled to this knowledge and live with it. Salome and Keti were caught up in the war for 50 days when most civilians were forced to leave the city. They stayed to take care of their father who, had suffered a major stroke during the war. But this was not the only reason they had not left. Salome recalls that they could not fully comprehend that they had to leave their home and the city—Sukhumi—behind. Their whole family refused to leave and decided to struggle together to survive there. They recall how their house was hit by a bomb, which destroyed half of it, but they did not think about living anywhere else. They recall passing streets full of dead and brutally injured combatants from both sides of the conflict. They had to take a street of this kind on their way to the airport area, where they expected to get vital medication for their father. They remembered seeing soldiers shot in full view, and how they 'had gotten used to and expected death each and every moment'.

In a very relaxed manner during our interview, they reflected on the remote acts of violence they had witnessed at the beginning of the 1990s, telling a nuanced, coherent story of various events in a very elaborate way, at the same time intentionally refraining from detailed descriptions of specific atrocities they had seen, and sharing only a summary of what had happened. In choosing not to revisit painful passages from her past, Salome often focused on amusing stories from the war, trying to illustrate the absurdity of joyful moments they experienced as the city was being shelled:

Coffee-breaks were sometimes followed by fortune-telling: were we going to die today or tomorrow, or maybe in an hour. As we did this, we could see the tanks in the streets, hear the shooting and bombing; we had no idea when the fighters would come after us... We literally faced death[6] and weren't afraid. Instead, we were joking, we couldn't have lived there otherwise.

As this interview excerpt demonstrates, Keti and Salome somewhat cheerfully shared with me the tactics they employed 'just to stay sane and adapt to our new reality'. Salome elaborated on why she prefers not to think about what happened in the past:

> Sometimes these memories come back to me, and, if I want, as I did today, I can recall and talk about everything in the tiniest detail, I even remember the expressions on the faces of people I met in the streets during the war, but I rarely think about that, because it hurts. I try really hard not to think about the past; instead I live in the present and look forward to tomorrow. I choose not to dwell on the past because this process of remembering is extremely painful.

The trauma of war in war-affected societies is, in Hirsch's words, experienced as 'a sense of inexorable repetition of the past in the present and future in which injury cannot be healed or repaired, but lives on, shattering worlds in its wake' (Hirsch 2016, p. 80). In the case of Keti and Salome, choosing not to dwell in the past does not mean their traumas are healed. It is possible that, after decades, this memory has been mediated 'by the manner in which the world is being presently inhabited' (Das 2000).

Keti reflects on the long-term effect on her of her wartime experiences. She says that 27 years after the war, up to the present, she still cannot and has not been able to live in a house, and she has never left the windows open since the war:

> I was always scared that someone would manage to crawl into the house while we were asleep, and there were some cases when combatants would pay us a visit to 'check on' us. I was in the house when it was bombed and I nearly died. Maybe this is the reason why I feel it's safer to live in an apartment than in a private house.

Marianne Hirsch in *Vulnerable Times* asks whether 'the retrospective glance of trauma might be expanded and redirected to open alternate temporalities that might be more porous and future-oriented and that also might galvanize a sense of urgency about the need for change, now, in our contemporary moment' (Hirsch 2016, p. 80). I consider Salome's approach/history a good illustration of the way that traumatic memory can be 'mobilized for a different future'. She reflects on the influence of her wartime experience on her current approach to life:

> Earlier, maybe because I was younger... I don't really know, I took everything I owned – home, family, relationships – for granted, as if it was the natural order of things. After we lost everything and faced death, I entirely reassessed my own approach to life. Now I appreciate each and every day, and every second of life. I am much more optimistic than before. I value friendships and human relationships more ... And I think, in general I appreciate and love life more now than I used to before the war. I can't say I was pessimistic, but I appreciate small things ten times more than before and overall my approach to life, to the world, has dramatically changed.

Keti and Salome are the only women in this study who witnessed violent events for over 50 days during the war, despite profound pain, and they showed extraordinary resilience during and after the war. At the same time, they have managed to transform their painful memories and traumatic experiences into something different that has helped them develop a greater appreciation and zest for life.

The Aftermath: Tactics of Survival and the *Talent for Life*

After the flight, IDPs start from a position of loss. Starting life from scratch under previously unimaginable circumstances is an extremely complex and difficult process. One of the key tasks in this research is to reveal what is masked and concealed in the aftermath of conflict behind relatively stable and normal times (Greenhouse 2002). In this regard, I am particularly interested in the ways that IDPs coped (some of them are still coping) with extremities of dramatic change and their outcomes after the war, in their situation of prolonged aftermath.

As noted by Vigh, for the increasing numbers of people living in extreme circumstances around the world life is 'unpleasant but not impossible' (Vigh 2008, p. 11), a description which applied to the women I interviewed. The experience of 'fragmentation or disruption of unity' in times of crisis has not necessarily led them to passivity. Instead, the women in this study notwithstanding their extreme emotional damage, loss and trauma, have not only survived, but thrived to develop 'the talent for life', as anthropologist, Nancy Shepherd-Hughes puts it (Scheper-Hughes 2008, p. 25).

Overall, for these women, recovery after the war, the trauma and loss, was possible, in the words of Das, through a 'descent into the ordinary' and not through escape from it. In her words 'there is a mutual absorption of the violent and the ordinary [...] and the event as always is attached to the ordinary and the everyday and anchors the event to it in some specific ways' (Das 2006). Similarly, in the aftermath of war most women had to worry about the everyday survival of their families and many of them emphasized that they did not have the luxury or time to worry about what had happened in the past; they had to face the new reality and do something to provide for their families. Thus, the ordinary, the mundane, in Das's words, absorbed the violent events of the past. In the discussion below, I give some examples of survival tactics and strategies based on the stories of Tamara, Nino and Mari and on a wide range of emotions entwined with developing the *talent for life*.

Tamara was 35 when she had to flee with her two daughters (aged 7 and 9) and an 8-month-old son. She had to leave her husband, who was killed in the fighting the following day. For most of the research participants in this study, the direction of flight was not linear. They often had to relocate from one place to another in order to escape from war and find refuge. Tamara had to walk, together with her children, through the mountains of Svaneti, in cold and rainy weather. It took three days' of walking up and down the hills until they reached a safe place, where they were offered temporary shelter. Tamara recalls:

> I was young when I became a widow. I was left with three little children, all by myself, I didn't have time to worry or think about my emotions. I had to do everything I could to provide for my children. The feeling of fear that they might be hungry gave me strength to act. … I started preparing food for sale on the streets, which basically helped us make ends meet.

Tamara was the only breadwinner in her family. In reflecting on the past, she says she feels proud of her resilience all these years. At the same time, she considers her life after the conflict wasted, and has deep regrets that mere suffering took up so much of her youth. Her struggle for survival continues, exacerbated by her inability to get used to her temporary 'home' of 26 years and her strong desire to return. 'I can't call it home; it will always be a former kindergarten for me.[7] They gave it a different address; it's not called a kindergarten any more, but it doesn't make any difference to me. For everyone else, this is a place where we, the IDPs, live. Even if I owned five houses here, I'd still have the status of a displaced person, in my own country'.

Like Tamara, Nino also became the sole breadwinner for her family, her husband and three children. 'My husband couldn't find a suitable job, there were more opportunities of jobs for women', she explained. Nino has worked for 11 years in different jobs, as a nurse, a salesperson, a baker. She recalls how sometimes she would exchange cigarettes for other products that her family needed. Other women also mentioned being involved in some kind of bartering, as some still are. Other research on gender roles and relations among IDPs in Georgia also confirms that the capacity to adapt to new circumstances in the aftermath of the armed conflict at the beginning of the 1990s was a highly gendered process (Regulska et al. 2017). Arjevanidze (2017b) and Regulska, Mitchnek and Kabachnik (2017) describe how displaced women could become more creative and adapt more than displaced men could:

> They tend to interact more with people (for example, through their children), they have more friends of their own, they take jobs that men would not necessarily take, and they keep busy attempting to fulfill their familial obligations. (Regulska et al. 2017, p. 146)

Scholars further elaborate on the ways in which women were taking any job opportunities while men were not willing to take on 'lowly' jobs. As a result, they idled away their time, their lost status as breadwinner increasing their passivity and sense of shame that comes with knowing that women have become economically creative and successful in these conditions (Regulska et al. 2017, p. 147). Likewise, as exemplified above, greater adaptability, resilience and creativity were found in the women in my study too. Yet further examination shows, as I illustrate, that their engagement in different 'lowly' activities has been provoked a wide array of emotions. To Mari, for example, the fact that she still has to barter for survival, besides preparing food to sell in the nearby street market—has been a source of shame and humiliation.

Nino recalls how hard it was for her to do physical work because of her health. But she feels very satisfied and proud to look back on managing to provide for her family. She stresses that she was resilient and strong, that she would never show signs of weakness in front of her children. Instead, she would cry at night and spend the hours considering what new ways and strategies she could come up with to better provide for her family.

All these women could usefully worry about was being able to meet the basic everyday needs for their family; thus, through the very *descent into the ordinary* life of new, previously unthinkable situations, through increased everyday responsibilities as caretakers and breadwinners in their households, these women came up with various tactics for dealing with life after the war. They manifested incredible strength and resilience, but at the same time they admit being vulnerable in various ways.

The process of developing coping and survival tactics, being able to improvise to survive and adapt to new circumstances was accompanied by complex emotions and feelings such as guilt, regret, anger, uneasiness, humiliation, fear, pride; at times similar actions by different women emotionally triggered different and often contrasting feelings. Most emotions that accompanied their attempts to rebuild their lives were to a great extent connected to their experiences of destitution, or living in poverty, which was in stark contrast to their former stable, peaceful, affluent lives. Some women whom I interviewed were capable of developing the 'talent for life' at the expense of profound emotional damage, which can be traced to the shame of being poor and destitute, or the shame of poverty. For example, Nino reflects on how humiliated she felt when she was referred to as a 'refugee' (and not an IDP) and treated poorly for this reason. Being a 'refugee' to Nino meant being an outsider, destitute and in need of food and shelter. Tamara recalls:

> I was ready to do everything within my power so that my children didn't feel humiliated ... their friends had everything they required, my children didn't. I couldn't afford to buy even books when they were studying ... I'd not let them visit our relatives for many years, and I didn't go anywhere myself ... I was afraid that our friends or relatives who were relatively well-off would feel obliged to help me and my children financially.

Useful for the analysis of these complex emotions is Walker's work *The Shame of Poverty*, in which he examines *shame* and its related emotions in the everyday experiences of poverty. He notes that in many cases people in poverty who experience shame do not refer to or identify this emotion as shame, insofar as for many of them the word itself is a taboo, and is seldom conceptualized under its proper name. He elaborates on other self-conscious emotions associated with shame: 'Shame is a very powerful self-conscious emotion that sometimes appears to operate by stealth, labeled as embarrassment, discomfort, shyness, or even as guilt' (Walker 2014, p. 47). Walker further notes that 'people in poverty are frequently, if not invariably, subjected to shame as a social sanction for transgressing the norm of self-sufficiency', the norm and expectation that adults should be able to provide financially for their children and families.

Similarly, the women in this study do not talk about being ashamed but tend to elaborate more on their feelings of regret, humiliation, marginalization, embarrassment, discomfort, uneasiness, guilt and fear. As noted by Walker, people who experience poverty are afraid of the failure to provide appropriate food and shelter—the basic items of subsistence for their families. Thus, the absence of resources in the cases of the women whom I interviewed, especially in the first years of displacement, was the trigger for the wide array of emotions listed above.

Conclusions

In their recollections of war and reflections on their post-displacement lives, the women in my interviews shared stories which revealed their extraordinary strength and 'human hardiness', in the form of everyday resilience and through the 'descent into the ordinary', that allowed them to deal with traumatic memories and rudimentary living conditions. It is not to suggest that being busy with mundane tasks and ever-increasing responsibilities made it possible to overcome and be healed from the trauma of the war and all the consequences that forced displacement entails. I have tried to illustrate this in the aftermath of the forced displacement caused by armed conflict, through the 'mutual absorption of the violent and the ordinary' (Das 2006, p. 7). The women in this study experiencing extreme emotional damage, loss and trauma have not only survived but striven to develop 'the talent for life' (Scheper-Hughes 2008, p. 25). And through this very descent into previously unimaginable conditions, through increased everyday responsibilities as caretakers, as sole breadwinners in their households, after human and material losses, these women have manifested incredible strength, resilience and variety in the tactics of getting what they needed after the war.

At the same time their stories are filled with pain and emotions such as regret and shame: they feel regret at wasting and losing their most valuable years to the war; they feel regret and sadness for not being able to provide for their children adequately, for being unable to pay for their proper education, they feel unhappy to have borne the status of an IDP for more than two decades, they feel miserable for living for almost 26 years in the same 'temporary' accommodation provided for IDPs, which, in the words of one of the interlocutors in this study 'persists as a constant reminder of being a "refugee" in your own country, and a reminder of the horrible years in the immediate aftermath of the war'.

As this analysis has shown, we need to consider ways in which to approach the lives of thousands of individuals living and striving in war-torn societies; insistence on their resilience in times of chronic crisis should not ignore their vulnerability, which would mean negating the severe circumstances in which the lives of socially disadvantaged groups become livable. At the same time, the admission of vulnerability for these women should not be read as 'a plea for protection that potentially signals weakness and the perpetuation of disempowerment' (Hirsch 2016, p. 82). Instead, as proposed by Scheper-Hughes, on the one hand, we should not 'underestimate the human capacity not only to survive, but to thrive' during and following crisis and extreme adversity

(Scheper-Hughes 2008, p. 42). On the other, we need to consider the ways in which individuals can be both 'resilient *and* frail' and acknowledge the human vulnerability in this very manifestation of extraordinary human resilience.

Notes

1. There were approximately 17,000 IDPs from the 2008 war (IDMC 2016, p. 3), 10,000 of them still remain displaced (IDMC/NRC 2012).
2. Part of the research was funded by the Swedish Institute Scholarship Programme for Ph.D. studies (2016–2017) and the ASCN scholarship Programme (2016).
3. One might think that being an ethnic Georgian would be a drawback in this analysis, but it was helpful for conducting an intimate ethnography because my research participants knew that my experiences of war and trauma resembled theirs.
4. 'The tradition of the oppressed teaches us that "the state of emergency" in which we live is not the exception but the rule' (Benjamin 1999, p. 248 *cited* in Vigh 2008).
5. Salome and Keti lived in their own small apartment where I interviewed them together. I had a follow-up interview with them a year later and later a conversation with both sisters in the same space again.
6. From the Georgian it literally translates as 'we looked death in the eyes'.
7. Since the beginning of the 1990s, IDPs continued to live for decades in deteriorating living conditions. More than 85% of IDPs were accommodated in 'collective' or public housing provided by the Georgian government (Buck et al. 2000). Most of these buildings—Soviet-era hotels, hospitals, schools, factories and other buildings—were transformed into living spaces which were seen as temporary living spaces for IDPs. These buildings were referred to as collective centres and more than 3600 of them were created across the country. Various reports considered these facilities—most of them, like the centres, overcrowded—inadequate for living because of deteriorating sanitary conditions, etc. (Buck et al. 2000). In 2007 after many years of acquiescence, 'a nationwide strategy was formed to handle the issues of displacement in a systematic manner – and the implementation of this started only after the August war of 2008' (Rekhviashvili 2012, p. 128).

References

Altinay, Ayşe Gül and Andrea Pető. 2016. *Gendered Wars, Gendered Memories.* London: Routledge.

Arjevanidze, Nargiza. 2017a. "Remembering the Past: Narratives of Displaced Women from Abkhazia." In *Gender in Georgia: Feminist Perspectives on Culture, Nation and History in the South Caucasus*, edited by Maia Barkaia and Alisse Waterston. New York: Berghahn Books.

———. 2017b. "Experiences of Protracted Displacement in Narratives of Internally Displaced Women from Abkhazia." Conference Materials. Heinrich Boell Foundation. South Caucasus Office of the Heinrich Boell Foundation, Tbilisi, Georgia.

Brooks, Abigail. 2007. "Feminist Standpoint Epistemology: Building Knowledge and Empowerment Through Women's Lived Experience." In *Feminist Research Practice: A Primer*, edited by Sharlene Nagy Hesse-Biber and Patricia Lina Leavy, 53–82. London: Sage.

Buck, Thomas, Alice Morton, Susan Allen Nan, and Feride Zurikashvili. 2000. "Aftermath: Effects of Conflict on Internally Displaced Women in Georgia." Working Paper No. 310. ReliefWeb. September 3, 2011. https://reliefweb.int/report/georgia/aftermath-effects-conflict-internally-displaced-women-georgia.

Chanfrault-Duchet, Marie-Francoise. 1991. "Narrative Structures, Social Models, and Symbolic Representation in the Life Story." In *Women's Worlds: The Feminist Practice of Oral History*, edited by Shernar Berger Gluck and Daphne Patai, 77–92. New York and London: Routledge.

Das, Veena. 2000. "The Act of Witnessing: Violence, Poisonous Knowledge, and Subjectivity." In *Violence and Subjectivity*, edited by Veena Das, Arthur Kleinman, Mamphela Ramphele, and Pamela Reynolds, 205–226. Berkeley: University of California Press.

———. 2006. *Life and Words: Violence and the Descent into the Ordinary.* California: University of California Press.

Dunn, Elizabeth. 2014. "Humanitarianism, Displacement, and the Politics of Nothing in Postwar Georgia." *Slavic Review* 73 (2) (Summer): 287–306. https://doi.org/10.5612/slavicreview.73.2.287.

Greenhouse, Carol J. 2002 "Introduction: Altered States, Altered Lives." In *Ethnography in Unstable Places: Everyday Lives in Contexts of Dramatic Political Change*, edited by Carol J. Greenhouse, Carol J. Elizabeth Mertz, and Kay B. Warren. Durham, NC: Duke University Press.

Hirsch, Marianne. 2016. "Vulnerable Times." In *Vulnerability in Resistance*, edited by Judith Butler, Zeynep Gambetti, and Leticia Sabsay, 76–96. New York: Duke University Press.

Human Rights Watch. 1995. "Georgia/Abkhazia: Violations of the Laws of War and Russia's Role in the Conflict." 7 (7). https://www.hrw.org/reports/1995/Georgia2.htm.

———. 2011. "Living in Limbo: Rights of Ethnic Georgians Returnees to the Gali District of Abkhazia." June 15, 2011. https://www.hrw.org/report/2011/07/15/living-limbo/rights-ethnic-georgians-returnees-gali-district-abkhazia.

International Committee of the Red Cross (ICRC). 1999. "Country Report Georgia/Abkhazia." https://www.icrc.org/en/doc/assets/files/other/georgia.pdf.

Internal Displacement Monitoring Centre (IDMC). 2016. "Global Report on Internal Displacement." https://reliefweb.int/sites/reliefweb.int/files/resources/2016-global-report-internal-displacement-IDMC.pdf.

———. 2018. "Georgia Global Report on Internal Displacement." http://www.internal-displacement.org/sites/default/files/2018-05/GRID%20 2018%20-%20Figure%20Analysis%20-%20GEORGIA.pdf.

IDMC/NRC. 2012. "Georgia: Partial Progress Towards Durable Solutions for IDPs Internal Displacement Monitoring Centre/Norwegian Refugee Council." http://georgia.idp.arizona.edu/docs/idmc_georgia_3_12.pdf.

Jackson, Michael. 2002. *The Politics of Storytelling: Violence, Transgression, and Intersubjectivity.* Portland: Museum Tusculanum Press.

Jacobsen, Karen. 2014. "Livelihoods and Forced Migration." In *The Oxford Handbook of Refugee and Forced Migration Studies*, edited by Elena Fiddian-Qasmiyeh, Gil Loescher, Katy Long and Nando Sigona, 99–111. New York: Oxford University Press.

Kabachnik, Peter, Joanna Regulska, and Beth Mitchneck. 2010. "Where and When Is Home? The Double Displacement of Georgian IDPs from Abkhazia." *The Journal of Refugee Studies* 23 (3): 315–336. https://doi.org/10.1093/jrs/feq023.

Kabachnik, Peter, Magda Grabowska, Joanna Regulska, Beth Mitchneck, and Olga V. Mayorova. 2013. "Traumatic Masculinities: The Gendered Geographies of Georgian IDPs from Abkhazia." *Gender, Place & Culture: A Journal of Feminist Geography* 20 (6): 773–793. https://doi.org/10.1080/09 66369X.2012.716402.

Light, Duncan, and Craig Young. 2015. "Local Memories in a Nationalizing and Globalizing World." In *Local Memories in a Nationalizing and Globalizing World*, edited by Marnix Beyen and Brecht Deseure, 221–243. London: Palgrave Macmillan.

Lundgren, Minna. 2016. "Boundaries of Displacement: Belonging and Return Among Forcibly Displaced Young Georgians from Abkhazia." PhD diss., Mid-Sweden University.

Meintjes, Sheila, Anu Pillay, and Meredeth Turshen. 2002. *The Aftermath: Women in Post-conflict Transformation*. London: Zed Books.

Mitchnek, Beth, Olga V. Mayorova, and Joanna Regulska. 2009. "Post-conflict Displacement: Isolation and Integration in Georgia." *Annals of the Association of American Geographers* 99 (5): 1022–1032. https://doi.org/10.1080/00045600903279408.

Palmberger, Monika. 2008. "Nostalgia Matters: Nostalgia for Yugoslavia as Potential Vision for a Better Future." *Sociologija* 50 (4): 355–370.

Regulska, Joanna, Beth Mitchnek, and Peter Kabachnik. 2017. "Displacement, State Violence and Gender Roles: The Case of Internally Displaced and Violence-Affected Georgian Women in Gender in Georgia." In *Gender in Georgia: Feminist Perspectives on Culture, Nation and History in the South Caucasus*, edited by Maia Barkaia and Alisse Waterston. New York: Berghahn Books.

Rekhviashvili, Lela. 2012. "Survival Strategies of the Poor and Marginalized— The Case of Internally Displaced People in Georgia." *SEER: Journal for Labour and Social Affairs in Eastern Europe* 15 (1): 123–135. https://www.jstor.org/stable/43293455.

———. 2015. "The Politics of Helping: Mobilizing Support for Internally Displaced Persons After the 2008 Russia-Georgia War." *Journal of Internal Displacement* 5 (2): 2–18.

Rydström, Helle. 2007. "Proximity and Distance: Vietnamese Memories of the War with the USA." *Anthropological Forum* 17 (1): 21–39.

Scheper-Hughes, Nancy. 2008. "A Talent for Life: Reflections on Human Vulnerability and Resilience." *Ethnos* 73 (1): 25–56. https://doi.org/10.1080/00141840801927525.

Toria, Malkhaz. 2015. "Remembering Homeland in Exile: Recollections of IDPs from the Abkhazia Region of Georgia." *Journal on Ethnopolitics and Minority Issues in Europe* 14 (1): 48–70. https://heinonline.org/HOL/P?h=hein.journals/jemie2015&i=48.

Turner, Victor. 1967. *The Forest of Symbols: Aspects of Ndembu Ritual.* Ithaca and London: Cornell University Press.

Vigh, Henrik. 2008. "Crisis and Chronicity: Anthropological Perspectives on Continuous Conflict and Decline." *Ethnos* 73 (1): 5–24. https://doi.org/10.1080/00141840801927509.

Walker, Robert. 2014. *The Shame of Poverty: Global Perspectives.* Oxford: Oxford University Press.

Waterston, Alisse, and Rylko-Bauer Barbara. 2006. "Out of the Shadows of History and Memory: Personal Family Narratives in Ethnographies of Rediscovery." *American Ethnologist* 330 (3): 397–412. https://doi.org/10.1525/ae.2006.33.3.397.

Zürcher, Christoph. 2007. *The Post-Soviet Wars: Rebellion, Ethnic Conflict, and Nationhood in the Caucasus.* New York: New York University.

8

The Politics of Widowhood in Nagorny Karabakh

Nona Shahnazarian and Ulrike Ziemer

Becoming a widow is completely contingent and leads to major changes in a woman's life. In many parts of the world, widows become victims of their circumstances due to structural inequalities and patriarchal gender norms (Sahoo 2014; Sengupta 2016). While accurate information is limited, it has been estimated that there are approximately 285 million widows around the world (UN Women 2017). Yet, there remains a need for more detailed research concerning their everyday struggles,

---

This chapter is a revised version of Shahnazarian and Ziemer. 2018. 'Women Confronting Death: War Widows' Experiences in the South Caucasus'. *Journal of International Women's Studies*.

As explained in the introduction to this edited volume (Note 2), this chapter uses the more common 'Nagorny Karabakh'. Following the constitutional referendum in February 2017, the unrecognized Nagorny Karabakh Republic was renamed the Republic of Artsakh.

N. Shahnazarian
The Institute of Archaeology and Ethnography,
National Academy of Sciences, Yerevan, Armenia

U. Ziemer (✉)
University of Winchester, Winchester, UK
e-mail: Ulrike.Ziemer@winchester.ac.uk

© The Author(s) 2020
U. Ziemer (ed.), *Women's Everyday Lives in War and Peace in the South Caucasus*,
https://doi.org/10.1007/978-3-030-25517-6_8

especially when it comes to publications on widows' agency and how societal gender norms impact upon their entitlements, statuses and vulnerability (cf. Ramnarain 2016). Female vulnerability and insecurity are heightened in conflict and post-conflict settings (Detraz 2011; Sjoberg and Gentry 2007). Thus, more recent literature on widowhood and violent conflict has begun to examine the various ways in which widowed women deal with life after the death of their husbands in the aftermath of war (Brown 2016; Finke and Shackel 2015; Nwadinobi 2016; Pannilage 2017). When it comes to research on widowhood in post-socialist societies torn by conflict or in prolonged conflict conditions, however, there is still a significant gap in the literature. Hence, exploring the everyday struggles of widows in the disputed region of Nagorny Karabakh in the South Caucasus, the present chapter is intended to open up the still neglected subject of widowhood in post-socialist societies affected by violent fighting.

As the literature and knowledge about widowhood and conflict are still relatively sparse (Bokek-Cohen 2014; Quayoom 2014; Qutab 2012), important aspects of widows' lived experience remain largely unexplored. This in turn makes it particularly difficult to advocate and design programmes targeting the specific needs of widows (UN Women 2012). While current studies on widowhood in Western countries provide important accounts of well-being and the psychological effects of loss and bereavement (Balkwell 1981; Bonanno et al. 2004; Ory and Huijts 2015), the information available on the subject of widowhood in previously war-torn post-socialist regions is limited to some brief mentions of widows in parts of former Yugoslavia as important for the national discourse of the newly emerged nations (Jacobs 2016; Mostov 2000; Nikolic-Ristanovic 1998). It is therefore a pressing need to consider the lived experiences of widows in other post-socialist regions in order to address and understand the socio-political and economic context.

The current literature on widowhood can be divided on the basis of its two main regional perspectives. First, there is the literature focusing on widowhood in developed Western countries and, second, there is the 'outsider' perspective of widowhood in developing countries (Lenette 2013). While the former largely discusses studies based on quantitative measures of bereavement and trauma and is limited to older groups

(Martin-Matthews et al. 2013; Ory and Huijts 2015), in the latter it is much more likely that the women supplying the data have experienced widowhood earlier in life than they would in a Western society (Mand 2005; Sabri et al. 2016). Many of the widowhood narratives in developing countries are marked by stories of isolation and humiliation and focus largely on female widows (Owen 1996; Sabri et al. 2016).

The study of widowhood in terms of armed conflict started with historical studies focusing on World War One war widows (Kuhlman 2012) or memories from widows after the Vietnam War (Fitzpatrick 2011). In recent years, due to the ongoing involvement of military personnel from Western countries in long-term wars, detailed qualitative analysis of experiences of widowhood has gained momentum and may continue to increase (Fitzpatrick 2011). Although still very much under-researched, of particular interest to scholars has been the study of young and middle-aged widowhood (Lenette 2013). Basnet et al. (2017, p. 10), for example, found increased levels of anxiety among young war widows in Nepal. Women who were young at the time of widowhood came across as much more nervous over their future and day-to-day life, whereas middle-aged women had significantly lower chances of anxiety.

In the context of armed conflict, widowhood is often combined with displacement and violence. Loss and bereavement are integral to displacement, yet only a few publications so far have examined how exactly the loss of a spouse affects widowhood in exile (Chou 2007; Lenette 2013). Violence against women is also integral to conflict and accordingly widows have not been spared from acts of violence (Koos 2017). In situations of armed conflict, the sense of frustration, anxiety and powerlessness may be manifested in a number of ways, but research has shown that women and children are disproportionately affected (Sjoberg 2014). Noteworthy here is that a conflict is often compounded by a polarization of gender roles (Qayoom 2014). Therefore, the way in which patriarchal power relations and the newly acquired identity as widow are negotiated on an individual level needs urgent analysis. How do widowed women in Nagorny Karabakh deal with their unwanted status as widows? How do some of them manage to overcome the limitations of their status?

The chapter proceeds as follows. After a description of the context and methodology, the results are presented thematically in three subsections. The first section discusses war widows facing societal marginalization and isolation. This is a topic that has been substantially discussed in many parts of the world, in the context of developed countries (cf. Ory and Huijts 2015; Panagiotopoulos et al. 2013) as well as developing ones (cf. Chitrali and Anwar 2013; Kotzé and Rajuili-Masilo 2012; Ng et al. 2016). Yet in the post-socialist context this is still an aspect of women's lives that is almost wholly absent from the literature. The second section considers remarriage as a strategy that widows use to reintegrate into society by achieving once more the status of married women. However, for widows in Nagorny Karabakh this strategy is not as straightforward as it might seem. While one choice is that of remarrying as a result of finding a new love, the other choice is levirate marriage. Levirate marriage is an ancient tradition and has received some attention in the previous literature on widows (cf. Nyanzi 2011; Sapir 1916; Sev'er and Bagli 2006). The final section examines widows' sexuality and social control. Previous literature exploring the topic of widows as sexually active persons has almost unanimously concluded that this is not an accepted phenomenon in developing countries (cf. Nyanzi 2011).

Study Context and Methodology

The chapter is based upon data from a larger ongoing ethnographic study exploring gender issues and political transformation in the protracted conflict zone of Nagorny Karabakh (cf. Shahnazarian and Ziemer 2012, 2014). Ulrike Ziemer has made three fieldwork trips to Nagorny Karabakh, one to Martuni in July 2009,[1] one to Stepanakert, the capital of Nagorny Karabakh in August 2015, and one to Shushi in August 2016.[2] Nona Shahnazarian is originally from Martuni but emigrated to Russia in the 1990s when the conflict over Nagorny Karabakh started. Recently she has returned to live in Yerevan. As part of her doctoral degree, she started her research in 2000 and has returned to Nagorny Karabakh every year since then.[3]

In this paper, we draw on biographical interviews, with a total of seven local widows and five widows who were formerly from Azerbaijan and had to resettle in Martuni and Shushi as a result of the conflict. In addition, we draw on interviews in Nagorny Karabakh with journalists and leaders of women's civil society organizations. Research participants were selected by means of purposive sampling (Marshall 1996). Nona Shahnazarian provided the local knowledge to contact widowed interviewees. The participation of these widows was voluntary and depended upon the willingness and availability of individuals to take part in the study. As in most cases, widowhood is for them a painful experience; our sample included only middle-aged and elderly women, because they had had enough time to overcome their distressing loss and were more open and reflective about their experience. The interviews and discussions were mainly held in Armenian or Russian and recorded. The interviewees were free to choose the location of their interviews. Very often the research participants chose their place and kitchen as the interview location.

The Conflict over Nagorny Karabakh

To date, the conflict between Armenia and Azerbaijan over the Nagorny Karabakh region[4] is a central obstacle to the political development of Armenia and Azerbaijan and a key impediment to the development of the South Caucasus region as a whole and its integration into the wider world. The conflict can be traced further back than the collapse of the Soviet Union and has long stood out as one of the world's more daunting diplomatic challenges (Cornell 2017).[5] Inspired by Gorbachev's slogans about democratization and promises of correcting mistakes made by previous Soviet leaders, Karabakh Armenians turned to Moscow with a petition for the re-establishment of Nagorny Karabakh under the jurisdiction of Armenia. In 1988, Armenian deputies in the local Soviet Assembly of Nagorny Karabakh voted to unite the region with Soviet Armenia. Following this vote, tensions between Armenians and Azerbaijanis living in Nagorny Karabakh escalated into interethnic violence between the two (Civil Society Monitoring Report 2014). The ethnic Armenians of Nagorny Karabakh strongly pursued the principle of self-determination, separated from Azerbaijan and subsequently declared themselves 'independent'. Unlike Armenia, Azerbaijan, despite losing the war as well as seven of its provinces surrounding Nagorny Karabakh, rejects the principle of self-determination, accepting only the opposing principle of territorial integrity (Cornell 2017).

In May 1994, after large-scale ethnic cleansing, a Russian mediated ceasefire came into effect, but no peace agreement was reached. Since then, the conflict has not moved any closer to a political solution. Overall, there has been a pronounced lack of political will from the main parties to the conflict and little effort to encourage peace talks, resulting more or less in diplomatic deadlock. In the meantime, the economic and political imbalance between the two countries has also grown. Armenia, the victor in the war, has suffered a decline in its population[6] and struggles economically, while the development of Azerbaijan's oil and gas resources has meant that its economy is now over six times larger than Armenia's, and for several years its official defence budget exceeded Armenia's entire state budget (ibid.).

In recent years, the unsettled nature of the conflict has been regularly reiterated, with a steady escalation of tension almost every month.[7] The most serious escalation of fighting in over two decades occurred on April 2016 with some serious combat and civilian fatalities on both sides (Sanamyan 2016). Since then, sporadic clashes on the Line of Contact (LoC) have continued and the tensions have not relaxed; in fact the risk of a further escalation in the conflict is, if anything, higher than before (Sanamyan 2017). In short, in the current circumstances, both societies continue to prepare for war and the best-case scenario is the continuation of low-intensity conflict along the LoC (Poghosyan 2017).

Model Mothers and Dutiful Wives: Armenian Gender Ideology

Gender roles, traditional gender roles in particular, receive heightened attention during wars and in post-conflict societies (Cockburn 1998; Elshtain 1987; Lorentzen and Turpin 1998). They serve as symbolic boundaries of the nation in the nationalist discourse of countries which have been shaken by violent conflicts. Mothers, wives and daughters signify the nation and national belonging (Turpin 1998). They are perceived as the property of the nation (Mostov 2000). Regarding the Armenian nation and its gender traditions, concepts such as motherhood play a significant role in the construction of Armenian femininity. As already discussed in Chapter 4, women are considered the nurturers of the nation; they have the childbearing responsibility to keep the nation growing. Particularly, in view of the security threats, the discourse of 'othering' Azerbaijan (and the Turks) in Nagorny Karabakh and Armenia necessitates an equally strong discourse of 'us' that underscores Armenianness as exclusive. Thus, Armenian women typically believe that the concept of motherhood is constructed to be an exceptional Armenian trait that distinguishes Armenian women from those of other nations.

Alongside 'motherhood', family and home (guardians of the hearth [*ojakh*]) also play an imperative role in the Armenian sense of national belonging. As in other patriarchal societies, women in Armenia and Nagorny Karabakh are supposed to concentrate on family related duties and, most importantly, on children's upbringing. In Nagorny Karabakh, mothers are required to care for and protect their patriotic sons. Daughters are brought up to lookout for a good marriage opportunity, to secure a respected future life and status within the community (Ziemer 2011, p. 135). As many studies on Armenians in the world have demonstrated, marriage and the family in Armenian culture is central, due to Armenia having little history of independent statehood and its long struggle to survive (Boulgourdjian-Toufeksian 2000; Komsuoğlu and Örs 2009). In addition, marriage carries a huge emotional weight in Armenian society because it is the culminating moment in a woman's life. Hence marriage is a fundamental aspect of Armenian society; the family that emerges through marriage processes is a microcosm of society. When a woman gets older she is given high social status, for instance, when she becomes a mother-in-law and has accomplished maternity and child-rearing. This stage as an 'older woman' is perceived as a reward for a life devoted to serving the interests of the family (Shahnazarian 2011; Ziemer 2011).

Societal Marginalization and Isolation of War Widows

Just as in other societies affected by war (Katz and Ben-Dor 1987), war widows in Nagorny Karabakh today represent powerful symbols of patriotism, since in most cases their husbands sacrificed their lives in the 1990s war, or in more recent years were killed in combat service along the border of Nagorny Karabakh. The Nagorny Karabakh authorities recognize this symbolism in the form of monthly state pensions. These war widows receive a small monthly pension of 30,000AMD (approximately 62USD) and an additional 70,000AMD (approximately 144USD) for each child younger than 18 years of age.[8] If a child decides to study at university this child support is paid until the age of 23 years. In addition, in honour of their husband's sacrifice, war widows three times a year receive 16,000AMD (approximately 33USD) on the Nagorny Karabakh Independence Day, New Year's Eve and Victory Day. They also receive 400USD for their fallen husband's gravestone (Interview, Artur Arystumyan, August 2015).[9]

This financial support from the government can also produce resentment in a widow's immediate neighbourhood as a conversation with a war veteran showed when he exclaimed: '*I wish I'd die as well, then my kids at least wouldn't be hungry*'.[10] In addition, this relatively generous support from the state generates considerable societal expectations that a widow will honour appropriately the great achievement of her fallen husband. Thus, according to patriarchal norms, widowhood demands further sacrifice. Joy and laughter should not be part of a widow's life; instead, with no husband, it is memory and grief that define it. Suddenly widows face a diminished status as they have 'lost their master' (*tar chonim*) or are 'left without their owner' (*andar mynal*) or pitifully are considered 'headless women' (*kylyoxy kytyrvatz kynegya*) (Shahnazarian 2004). In short, all these linguistic phrases allude to the patriarchal norm of a complete family where the father is the head of the family and the breadwinner. Maria[11] remembers:

> When my father was seriously injured and his life hung on a thin line, my grandmother loudly prayed to God and asked him 'even if crippled, even

if without hands or feet, let him stay alive, don't let my daughter remain without her master. (*andar-ynderyu*)

A widow's isolation and marginalization can also come from the fact that widows keep their husband's memory alive and thus to some extent it continues to control their life. Susanna describes how she keeps the memory of her husband alive: '*The portrait of my husband hangs on the wall in my house ... I'll never remove his portrait, never...*' Some widows have talked about waiting for signs from their husband when they face difficult tasks. Furthermore, some widows assume that their husband is embodied in their children, especially if he died at the birth of their child (which happened often during the war in the 1990s). As Anush maintains: '*my husband died but he is alive in his child*'. This is specifically the case when the child is a boy and gets given the role of a male adult, the perished father. Thus, every so often a son at an early stage of his life is treated as the head of the family because he is perceived to be the incarnation of his father. In other words, some widows create their own reality to make sense of their life according to patriarchal norms which stipulate a woman's subordinate role in the shadow of her husband.

In addition to the societal demand on widows to live a withdrawn and quiet life in honour of their perished husband,[12] widows are also marked by superstition, connected to their social stigmatization. This phenomenon has been especially discussed in publications focusing on widows in developing countries (Courtney 2014; Soussou 2002). Nune, a widow with three children, has experienced this marginalization as a result of stigma and superstition. Nune is not a war widow, thus received less state support and found herself at the bottom of the hierarchy of widows. Before her husband's death, she provided some additional family income by baking from home (wedding cakes, birthday cakes, etc.). Together with her husband's income, her small additional earnings secured a good income for the family. However, when she became a widow, the number of orders decreased substantially, especially for weddings and birthday cakes, because people felt superstitious about placing orders with a widow.

Another facet of the isolated and marginalized status as a widow is that, according to Karabakh Armenian traditions, it is not customary to invite widows to birthday parties or other celebrations such as weddings or the ancient community tradition of *midzhi*.[13] If they are invited out of politeness, they know that they should not attend because of their social stigma and their grieving status. Birthdays and weddings are about celebrating the next stage in life; widows are about grief and remembering the past with their husbands. This stigma about their status does not seem to leave them; Seda, who has been a widow for many years, told us with regret how she had been excluded from the *midzhi* for her young niece in 2006, just because her husband died in 1993.

Life Choices: Respect and Status or Second Love?

For most of the war widows we interviewed, returning to their former social group and integrating again is hardly possible, although they are not subject to a sharp decline in their economic position, as widows in other countries experience (Cavallow and Warner 2014; Owen 1996; Soussou 2002) thanks to the relatively generous state pension. In Karabakh society, three factors determine the next life stage of widows—motherhood, patrilocality and strict social control. Many of the widows interviewed became largely dependent on their husband's family after his death. This dependence is especially strong when they have already lived with the husband's family during his lifetime. According to Armenian tradition, it is expected that the wife of the youngest (or only son) lives with his family. Given this dependency on their husband's family, widows are faced with a choice between a more predictable (approved) and a less predictable (risky) future. If they choose the latter and get married a second time, they would lose the help and support of their parents-in-law, as well as other relatives of their perished husband. The choice of the former, i.e. remaining a widow for the rest of their life and forgetting about their own personal desires, would ensure them a safe and accepted status in society but under strict social control. This option is more likely to be chosen by widows with children, because they prefer to ensure a respected societal position for their children.

Getting married again? I couldn't risk the well-being of my children … it's very difficult with children to get married again anyway, and also generally it's difficult to find a good husband. Often even young girls have difficulty finding a husband. Those who didn't get killed in the war were often either disabled war veterans or in the best case scenario shell-shocked … many of them didn't have work. Well, what kind of life would that be? … Yes, of course, it would be easier for my kids … then people can't look down on them or talk about us. Well, not long ago someone proposed to me, but I said no straightaway … Well I'm actually not a *songsuz*,[14] why do I need a husband? My daughter is married, my son is grown up. He came back from the army recently. That's a comfortable life, isn't it?

As becomes obvious from this interview excerpt, Marietta refers to the deep-rooted Armenian gender ideology that a respected family has a husband, the head of the household. She implies that people would look down on her because she lives without a husband and thus has not got a complete family as the societal discourse demands. Yet she concludes by highlighting that she has done her duty as a wife, she has brought up two children who now can take care of her. Hence, she questions the importance of finding another husband, implying the Armenian gender ideology that almost the only purpose of marriage is to create a family. Narine also explains how she decided to live with her parents-in-law in order to avoid the risk of an unpredictable insecure future:

It was me who decided after the death of my husband to live with my mother-in law for another twenty years until she died. And yes, there were five men who wanted to marry me … My husband was killed by a mine … I decided to live with his parents in his house … Where else could I go? If I was to get married again, I'd lose the support of his parents. But how would life be with a new husband, who knows? …

Levirate: A Strategy for Reintegration?

In connection with the issue of marginalization of widows, it is interesting to examine the phenomenon of levirate among Karabakh Armenians. Levirate is a very old marriage institution which has been discussed in other publications as a solution to widows' isolation and impoverishment (cf. Nyanzi et al. 2009; Sev'er and Bagli 2006). It is an ancient form of marriage, in which when a married man dies his widow marries one of his brothers (Sapir 1916). This tradition is often explained as an expression of patrilinearity, which suggests that a married woman is perceived as the property of the husband, eternally linked to him even after his death. Levirate in Nagorny Karabakh presents a legitimate and accepted solution to the lonely status of widows and had been practised as early as the 1917 Russian Revolution and the Second World War, long before the war over the Nagorny Karabakh region in the 1990s (Shahnazarian 2004). Nonetheless, in the Soviet era this tradition lost importance and was almost forgotten, but when the war started in 1991 and the number of widows in Nagorny Karabakh sharply increased, this tradition experienced a revival. However, this does not mean that the revival was accepted without any criticism from the individuals affected by it.

In one of our informal conversations with a group of young men in Martuni in 2009, we heard of a case showing that even for men it is not easy to practice levirate. We were told that one young man whose brother had died and whose mother wanted him to marry his brother's wife ran away from home to avoid this, because he was in love with another woman. However, before he ran away he promised his brother's wife that he would take financial care of her and his nephew. In other words, this young man, aware of his responsibilities as a provider for his dead brother's family, was trying to find a middle way.

Gohar, who married a second time via the levirate practice, told us how difficult this was for both parties:

> My mother-in-law, when she received the letter (from the army) that her son had vanished, forced her younger son, my husband (but we weren't married then), to marry me because I had a son from his brother, basically his nephew. Initially, he rejected this suggestion in every possible way, saying 'how can I share a bed with my brother's wife, how can I look at her when he might re-appear.' In response, my mother-in-law suggested to me that I could choose any part of her house to live in with her second son ... and this is how we grew together.

In this way, because Karabakh society is a society where women's social status and welfare depend on their relationship to men, the practice of levirate fulfils the function of protecting its widowed women. By means of this practice, widows and their children in a patriarchal society can without conflict secure their social status as a complete family headed by a husband. However, while the above interview excerpts demonstrate a degree of resistance from the men involved and to a lesser extent resistance from the widows themselves, the next interview excerpt with Mariam shows that even widows do not always approve of this practice. Sometimes it is other family members who enforce it, for instance, mothers-in-law, who as older women have acquired a very high and almost unquestioned status in society. Mariam tells us how she resisted this practice:

> In 1992, we got bombarded. My husband was killed and our house burnt down. My husband's cousin planned to get married to me, but I didn't want to. Simply because he is a rude person and an alcoholic and he is an *azaph*.[15] I can't imagine being his subordinate and serving him. Why do I need such a man? ...

Here it becomes obvious that for some widowed women, widowhood offers a certain freedom to choose what will happen next and the possibility of rebuilding their own life. In this interview excerpt, Mariam prefers the status of a grieving widow. She used some money from a government fund and with the support of her children rebuilt her home. Thus, she chose the predictable future of a single widowed woman rather than getting entangled with a man who, according to her, was not trustworthy enough.

Widows' Sexual Desires and Social Control

Social control is perhaps the biggest influencing factor for a widow's further decisions in the next stage of her life. Neighbours and their controlling behaviour can affect widows as much as their children. In August 2015, the Director of the Women's Resource Center in Shushi,

Gayane Hambardzumyan, explained that perhaps 'the smaller the territory, the more important neighbours are', and this is how they can assert so much social control. As important as it is for neighbours to watch out for each other in the insecure circumstances of Nagorny Karabakh, their vigilance also has the effect of controlling other women's lives to a degree that severely limits women's freedom. Thus, social control structures a widow's life strategies and choices—they do not want to be ostracized by their neighbourhood for one wrong move. Following the unspoken discourse of traditional widowhood, to live with the memory of a deceased husband means prestige and honour for one's family and children. However, some widows openly criticize these social control mechanisms and what they entail for them:

> I'm not against thinking of my own individual life. Everyone's organism has desires. And really one can potentially do anything within boundaries (*sahmanaphak*). Here in Karabakh, adhering to traditions (*orenkhav*) would be like burying oneself alive. It shouldn't be like this. I'm a little older, but there are also younger widows, how can they completely forget about their own desires? ... these desires are given by nature and don't depend on the person. Really, widows have only got two choices in this situation: either they don't care about society, and go from one man to another and follow their heart, in this way risking their children's future; or they remain alone and live as society expects ... and their children will suffer less.

As Hasmik describes in this interview excerpt, there are only a few options for widows: there is the option of accepting their widowed status according to societal norms or the option of ignoring societal norms and once more becoming sexually active. The latter option, however, would entail great risk of further marginalization, since sexual relationships outside marriage are not as accepted, as Hasmik explains further:

> ... three years ago I went to see a doctor because I thought I was ill with a women's problem.[16] But the doctor said: 'you aren't ill, you just need to get married again.' My daughter, however, didn't allow me to listen to what the doctor said because she didn't want me to get married again. She admitted that she didn't want me to get ill, but in this town (Martuni),

she said, you couldn't find even five men who would keep it a secret if they had been with you.

As Hasmik's daughter's comment demonstrates, having a secret sexual relationship would mean sacrificing a widow's reputation, for it is not an accepted practice outside marriage. Accordingly, with a damaged reputation a widow could then experience losing the support and help from her neighbours which is essential in uncertain circumstances such as in Nagorny Karabakh, as Gayane Hambardzumyan explained at the beginning of this section. Nonetheless, the idea of a second marriage seems to be unbearable for some widows, even if it was done to resolve their insecure status by conforming to societal expectations, as Shushan tells us:

This isn't possible (second marriage), this is a desecration of the husband's memory and I'll never get married again. I don't want to experience again what I experienced when I got married for the first time. It was all perfect with him (her husband), even very perfect.

Conclusions

The widows' experiences explored in this chapter have highlighted the various ways in which war widows in Nagorny Karabakh can become marginalized and how they navigate the challenges linked to their status as widows. Even though as war widows they have a respected societal status and receive substantial governmental support, it places societal expectations on them which may marginalize them in everyday life. We have documented how research participants have dealt with their unwanted status. Our discussion has shown that although in public most war widows conform to societal expectations, they are critical of Karabakh society's demanding exigent expectations of them. The most significant finding of our research is that marginalization for widows in Nagorny Karabakh is not so much related to a worsening of their economic position as it often is in other parts of the world, but that it is the patriarchal discourse in society that marginalizes them. Due to the heightened militarization of society in the region, most widows would rather comply than openly challenge the patriarchal discourse, as 'women are simply not ready yet to challenge' (Anahit Danielyan, independent journalist, August 2015). Hence, although one may be tempted to read these narratives as stories of powerless female victims of male patriarchy in need of support, we are instead inclined to read these stories as narratives of resourcefulness. They show the search for a middle way that satisfies both their families and society and does not entirely marginalize them. As we have demonstrated, for example, refusing the options of second marriage or levirate turns widows into agents in charge of their future. This agency could perhaps be interpreted as a sign of social change, although one which may be very slow, especially since these widows' narratives also show, as other studies do, that the protracted conflict over Nagorny Karabakh has led to a polarization of gender roles.

Evidently, conditions for war widows in Nagorny Karabakh can be vastly different, even in such a small region. Still, the challenges that face our research participants demonstrate that detailed explorations of widowhood deserve more attention. Although we have discussed the experiences of middle-aged and older war widows, their experiences can provide useful examples of the difficulties that widows under the age of 30 encounter. Thus, the topic of widowhood and how to deal with marginalization needs a much deeper understanding and further exploration in order to identify ways and strategies that can empower widows in general, and younger widows in particular.

Notes

1. This fieldwork trip was funded by the Centre for East European Language Based Area Studies (CEELBAS) and was conducted as part of a CEELBAS Postdoctoral Research Fellowship on Migration and Diasporic Citizenship (2009–2011).
2. These fieldwork trips were funded by the University of Winchester internal REF fund (2014–2015 and 2015–2016).
3. Since 2000, Nona Shahnazarian has conducted more than 80 interviews with women living in Nagorny Karabakh. Most of her fieldwork trips were self-financed.

4. The Nagorny Karabakh region comprises an area of 4400 square kilometres. The population of Nagorny Karabakh was estimated at 145,200 in 2016 (http://stat-nkr.am). The capital of Nagorny Karabakh has a population of 55,000 (www.karabakh.travel/en).
5. The main causes and developments of the Armenian–Azerbaijani conflict over Nagorny Karabakh have been examined in great detail. Thomas De Waal's (2013) book provides perhaps the most detailed analysis.
6. According to World Bank data, Armenia's population has decreased from approximately 3.5 million in 1990, to roughly 2.9 million people in 2016, whereas Azerbaijan's population has increased from approximately 7.1 million in 1990, to 9.7 million people in 2016.
7. For data on fatalities, see, for example, Broers (2016, p. 8).
8. In comparison, according to the Republic's National Statistical Service, the average salary in Nagorny Karabakh was estimated at 46,409 AMD (approximately 96USD) in 2016 (http://stat-nkr.am/en, p. 53).
9. Director of the Union for Relatives of Fallen Soldiers [*Soyuz rodstvennikov pogibshchikh voinov*] (Stepanakert, August 2015).
10. This interview quote also relates to the difficult socio-economic conditions in Nagorny Karabakh. Unemployment rates vary across the region but can be as high as 30% in some parts according to the National Statistical Service (2017). In the capital of Nagorny Karabakh, unemployment was estimated at 22.3% in 2016 (http://www.haynews.am/hy/karabakh-1326286593). According to the Republic's National Statistical Service (2017, p. 26), 23.3% of the population in Nagorny Karabakh live in poverty and 6.2% of the population in extreme poverty.
11. In this chapter, interviewed women are referred to by pseudonyms to ensure complete confidentiality.
12. In Nagorny Karabakh, their solitary being is simply expressed in their everyday dress which is meant to be black for at least six months after the death of their husband.
13. The *midzhi* support network is used in Nagorny Karabakh villages to help families to complete big tasks, for example, building a house or organizing a very big wedding with more than 200 guests. Today, *midzhi* in Karabakh society is mostly held to prepare for the dowry of young girls and thus has become a type of young women's gathering before the wedding takes place, but one to which widows are never invited. Young women take part in this event and also married

women, if wealthy, to help add to the stock of married women's wisdom (Shahnazarian 2004).
14. A woman without children or infertile.
15. Translates as bachelor.
16. Most of Nagorny Karabakh's infrastructure was destroyed during the war in the 1990s, including hospitals and health clinics. Women were most affected by this, since they were not able to access adequate healthcare. Even today, most towns and villages lack adequate health facilities and women have to travel a long way to get medical care. Therefore, in Shushi, for example, women organize among themselves that one of them visits the gynaecologist in the capital Stepanakert (by bus 30 min from Shushi), gets a prescription for contraceptive pills and shares the prescription with her friends. This can potentially harm women's health, as they mostly take medication without any prior consultation (Civil Society Monitoring Report 2014).

References

Artsakh Republic National Statistical Service. 2017. "Poverty and Social Panorama of the NKR." http://stat-nkr.am/en/publications/756--2017.

Balkwell, Carolyn. 1981. "Transition to Widowhood: A Review of the Literature." *Family Relations* 30 (1): 117–127. https://www.jstor.org/stable/584245.

Basnet, Syaron, Pragya Kandel, and Prabhat Lamichhane. 2017. "Depression and Anxiety Among War-Widows of Nepal: A Post-Civil War Cross-Sectional Study." *Psychology, Health & Medicine* 23 (21–13). https://doi.org/10.1080/13548506.2017.1338735.

Bokek-Cohen, Ya'arit. 2014. "Remarriage of Terror Widows: A Triadic Relationship." *Death Studies* 38 (10): 672–677. https://doi.org/10.1080/07481187.2013.844747.

Bonanno, George A., Camille B. Wortman, and Randolph M. Nesse. 2004. "Prospective Patterns of Resilience and Maladjustment During Widowhood." *Psychology and Aging* 19 (2): 260–271. http://dx.doi.org/10.1037/0882-7974.19.2.260.

Boulgourdjian-Toufeksian, Nelida. 2000. "Armenians in Argentina: Women and the Preservation of Identity." In *Voices of Armenian Women*, edited by Barbara Merguerian and Joy Renjilian-Burgy, 242–253. Belmont, MA: AIWA Press.

Broers, Laurence. 2016. "The Nagorny Karabakh Conflict: Defaulting to War." *Chatham House*, July 11. https://www.chathamhouse.org/publication/nagorny-karabakh-conflict-defaultingwar?dm_i=1TYG,4CQR2,NFH11P,-FYZTH.

Brown, Sara. E. 2016. "Reshaping Gender Norms in Post-Genocide Rwanda." *Genocide Studies International* 10 (2, Fall): 230–250. https://doi.org/10.3138/gsi.10.2.06.

Cavallo, Sandra, and Lyndon Warner. 2014. *Widowhood in Medieval and Early Modern Europe.* London: Routledge.

Chitrali, Jamil A., and Mussarat Anwar. 2013. "Socio-psychological Consequences of Spouse's Death on Widows of Khyber Pakhtunkhwa." *Putaj Humanities & Social Sciences* 20 (1): 147–156. http://putaj.puta.pk/index.php/hss/article/view/85.

Chou, Kee-Lee. 2007. "Psychological Distress in Migrants in Australia over 50 Years Old: A Longitudinal Investigation." *Journal of Affective Disorders* 98 (1–2): 99–108. https://doi.org/10.1016/j.jad.2006.07.002.

Civil Society Monitoring Report. 2014. "Nagorno-Karabakh: Women Count—Security Council Resolution 1325: Civil Society Monitoring Report 2014." http://gnwp.peacegeeks.org/tags/nagorno-karabakh.

Cockburn, Cynthia. 1998. *The Space Between Us: Negotiating Gender and National Identities in Conflict.* London: Zed Books.

Cornell, Svante E., ed. 2017. *The International Politics of the Armenian-Azerbaijani Conflict: The Original "Frozen Conflict" and European Security.* New York: Palgrave.

Courtney, Sheleyah A. 2014. "Savitri, the Unshackled *Shakti*: Goddess Identification, Violence and the Limits of Cultural Subversion of Widows in Varanasi." *South Asia: Journal of South Asian Studies* 37 (2): 268–280. https://doi.org/10.1080/00856401.2014.884987.

Detraz, Nicole. 2011. *International Security and Gender.* Cambridge: Polity Press.

De Waal, Thomas. 2013. *Black Garden: Armenia and Azerbaijan Through Peace and War, 10th Year Anniversary Edition.* New York: New York University Press.

Elshtain, Jean B. 1987. *Women and War.* Chicago: University of Chicago Press.

Fiske, Lucy, and Rita Shackel. 2015. "Gender, Poverty and Violence: Transitional Justice Responses to Converging Processes of Domination of Women in Eastern DRC, Northern Uganda and Kenya." *Women's*

Studies International Forum 51: 110–117. https://doi.org/10.1016/j.wsif.2014.11.008.

Fitzpatrick, Paul. 2011. "Widows at the Wall: An Exploration of the Letters Left at the Vietnam War Memorial." *Mortality* 16 (1): 70–86. https://doi.org/10.1080/13576275.2011.536372.

Jacobs, Janet. 2016. "The Memorial at Srebrenica: Gender and the Social Meanings of Collective Memory in Bosnia-Herzegovina." *Memory Studies* 10 (423–439). https://doi.org/10.1177/1750698016650485.

Katz, Ruth, and Nitza Ben-Dor. 1987. "Widowhood in Israel." In *Widows: The Middle East, Asia, and the Pacific*, vol. 1, edited by Helena Znaniecka-Lopata, 133–147. London: Duke University Press.

Komsuoğlu, Ayşegül, and Birsen Örs. 2009. "Armenian Women of Istanbul: Notes on Their Role in the Survival of the Armenian Community." *Gender, Place & Culture: A Journal of Feminist Geography* 16 (3): 329–349. https://doi.org/10.1080/09663690902836425.

Koos, Carlo. 2017. "Sexual Violence in Armed Conflicts: Research Progress and Remaining Gaps." *Third World Quarterly* 38 (9): 1935–1951. https://doi.org/10.1080/01436597.2017.1322461.

Kotzé, Elmarie, Lishje Els, and Nstiki Rajuili-Masilo. 2012. "'Women… Mourn and Men Carry On': African Women Storying Mourning Practices—A South African Example." *Death Studies* 36 (8): 742–766. https://doi.org/10.1080/07481187.2011.604463.

Kuhlman, Erika. A. 2012. *Of Little Comfort: War Widows, Fallen Soldiers, and the Remaking of Nation after the Great War*. New York: New York University Press.

Lenette, Caroline. 2013. "'I Am a Widow, Mother and Refugee': Narratives of Two Refugee Widows Resettled to Australia." *Journal of Refugee Studies* 27 (3): 403–421. https://doi.org/10.1093/jrs/fet045.

Lorentzen, Lois. A., and Jennifer E. Turpin. 1998. *The Women and War Reader*. New York: New York University Press.

Mand, Kanwal. 2005. "Marriage and Migration Through the Life Course: Experiences of Widowhood, Separation and Divorce Amongst Transnational Sikh Women." *Indian Journal of Gender Studies* 12 (2–3): 407–426. https://doi.org/10.1177/097152150501200211.

Marshall, Martin N. 1996. "Sampling for Qualitative Research." *Family Practice* 13 (6): 522–526. https://doi.org/10.1093/fampra/13.6.522.

Martin-Matthews, Anne, Catherine E. Tong, Carolyn J. Rosenthal, and Lynn McDonald. 2013. "Ethno-cultural Diversity in the Experience of

Widowhood in Later Life: Chinese Widows in Canada." *Journal of Aging Studies* 27 (4): 507–518. https://doi.org/10.1016/j.jaging.2012.12.011.

Mostov, Julie. 2000. "Sexing the Nation/Desexing the Body: Politics of National Identity in the Former Yugoslavia." In *Gender Ironies of Nationalism: Sexing the Nation*, edited by Tamar Mayer, 89–112. London: Routledge.

Ng, Petrus, Wing-Chung Ho, Angela Tsun, and Daniel K. W. Young. 2016. "Coping with Bereavement of Widows in the Chinese Cultural Context of Hong Kong." *International Social Work* 59 (1): 115–128. https://doi.org/10.1177/0020872813509395.

Nikolić-Ristanović, Vesna. 1998. "War, Nationalism, and Mothers in the Former Yugoslavia." In *The Women and War Reader*, edited by Lois A. Lorentzen and Jennifer Turpin, 234–239. New York: New York University Press.

Nwadinobi, Eleanor Ann. 2016. "Conflict Intervention on Behalf of Widows: Notes from Enugu State in Nigeria." In *Moving Toward a Just Peace*, edited by Jane Mary Fritz, 167–188. London: Springer.

Nyanzi, Stella. 2011. "Ambivalence Surrounding Elderly Widows' Sexuality in Urban Uganda." *Ageing International* 36 (3): 378–400.

Nyanzi, Stella, Emodu-Walakira, Margaret, and Wilberforce Serwaniko. 2009. "The Widow, the Will, and Widow Inheritance in Kampala: Revisiting Victimisation Arguments." *Canadian Journal of African Studies/La Revue canadienne des études africaines* 43 (1): 12–33. https://doi.org/10.1080/00083968.2010.9707581.

Ory, Brett, and Tim Huijts. 2015. "Widowhood and Well-being in Europe: The Role of National and Regional Context." *Journal of Marriage and Family* 77 (3): 730–746. https://doi.org/10.1111/jomf.12187.

Owen, Margaret. 1996. *A World of Widows*. London: Zed Books.

Panagiotopoulos, Georgia, Ruth Walker, and Mary Luszcz. 2013. "A Comparison of Widowhood and Wellbeing among Older Greek and British-Australian Migrant Women." *Journal of Aging Studies* 27 (4): 519–528. https://doi.org/10.1016/j.jaging.2013.03.005.

Pannilage, Upali. 2017. "Prejudice-Based Discrimination Encountered by Women War Widows in the Post-War Society of Sri Lanka." In *Papers on Peace, Reconciliation and Development Challenges; Proceedings of the 2nd International Conference on Humanities and Social Sciences*, edited by Upali Pannilage, E. A. Gamini Fonseka, and P. K. M. Dissanayake, 40–56. Matara, Sri Lanka: University of Ruhuna.

Poghosyan, Benyamin. 2017. "Commentary: Little Hope for a Negotiated Solution to the Karabakh Conflict in the Short-Term." July 27. http://commonspace.eu/index.php?m=23&news_id=4308.

Qayoom, Farah. 2014. "Women and Armed Conflict: Widows in Kashmir." *International Journal of Sociology and Anthropology* 6 (5): 161–168.

Qutab, Soudiya. 2012. "Women Victims of Armed Conflict: Half-Widows in Jammu and Kashmir." *Sociological Bulletin* 61 (2): 255–278.

Ramnarain, Smita. 2016. "Unpacking Widow Headship and Agency in Post-Conflict Nepal." *Feminist Economics* 22 (1): 80–105. https://doi.org/10.108 0/13545701.2015.1075657.

Sabri, Bushra, Shrutika Sabarwal, Michele R. Decker, Abina Shrestha, Kunda Sharma, Lily Thapa, and Pamela J. Surkan. 2016. "Violence Against Widows in Nepal: Experiences, Coping Behaviors, and Barriers in Seeking Help." *Journal of Interpersonal Violence* 31 (9): 1744–1766. https://doi. org/10.1177/0886260515569058.

Sahoo, Dipti Mayee. 2014. "An Analysis of Widowhood in India: A Global Perspective." *International Journal of Multidisciplinary and Current Research* 2: 45–58.

Sanamyan, Emil. 2016. "April 2016 War in Karabakh: A Chronology." April 6. http://yandunts.blogspot.fi/2016/04/april-2016-war-in-karabakh-chronol-ogy.html.

———. 2017. "Coming Military Escalation in Karabakh." February 25. http://armenian.usc.edu/focus-on-karabakh/analysis/coming-military-escalationkarabakh-considerations-nature-timing/.

Sapir, E. 1916. "Terms of Relationship and the Levirate." *American Anthropologist* 18 (3): 327–337.

Sengupta, Anasuya, and Muriel Calo. 2016. "Shifting Gender Roles: An Analysis of Violence Against Women in Post-conflict Uganda." *Development in Practice* 26 (3): 285–297. https://doi.org/10.1080/09614524.2016.1149 151.

Sev'er, Aysan, and Mazhar Bagli. 2006. "Levirat & Sororat Marriages in Southeastern Turkey: Intact Marriage or Sanctified Incest?" https://tspace. library.utoronto.ca/bitstream/1807/9398/1/sever_bagli.pdf.

Shahnazarian, Nona. 2004. "Pokhoronennaya zazhivo (vdova v obshchestve karabakhskikh armyan." *Bulletin: Anthropology, Minorities, Multiculturalism* 6: 89–96.

———. 2011. *V tesnykh obyatiyakh traditsii: voyna i patriarkhat.* Sankt Peterburg: Izdatel'stvo Aleteya.

Shahnazarian, Nona, and Ulrike Ziemer. 2012. "Young Soldiers' Tales of War in Nagorno-Karabakh." *Europe-Asia Studies* 64 (9): 1667–1683. https://doi.org/10.1080/09668136.2012.718423.

———. 2014. "Emotions, Loss and Change: Armenian Women and Post-socialist Transformations in Nagorny Karabakh." *Caucasus Survey* 2 (1–2): 27–40. https://doi.org/10.1080/23761199.2014.11417298.

———. 2018. "Women Confronting Death: War Widows' Experiences in the South Caucasus." *Journal of International Women's Studies* 19 (2): 29–43. http://vc.bridgew.edu/jiws/vol19/iss2/3.

Sjoberg, Laura. 2014. *Gender, War, and Conflict*. London: Wiley.

Sjoberg, Laura, and Caron E. Gentry. 2007. *Mothers, Monsters, Whores: Women's Violence in Global Politics*. London: Zed Books.

Sossou, Marie-Antoinette. 2002. "Widowhood Practices in West Africa: The Silent Victims." *International Journal of Social Welfare* 11 (3): 201–209. https://doi.org/10.1111/1468-2397.00217.

Turpin, Jennifer. 1998. "Many Faces: Women Confronting War." In *The Women and War Reader*, edited by Lois A. Lorentzen and Jennifer Turpin, 3–18. New York: New York University Press.

UN Women. 2012. "UN Women and the Loomba Foundation Join Forces to Empower Widows in Three Continents." http://www.unwomen.org/2012/11/un-women-andthe-loombafoundation-join-forces-to-empower-widows-in-three-continents/.

———. 2017. "Statement: Widows' Rights to Independent Life and Livelihood After Loss." *UN Women Statement for International Widows' Day*. June 23, 2017. http://www.unwomen.org/en/news/stories/2017/6/statement-un-women-internationalwidows-day.

Ziemer, Ulrike. 2011. *Ethnic Belonging, Gender, and Cultural Practices: Youth Identities in Contemporary Russia*. Stuttgart: ibidem Verlag.

Part III

New Beginnings and Old Challenges: Feminism and Women's Identities

9

Invisible Battlefield: How the Politicization of LGBT Issues Affects the Visibility of LBT Women in Georgia

Natia Gvianishvili

Georgia's decision to work towards EU integration hastened the government's implementation of new democratic reforms and initiatives in close collaboration with civil society organizations. Thanks to the country's political aspirations and development assistance from the West, the non-governmental sector has recently become stronger and more vocal, adopting a human rights agenda similar to that of established Western democracies. During this process, closer ties with international human rights organizations have also been strengthened. Thus, in Georgia today NGOs are much more capable of putting pressure on the Georgian government. Alongside these positive developments, the more recent economic and political shifts and subsequent crises, as well as military conflicts over Georgia's breakaway regions, still delay the strengthening of a democratic vision of Georgian society and the way that it should function. This chapter seeks to demonstrate that, just as it was a characteristic of Soviet Georgia, the capitalizing on the strict division between 'us' and 'them' in Georgia's political discourse is still

N. Gvianishvili (✉)
Stockholm, Sweden

© The Author(s) 2020
U. Ziemer (ed.), *Women's Everyday Lives in War and Peace in the South Caucasus*,
https://doi.org/10.1007/978-3-030-25517-6_9

prevalent today, in particular, at times when social and political anxieties intensify, such as during elections.

The Georgian government is quickly adopting new democratic laws, strategies and action plans, but is still reluctant to engage in re-shaping public opinion into something less violent and more inclusive. Instead, together with oppositional parties, the Orthodox Church and other public actors it is still using marginalized groups, such as LGBT people, as tokens to serve its narrow interests. Media monitoring conducted by various NGOs shows that hate speeches against LGBT people (as well as ethnic minorities) escalated around the time of elections or other important events that involve the distribution of power (Aghdgomelashvili 2012; Kintsurashvili 2016). It is problematic that, while politicians and government officials may differ about the homophobic initiatives or statements of their colleagues, the official discourse remains purely related to party politics and hardly anyone inside the political elite raises the question of the human rights of lesbian, gay, bisexual and transgender persons, showing complete disregard for the correlation between hate speech, discriminatory language and hate crimes.

Exploring the politicization of LGBT issues and how it affects the visibility of LBT women, I argue that Georgia is still recovering from its recent traumatic past and here (just as in many other countries) the conversation around conflict and security is for the most part dominated by the military and physical dimensions of these two concepts. Although the idea of human security has been more publicly discussed lately, little research has been done on the political use of marginalized groups in post-war (or post-armed conflict) societies and identity building. Noteworthy here is that there is no empirical data on the impact of such politicization on lesbian, bisexual and transgender women, who in Georgian society today often end up at the bottom of the social ladder. While the lives of lesbian and bisexual women have remained under-researched, however, the experiences of transgender women, for example, have become more visible, due to the recent rise in everyday violence against them. Issues involving LBT women have become more politicized, yet stories of violence and discrimination, which affect their mental health and well-being, have been largely absent from public discourse and have not been addressed in the media either. To close this gap, this chapter analyses instances of the politicization of LGBT rights and its impact on the lives of LBT women in Georgian society. First, this chapter provides some background information on the everyday struggles of LGBT people in Georgia. Second, it analyses the politicization of LGBT issues in public discourse. It goes on to show how this politicization makes LBT women invisible in public discourse, which then impacts negatively on their everyday lives. The chapter concludes by exploring the possible reasons for the invisibility of LBT women and calling for systematic research on the issue in the future.

LGBT People in Georgia

Georgia is often praised as a successful example of transition from communism to a system of democratic governance with a market-oriented economy. In its aspiration to move politically and economically close to the European Union, the country has made improvements on many levels of governance including the legislation related to human rights. Significant success was achieved in fighting corruption and crime, reforming the law enforcement agencies, improving the educational system and making the country safer for both residents and tourists.[1] Yet, to date, closer regular communication between civil society activists and the government still needs to improve, especially in regard to the human rights issues of such social groups as LGBT people, in Georgian society.

In line with the improvement of human rights legislation following the efforts to focus on EU integration, homosexuality was decriminalized with the adoption of the revised Criminal Code but only in 2000 (Women's Initiatives Supporting Group 2012, p. 54). Since then legal protection on the basis of sexual orientation and gender identity has been improved by various laws, such as the Labour Code or the Law on Patients' Rights as well as the Criminal Code—which lists homo/bi/transphobic bias as an aggravating circumstance (Ratiani et al. 2015). In 2014, Georgia adopted a widely debated law on the Elimination of All Forms of Discrimination, which, unlike similar laws in Moldova and Ukraine, protects people from discrimination on the grounds of sexual orientation and gender identity not only in employment, but in most other spheres of life (Civil Georgia 2014). Moreover, the National Human Rights Strategy and action plan were introduced in the same year. These two new strategies explicitly address the rights of LGBT people and can be seen as a public declaration of the government's will to work on improving the human rights situation in the country (Jalagania 2016).

Many of these changes, however, turned out to be more cosmetic and the actual daily fate of those belonging to a minority social group has not significantly improved. For example, the Law on the Elimination of All Forms of Discrimination has a very weak implementation mechanism. The main difficulty is that a person facing discrimination has either to file a lawsuit and maintain the burden of proof, or to address the Public Defender's Office, which tries to be more sensitive to the discrimination against marginalized groups, but cannot make legally binding recommendations either to the State or the private sector. The same applies to cases of hate crime, where law enforcement agencies repeatedly show their ineptitude and unwillingness to seriously address the wrongdoing. Often their investigation of incidents is biased from the first instance. Noteworthy here is that transgender people are almost barred from the reforms since full recognition officially restricts them to legally filing a case only as a man or a woman. To do so, they would need to identify themselves as one or the other, which requires full gender reassignment surgery, because the law does not recognize the transgender category. In short, the law, discriminatory in itself, precludes the very people who need it from invoking it.

In order to sign the Association Agreement with the EU and get access to visa-free travel, Georgia had to enact a list of reforms, including an improved legal framework and a higher level of inclusiveness of minorities (EU-Georgia Relations Factsheet 2017). But as soon as one looks beyond this numerous gaps appear in the implementation mechanisms (Jalagania 2016), as well as inconsistencies in political rhetoric. Despite the legal progress, members of Parliament and government officials are still making homophobic comments and the media keep reproducing the distorted image of so-called 'sexual minorities' that the

Church[2] and state promote. This image of LGBT people as sick and perverted is contrasted with the values of the traditional, nuclear family propagated by the Church and many groups connected to it. They act, for instance, by lobbying to have marriage defined in the Constitution as a union between a man and a woman,[3] opposing an introduction of courses in school that would speak of gender equality and liberal politics (Minesashvili 2017) and appropriating May 17 as a day for 'family purity' (Civil Georgia 2014) specifically in opposition to the LGBT activists who year after year try to use this day for peaceful rallies. Since there is rarely any political opposition to the Church's stance on minority issues, it becomes clear to many Georgian citizens that the commitment to protecting marginalized communities is slight. Some of them, of course, interpret this in the way that best suits either their political interests or xenophobic beliefs. The double message of adopting LGBT-inclusive laws and policies, but never condemning violence against this community or taking any proactive steps to tackle the problems facing it results in a sense of impunity, which in turn permits, and may even encourage, violence and discrimination against LGBT people.

The lack of commitment mentioned above, is also evident in the fact that law enforcement agencies in Georgia keep no data on violence and discrimination against LGBT people and human rights defenders have to rely heavily on data collected by NGOs. According to research conducted by the Women's Initiatives Supporting Group (WISG) in 2012, every third member of the LGBT community faces violence due to sexual orientation and gender identity. This dynamic had fallen slightly in terms of physical violence by 2014, but was replaced by the increased frequency of physical assaults per person (Aghdgomelashvili 2016). At the same time, 72% of the surveyed community members were afraid to come out because of increasingly hostile public opinion (ibid.). Indeed, major opinion polls and other research on values in Georgian society indicate that LGBT people form one of the most hated groups here. The results of the World Value Survey Study Five (2008) and Six (2014) show that the number of people who feel that 'homosexuality is never acceptable' drastically increased between 1996 and 2008. The sections of this research that measure the distance between different social groups showed that in 1996, 77% of the respondents were opposed to having homosexuals as their neighbours. This percentage increased by 2008, reached 92% and had gone down again to 86.6% by 2014 (ibid.).

It is assumed that this reduced percentage between 2008 and 2014 may have been caused by an attack in 2013 on May 17 (Civil Georgia 2013) on a group of LGBT activists and allies, who had planned a peaceful demonstration to mark the International Day against Homo/bi/transphobia. The fact that a crowd of approximately 20,000 people, led by the orthodox clergy, attacked a group of not quite 100 activists and their friends, injuring many people (including police officers, journalists and of course the activists), caused a strong social outcry. The scale of the violence managed to shake up the segment of the Georgian society that hitherto had usually chosen to remain neutral when it came to the rights of different marginalized groups; many more public figures than usual condemned this act of violence.

Since then, freedom of assembly for LGBT people has become one of the most widely discussed topics in Georgian society. As opposed to the 1990s, when LGBT issues were not part of public discussion and homosexuality was mentioned only as one way of insulting politicians or public figures (Aghdgomelashvili 2012), in 2006 an LGBT movement was established, starting with the first community-based NGO; it addressed a range of issues concerning the situation of LGBT people. Raising these issues in public debates raised public awareness and the visibility of LGBTs in everyday life. In addition, non-governmental organizations working with the community started systematically to review the Georgian legislation on sexual orientation and gender identity, researching different aspects of the lives of LGBT people (including violence, discrimination, access to healthcare and access to legal gender recognition).[4] Alongside freedom of assembly, the main questions raised and debated have included discussions about hate crimes and discrimination and, most recently, the legal gender recognition of transgender identities.

However, while LGBT people have all of a sudden stopped being a mythical faceless group, their activism has met even greater resistance or backlash. Research exploring the correlation between attitudes to LGBT people and the belief systems and social situation of Georgians shows that 67% of the survey participants believe that LGBT people should not work with children, 74% disagree that same-sex couples should be allowed the right to adopt a child that other couples have, 82% disagree that marriage should be accessible to LGBT people and 66% believe that LGBT rallies should be banned by law (Aghdgomelashvili 2016). The above numbers speak of the situation of LGBT people in Georgia in practice, illustrating the vicious cycle in which events move. While the same research showed that acquaintance with a member of LGBT community is negatively correlated with a high level of homophobia, most of the community members, as mentioned above, are not able to come out even to their closest social circle, because of the high level of stigma (ibid.).

The Politicization of LGBT Issues

The negative public opinion and opposition to allowing LGBT people to enjoy their guaranteed rights and freedoms are partly the result of a lack of general knowledge and awareness of gender and sexuality (neither the Georgian educational system nor the media provides adequate information on the matter). The high politicization of these issues also seems to play a crucial role. According to Rubin (2011), conflicts over sexuality have become 'the vehicles for displacing social anxieties' and thus it is argued that, in Georgia, the cause of such anxieties has been the country's political and economic transformations, as well as the ongoing armed conflicts in Abkhazia and South Ossetia. In other words, in the past two decades, Georgia has experienced major changes in its political and economic system (including an economic crisis), a civil war and two armed conflicts in the breakaway regions of Abkhazia and South Ossetia. It should be remembered, too, that Georgian society spent the first 15 years after the collapse of the Soviet Union in a precarious state, meeting challenges to its security at all levels.

Given these challenges, it is not surprising that the making of the 'other' (de Beauvoir 1997), in attempts to shape and manipulate the idea of Georgian identity, has been used successfully by conservative and populist politicians and the Church, which all tend to use the emotions of their adherents to stir them in specific directions. The leader of the Georgian Orthodox Church, Ilia II, has repeatedly stated that homosexuality is an 'anomaly and disease' (McLaughlin 2013). The Georgian Orthodox Church is an important political actor and opinion-maker in Georgian society (BBC News 2013), so it is no wonder that over time more clerics and public figures have begun to employ more and more populism, building on the general fear and doubts that people have about homosexuality and portraying it as damaging for the moral fabric of the country's identity.

A similar strategy was employed in the Soviet Union, after consenting male homosexual relations were re-criminalized in 1933 and the regime decided to change its liberal attitude to marriage and citizens' private lives and strictly enforce the norm of the nuclear family (Stella 2016). Yet, in contradistinction to Soviet Georgia's silence about female homosexuality, before Stalin came to power, female homosexuality received substantial attention from doctors and researchers, fascinated by the attempts of their Western (especially German) counterparts to 'cure' homosexuality through therapy and various kinds of surgery (Healey 2001). Lesbian women were also more widely represented in literary circles in Soviet Russia than in Soviet Georgia, with Lidia Hannibal and Marina Tsvetaeva, to name only two prominent figures.

After this re-criminalization, the Communist propaganda machine started to use male homosexuality to typify Western decadence. During Stalin's repressions homosexual men were declared 'spies', 'enemies of the revolution' and 'declassified elements, while women were accused of asocial behaviour and continued to be treated by psychiatrists (Healey 2001). In 1934, one of the most popular Soviet writers, Maxim Gorky, who was also very popular in Georgia, declared that homosexuality was one of the results of fascism's detrimental effect on European youth and that a country that is bravely and successfully ruled by the Proletariat finds such behaviour criminal and unacceptable. He ends his pronouncement with the phrase 'Exterminate homosexuals and fascism will disappear'. With this level of propaganda, we can understand how Article 121 of the USSR Criminal Code was used not only against men who had sex with other men, but often against political activists and others undesirable to the regime (Healey 2001). Just as in Georgia today, homophobic anti-Western rhetoric accompanied a stronger promotion of the nuclear family, stricter control on women's reproductive rights and strict limits on women's gender role, serving a double shift for the motherland and for their husbands. This was enough to force lesbian women back into invisibility.

In the Georgian media, public discussions on homosexuality started only in the 1990s. Nonetheless, to date, the Soviet myth of the Western origins of homosexuality has remained strong. Starting from 1998, in Georgia, the idea of homosexuals/homosexuality was transformed into something 'foreign' and 'sick' and is then portrayed as a social deviation. Between 1998 and 2003 homosexuality joined a list of objects for political speculation, such as ethnic and religious minorities, and the myth of the 'homosexual conspiracy' emerged. The panic about this 'conspiracy', soothed after the Rose Revolution in 2003, had reappeared with renewed force by 2011–2012 (Aghdgomelashvili 2012). The reason for this lies in the higher level of politicization of the issue, as well as the increased visibility of the LGBT movement itself. This visibility was gained through its public rallies in 2012 and 2013 and the appearance of LGBT activists on public television and certain public platforms (Gvianishvili 2017).

Media monitoring conducted at various stages between 1999 and 2011 shows that the media's interest in homosexuality was not stable; the peak of hate speech coincided with important political events and times of the distribution of power (ibid.). It is interesting to note that while between 1999 and 2003 the arguments against homosexuality were at least rational on the surface, after this period the Church began actively to spread the idea of homosexuality as opposed to Orthodox Christian values. This is the same argument used by the Church in its war to 'clear the public space from sin' (ibid.). It is also not surprising to find the Church's stance on issues related to sexuality affecting public opinion, given that, as the World Values Survey shows the importance of religion for Georgians increased from 49% in 1996 to 84% in 2014 whereas the importance of politics, which at the best of times has never been high enough dropped from 13.2% in 1996 to 10.2% 2014.

This makes the use of discriminatory language and homophobic hate speech all the more acceptable for politicians and public figures as well as certain types of media. Hateful rhetoric is employed to stereotype, humiliate, create negative images, blame members of a social group for their negative impact on society, accuse them of treason and the abuse of power (in their secret domination of politics and/or show business, propaganda, etc.) and call covertly or openly for violence and discrimination. Although the media have changed significantly in the last decade and journalists oppose hate speech and discriminatory language more strongly, the main problems are still that the media confuse the terminology (for instance, mixing up sexual orientation and gender identity), quote homophobic texts, point out or emphasize someone's sexual orientation or gender identity when not necessary, and most importantly choose respondents who are aggressively homophobic and make little or no attempt to restrain them (Khorbaladze 2015).

In the last three years, unfortunately, the tendency of politicization has shown no sign of receding, despite the active work of the LGBT movement, increased access to information and steady dialogue between government and civil society. This resistance to change can be found in reports on political hate speech. According to the regular media monitoring conducted by the Media Monitoring Fund (MDF) in 2012–2015, 331 cases of homophobic hate speech were documented in the printed media, internet media and TV, hereby TV being the most important outlet for hate speech. Homophobic statements were made by media representatives (100), political parties (70), officials (6), former officials (9), clerics (42) and other public figures (96). Among the political parties, Georgian Dream Coalition (the ruling coalition at the time), *Burjanadze*—United Democrats and Patriot Alliance held the top three positions.

The situation grew worse as 2016 approached, especially in the period before the parliamentary elections (Kintsurashvili 2016), when out of 868 cases of hate speech 52% (454) were related to homophobia. Political parties (139) and the media (152) were the top two sources of hateful statements. With the political parties, things were similar to the previous cycle, *Burjanadze*—United Democrats and Patriot Alliance, Georgian Dream (a party holding the constitutional majority in the Parliament from October 2016) and *Erovnulebi* being the top three. Another study conducted by the MDF shows that one of the most popular ploys was to equate the West with the promotion of homosexuality, incest and paedophilia, along with the false dichotomy of homosexuality vs Euro Atlantic integration employed by xenophobic media and politicians.

Many of the examples mentioned above were connected to the initiative of the ruling coalition to amend the constitution and include a gender-specific definition of marriage (Civil Georgia 2016; Synovitz 2017). This is a very interesting example, since the initiative was and remains purely related to party politics. It was not a conservative response to the agenda of the LGBT movement, since none of the LGBT groups has so far advocated marriage equality. The official explanation of the government's deciding to take up this issue was allegedly to avoid any further speculations about allowing gay marriage as a prerequisite for Georgia's Euro Atlantic integration (Morrison and Waller 2016). Thus, one can say that the main discourse around sexuality in Georgia is a political one. It uses sexualized identities to present an image of a threat to the nation, culture and religion, as well as, very specifically, to demography (Tsereteli 2010) and makes it acceptable to 'sacrifice' these identities for the 'greater good'.

Invisible Women—Invisible Battlefields

It is true that in discussing the politicization of LGBT issues we did not touch upon specific identities. Public discourse still does not discriminate between different sub-groups of the community. Generally speaking, however, the sexualized identities of women have a history of being invisible. Even in Soviet times, the more overt punishment was given to men who had sex with men, leaving female homosexuality to the sphere of psychiatry and 'sexopathology' (Stella 2016). While we now witness increasing attention to the situation of transgender women, very few empirical data have been collected in relation to lesbian and bisexual women in Georgia and these sub-groups literally have no agenda inside the movement. Most research done in the field is dedicated to exploring general, or policy—and advocacy-related, experiences of violence and discrimination, leaving out social practices and other issues relevant to LB women and transgender persons.

Gabunia (2010) conducted research on the use of virtual platforms by lesbian residents in Tbilisi and showed that lesbian women are often closeted and tied to virtual spaces (which they use to create and maintain relationships with each other) and indoor spaces. These findings suggest that such practices contribute to their general invisibility. This tendency is connected to their need to maintain social status, depending also on financial factors (ibid.). In addition, it is argued that their absence from the public sphere also depends on the gendered socialization of men and women in Georgia. Gay men have cruising areas outdoors (Gabunia 2009) but women do not, since their lives are usually more controlled by their family members. Research conducted in 2014, endorses this argument by reporting that, in terms of socialization, 68% of lesbian and bisexual women preferred 'visiting a friend at home' and/or attending regular meetings organized by the community-based organization (58%), while 78% of gay and bisexual men who were interviewed preferred frequenting LGBT-friendly clubs/bars (78%) and used the Internet for dating (76%) (Aghdgomelashvili 2016).

An article exploring the representation of lesbians in public discourse in Georgia argues that (generalized and abstract) sexualized identities other than those of gay men are almost completely excluded from public discourse (Kharchilava 2010). Kharchilava (2010) states that lesbian identities are subjected to the logic of representation which is based on legitimization through building stereotypes upon experienced social phenomena. Lesbians (on the rare occasions when they are mentioned in public discourse) go through this process of legitimization transferring from completely marginalized spaces to the new semiotic zones where they are considered along the lines of heterosexuality and not in opposition to them. This logic of representation is in line with patriarchal principles. Since the roles and functions of men and women are seen as 'given' and any deviation is perceived as a social problem, women and men are charged with maintaining both biological and symbolic reproduction.

However, since female sexuality in general is seen as passive (recipient), lesbianism is not taken as seriously or tragically as male homosexuality, since a lesbian can still 'find a right way' and have a 'normal' family (Kharchilava 2010). This gives the impression that as far as lesbian or bisexual women are concerned, there is not much to talk about. This argument is supported by a recent research project *From Prejudice to Equality* conducted by the NGO WISG to examine respondents' attitudes to LGBT people and the various stereotypes connected to these identities. It is interesting to see that while participants are more decisive when it comes to the stereotypes that target gay men, their usual response to the stereotypes surrounding lesbians is '*I don't know*' (Aghdgomelashvili 2016).

Despite the general closeted nature of lesbianism and the absence of lesbian identities from public discourse, there seems to be quite a strong activist base of lesbian, bisexual and queer women. A study conducted by WISG in 2015 reports that lesbian and bisexual women show greater readiness to engage in activism (50% of the LB group vs. 40% of the GB group) than in their gay male counterparts. In addition, 58 and 40%, respectively of the interviewed lesbian and bisexual women attend regular meetings and are involved in the activities of the organizations, a number that is three times higher than the number of their gay and bisexual counterparts (Aghdgomelashvili 2016). This can be explained by the fact that women in general represent the core of many social movements in Georgia and are on the front line when it comes to alternative forms of activism. For instance, the first activist group in Georgia refusing to become an NGO in order to respond to sexism and homophobia without formal constraints was the *Independent Group of Feminists*. The reason why it refused was that NGOs were not vocal in challenging the public expressions of sexism, for instance, by politicians, and also did not pursue an explicitly feminist agenda. The core of this group was represented both by straight and queer women. It is also interesting that lesbian, bisexual and queer women show a higher level of public identification with their sexual orientation than is shown in the gay male community (Gvianishvili 2012). This is confirmed by looking at the coming out dynamics, which show that lesbian and bisexual women are mostly out with their friends (also present in the activist groups), but the two most stressful spaces for them are the work environment and the family and they avoid coming out there (Aghdgomelashvili 2016). Thus, it is argued that the active segment of the LBQ community balances concealment in certain spaces by openness in other circles especially tied to activism, given that both concealment and coming out are considered to be at the same time stress factors and coping mechanisms (Gvianishvili 2012).

While lesbian and bisexual women are invisible, the visibility of transgender women has increased over the past 3 years, but it has done so at the expense of the extreme victimization of trans identities. Violence against transgender women has been highlighted recently (very much thanks to the increasingly active role of trans sex workers in the movement). However, the brutal violence that they constantly face has prevented much reporting on the lives of lesbian and bisexual women. The public discussion around the lives of transgender women started in 2014 when a young trans woman was murdered in Tbilisi (Popovaite 2014). Another trans woman shared the same fate in 2016 (DFWatch 2017). Both were brutally murdered by men who were arrested and tried, but bias as a motive was neither investigated properly, nor, of course, proven. After this case, the number of trans women speaking openly about the violence and discrimination they face increased. Transgender men and non-binary transgender people (especially those assigned female sex at birth) are also left out of public discourse. Because Georgian society is very patriarchal and men (biologically speaking) are the primary recipients of aggression outdoors (the situation in the family is wholly different), the problems that lesbian and bi women face remain largely invisible.

The issues regarding the agenda of the LGBT movement and its public reception form a hierarchy: if you are brutally attacked outdoors, your issue ends up in the spotlight but if the same thing is threatened at home, you either do not come out or you deal with the whole range of problems on your own. While violence against women in the LGBT community is often underestimated, research shows that by 2014 violent incidents against LBT women, especially in correlation with activism, had exceeded that in previous years. The frequency of physical violence against LB women in terms of the number of violent incidents per person outran the violence against the gay and bisexual community (LB women—36%; GB men—22%) (Gvianishvili 2012). In this hierarchy, the mental and emotional well-being of lesbian, bisexual women and transgender persons is scarcely addressed. Yet several studies suggest that stigma and discrimination damage these areas of LBT lives. For instance, along with concealment of one's identity and difficulties in coming to terms with one's sexuality, the constant expectation or actual experience of physical and psychological violence based on one's sexual orientation or gender identity remains an important stress factor for the LBT community (Gvianishvili 2012).

In a research project exploring the situation of transgender persons in Georgia, we see that the index of depression in the community is higher than normal (Gvianishvili 2014). Each of the respondents who scored high on the Depression Scale were in the years preceding or concurrent with the research, experiencing depression to which physical and psychological violence, based on their gender identity and expression, contributed. Another research project which explores the needs of LGB persons in terms of healthcare showed that lesbian and bisexual women showed greater inclination to suicidal ideation and self-harm than their male counterparts did (Aghdgomelashvili 2016) According to the results 44% of all the respondents had had suicidal thoughts (56% lesbian and bisexual women and 32% of gay and bisexual men) in the years before the research, of whom 7% had attempted to take their own lives and 16% had engaged in self-harm behaviour. Lesbian and bisexual women reported higher numbers of attempted suicides and forms of self-harm behaviours (32%) than their male counterparts (8%) (ibid.).

The data reported above show that the environment of hostility and politicization of LGBT issues has directly affected the lives of lesbians, bisexual women and transgender persons, despite the fact that these identities remain to a large extent invisible. This invisibility is caused by the general disregard for female sexuality and gender variance both inside and outside the movement. The concerns are higher as regards legal frameworks and more overt expressions of violence, leaving low emotional well-being and stigma, together with discriminatory social practices, unaddressed and stifling many women. There is still no explicit agenda for women in the community, even though the above studies speak of the closer attachment to the community among LBQ women, which could be connected to the lack of variety in women only spaces. We can argue that because lesbian, bisexual and queer women are more open to the diversity in the community, and show higher empathy for various gender expressions (Gvianishvili 2012), they too readily accept the given hierarchy of problems and take on an agenda which is more important to other social groups instead of paying attention to working on their own representation and positive visibility.

Conclusions

This chapter contributes to the growing, yet still sparse, literature on LGBT people in the South Caucasus. It has explored the dynamics of the politicization of LGBT issues in Georgia and how it impacts on the everyday life of lesbian, bisexual women and transgender persons. The foregoing discussion brings out four concluding observations to be made. First, as yet the issues relating to LGBT people's rights are highly politicized in Georgia. The discourse on homosexuality dominating the public space in recent years consists of tactics, such as the portrayal of homosexuality as abnormality, deviation; making parallels between homosexuality and behaviour perceived as deviant in the society; statements saying that homosexuality is a vice originating in the West, which puts traditions and religion at risk; discussions about same-sex marriage as a threat to the moral fabric of society; calls for discrimination and violence against LGBT people and a generally implied message that, while homosexuals may be allowed to exist, they should not express themselves in public space (Khorbaladze 2015).

Second, this discourse follows a patriarchal logic of making women invisible and focusing on male homosexuality and everything that is perceived to express the 'loss of manhood'. The instances in which the most socially marginalized subgroup of the community—transgender women—is able to gain some visibility point to the overtly brutal violence that they face. The cause for such visibility has been two murders of transgender women in Tbilisi in 2014 and 2016, which caused both the higher engagement of NGOs in the issue and the more active participation and criticism of transgender women themselves. However, the representation is very seldom empowering, since it is based primarily on the victimization of transgender identities.

The third observation, which follows from the first two, is that lesbian, bisexual and queer women, while being very active inside LBT, form a movement which continues to be invisible, since the general agenda of the movement does not cover issues that are more significant to individual identities; rather, they act in general. So, in a way the agenda of the movement (or different components of it) follows the dominant discourse leaving the battles of LB women and most of the trans community tied into the hidden domestic sphere.

The final observation relates to avenues for future research. Acknowledging the limitations of this chapter, it has become clear that more empirical research is needed to document the everyday experiences of lesbian, bisexual women and transgender persons in connection with politicization and their hostile environment. Such research should also serve the purpose of bringing out the perspective of these groups and increasing the positive visibility of their identities, thus shaping an agenda that is more inclusive of the issues that matter to the sub-groups of the community.

Notes

1. After the so-called Rose Revolution in 2003, the Georgian government implemented important reforms including one of the police and one of the taxation laws. The government imposed zero tolerance of corruption and gang violence, which helped improve the situation (World Bank 2012).
2. According to the World Value Survey (2014) and Pew Research Centre (2017) religion is very important for Georgians and the Georgian Orthodox Church is named as the people's most trusted institution. The Church and the State in Georgia are formally separated. However, the Orthodox Church has privileges defined by a special contract with the State, which include receiving significant annual contributions from the state budget, as well as full tax exemption. The Orthodox Church is currently an important political player, expressing strictly conservative opinions and providing inputs on a variety of subjects from education to women's reproductive health and rights. The Church's power over politics is also quite strong.

3. The initiative came from the Church and traditionalist groups and was endorsed by the Georgian Dream Coalition and later the Georgian Dream party. Despite fierce opposition from civil society and a very few politicians, the amendment was adopted. This happened despite the fact that none of the Georgian LGBT organizations or activists ever advocated marriage equality or civil partnerships. Some politicians from the ruling party stated that the amendment was intended to prevent marriage equality in future, while others stated that it would put an end to polarizing political speculations on the issue of Western values and same-sex marriage.

4. Organizations such as the Women's Initiatives Supporting Group (WISG), *Identoba* and Human Rights Education and Monitoring Centre EMC, have regularly researched the situation of LGBT people in Georgia since 2012, with separate research on the situation of transgender people, and also prepared a number of reports on the legal conditions and implementation of laws that apply to SOGI issues.

References

Aghdgomelashvili, Ekaterine. 2012. "Homophobia and Regulation Mechanisms—Public Policy Paper." *South Caucasus Office of the Heinrich Boell Foundation*. Tbilisi.

———. 2016. "From Prejudice to Equality—Study of Societal Attitudes, Knowledge and Information Regarding the LGBT Community and Their Rights." *Women's Initiatives Supporting Group (WISG)*. Tbilisi, Georgia.

BBC News. 2013. "Georgia's Mighty Orthodox Church." https://www.bbc.co.uk/news/world-europe-23103853.

de Beauvoir, Simone. 1997. *The Second Sex*. London: Vintage Classics.

Civil Georgia. 2013. "Violence Against Anti-homophobia Rally." *Daily News Online*, May 18. https://old.civil.ge/eng/article.php?id=26073.

———. 2014. "Georgian Church Calls for Family Day on May 17." *Daily News Online*, May 11. https://old.civil.ge/eng/article.php?id=27221.

———. 2016. "MPs Launch Proceedings for Setting Constitutional Bar to Same-Sex Marriage." *Daily News Online*, March 18. http://www.civil.ge/eng/article.php?id=29049.

DFWatch. 2017. "Georgian Sentenced to 13 Years for Killing a Transgender Woman." *Democracy Freedom Watch*, February 7. https://dfwatch.net/georgian-sentenced-to-13-years-for-killing-a-transgender-woman-47558.

EU-Georgia Relations Factsheet. 2017. https://eeas.europa.eu/headquarters/headquarters-homepage_en/23634/EU-Georgia%20relations,%20factsheet.

Gabunia, Shorena. 2009. "Homosexuality in Tbilisi's Urban Culture." *South Caucasus Office of the Heinrich Boell Foundation*. Tbilisi, Georgia.

———. 2010. *Role of Virtual Communication in Lives of Lesbians Living in Tbilisi*. Women's Fund of Georgia, Tbilisi, Georgia.

Gvianishvili, Natia. 2012. "Internalized Homophobia in Georgian LGBQ Community." *South Caucasus Regional Office of the Heinrich Boell Foundation*. Tbilisi, Georgia.

———. 2014. "Situation of Transgender People in Georgia." *Women's Initiatives Supporting Group*. Tbilisi. https://women.ge/en/publications/40/.

———. 2017. "Being Transgender in Georgia." In *Gender in Georgia: Feminist Perspectives on Culture, Nation, and History in the South Caucasus*, edited by Maia Barkaia and Alisse Waterston, 194–204. New York: Berghahn Books.

Healey, Dan. 2001. *Homosexual Desire in Revolutionary Russia: The Regulation of Sexual and Gender Dissent*. Chicago: University of Chicago Press.

Jalagania, Lika. 2016. *Legal Situation of LGBTI Persons in Georgia*. Human Rights Education and Monitoring Centre (EMC), Tbilisi, Georgia.

Kintsurashvili, Tamar. 2016. *Hate Speech—Report for 2016*. Media Development Foundation, Tbilisi, Georgia.

Kharchilava, Nino. 2010. "Representation of Female Homosexuality in Georgian Printed Media." PhD diss., Tbilisi State University, Tbilisi, Georgia.

Khorbaladze Tamar. 2015. "Homophobia and Gender Identity." *Media Monitoring Report 2014–2015*. Media Development Foundation, Tbilisi, Georgia. http://mdfgeorgia.ge/uploads/library/Homophobia-ENG-web%20(1).pdf.

McLaughlin, Daniel. 2013. "EU Condemns Attack on Gay Rights Rally in Tbilisi, Georgia." *Irish Times*, May 21. https://www.irishtimes.com/news/world/europe/eu-condemns-attack-on-gay-rights-rally-in-tbilisi-georgia-1.1400440.

Minesashvili, Salome. 2017. "The Georgian Orthodox Church as a Civil Actor: Challenges and Capabilities." Policy Brief No. 8. Tbilisi, Georgia.

Morrison, Thea, and Nicholas Waller. 2016. "NGOs Condemn Attack on Tbilisi Transgender Woman." *Georgia Today*, October 17. http://georgiatoday.ge/news/4940/NGOs-Condemn-Attack-on-Tbilisi-Transgender-Woman.

Pew Research Centre. 2017. *Religious Belief and National Belonging in Central and Eastern Europe: Social Views and Morality*. May 10. https://www.pewforum.org/2017/05/10/social-views-and-morality/.

Popovaite, Inga. 2014. "Transwoman killed and Flat Set on Fire in Tbilisi." *Democracy & Freedom Watch Net*, November 11. http://dfwatch.net/transwoman-killed-and-flat-set-on-fire-in-tbilisi-24236-32143.

Ratiani, Tsiala, Ekaterine Aghdgomelashvili, and Rusudan Gotsiridze. 2015. *Discrimination and Hate Crimes Against LGBT People in Georgia*. Women's Initiatives Supporting Group (WISG), Tbilisi, Georgia.

Rubin, Gayle, S. 2011. *Deviations: A Gayle Rubin Reader*. Durham, NC: Duke University Press.

Stella, Francesca. 2016. *Lesbian Lives in Soviet and Post-Soviet Russia: Post/Socialism and Gendered Sexualities*. London: Palgrave Macmillan.

Synovitz, Ron. 2017. "Georgian Dream Doubles Down on Same-Sex Marriage Ban." *Radio Free Europe, Radio Liberty*, June 24. https://www.rferl.org/a/georgian-dream-doubles-down-same-sex-marriage-ban/28577114.html.

The World Bank. 2012. *Fighting Corruption in Public Services: Chronicling Georgia's Reforms*. http://documents.worldbank.org/curated/en/518301468256183463/pdf/664490PUB0EPI0065774B09780821394755.pdf.

Tsereteli, Tamar. 2010. "Nationalism and Representation of Gays and Lesbians in Post-Soviet Georgia." PhD diss., Central European University, Budapest, Hungary.

Women's Initiatives Supporting Group (WISG). 2012. "Situation of LGBT Persons in Georgia 2012." http://women.ge/data/docs/publications/WISG_situation-of-lgbt-persons-in-Georgia_ENG-www.pdf.

World Value Study Survey. 2014. "Findings and Insights 2008–2015." http://www.worldvaluessurvey.org/WVSContents.jsp?CMSID=Findings.

10

Exploring Two Generations of Women Activists in Azerbaijan: Between Feminism and a Post-Soviet Locality

Yuliya Gureyeva Aliyeva

This chapter explores two different periods of engagement with gender equality and women's rights issues in post-Soviet Azerbaijan. It begins by illustrating scholars' engagement between 1990 and 2010 with Western gender studies and feminism after the collapse of the Soviet Union, and the importance of these for the advancement of feminist activism in twenty-first century Azerbaijan. Although during the 1990s gender equality and women's emancipation were central to the academic community in Azerbaijan, many avoided identifying themselves with the global feminist movement. In fact, these scholars were more comfortable to identify themselves as 'genderologists' or experts in gender studies. In contrast to these 'hesitant' feminists, a group of young feminist activists in the twenty-first century Azerbaijan is examined in the second part of this chapter. These are young women who are more open about identifying themselves as feminists and can be seen as belonging to the second wave of women's empowerment in Azerbaijan. Born for the most part in the 1980s and early 1990s, these women belong to a generation which has grown up in independent Azerbaijan. They have

---

Y. G. Aliyeva (✉)
Syracuse University, Syracuse, NY, USA

© The Author(s) 2020
U. Ziemer (ed.), *Women's Everyday Lives in War and Peace in the South Caucasus*,
https://doi.org/10.1007/978-3-030-25517-6_10

enjoyed relative political stability and economic growth in the first quarter of the twenty-first century. The new generation was born, as a rule, to well-educated middle-class families, speaks foreign languages (mostly English and other languages spoken in Western Europe), has access to the Internet, enjoys wider geospatial mobility and thus has higher exposure to 'Western values'. They symbolize a new class of empowered women and men who have developed strong personal ambitions and greater confidence. They are ready to question restrictive social practices that are at odds with their personal and professional goals. However, their outreach is often limited to urban middle-class educated groups and the prospects for their ability to influence the nature of the country's gender equality policies remain uncertain in the absence of open democratic processes.

This research draws on qualitative interviews, semi-structured, in-depth and open-ended, conducted in Baku, the capital of Azerbaijan, in 2006 and 2017. In 2006, the 'founders' of Gender Studies as an academic discipline in Azerbaijan gave me a series of in-depth interviews. These seven female and three male scholars were active in producing and institutionalizing the new academic discourse of Gender Studies in their academic centres.[1] The respondents were selected from the representatives of the four principal hubs for the development of Gender Studies in Azerbaijan.[2] In my analysis, I also use some publications that were produced by these centres in the second half of the 1990s and the early years of the twenty-first century.

The second part of this chapter is based on semi-structured interviews conducted in the period July–September 2017 with young people who identified themselves as 'feminists'. These interviews were based on set interview questions but allowed for flexible discussion, not restricting the respondents to any particular format. In total, seven women and one man were interviewed, representing the millennials generation, which in the Azerbaijani context is a post-Soviet generation born since the end of the Soviet Union. I also draw upon participant observation of the various cultural events that were taking place in Baku in 2017, as well as social media debates related to the issues of gender equality in Azerbaijan.

A Gender Framework Without Feminism

In 1991, Azerbaijan declared its independence from the rapidly collapsing Soviet Union and faced significant social transformations instigated by war, economic hardships and political instability. The situation started to improve slowly from the mid-1990s onwards, with the inflow of direct foreign investment mainly to the oil industry of Azerbaijan and the establishment of an authoritarian regime (Guliyev 2013). But the economy of Azerbaijan was not the only domestic domain that received foreign investments. The end of the iron curtain amplified the flow of Western ideas, ideals and practices and opened the possibility of academic exchange and collaboration. Concepts of 'gender' and 'gender equality' swiftly entered the domains of scientific inquiry and civic activism and Azerbaijani professional women became both explorers and the objects of inquiry.

Following the collapse of the Soviet Union, Western scholars turned to the unexplored field of post-Soviet Muslim Republics. These geographical areas had often been omitted from so-called Soviet Studies or Sovietology, although scholars differ over the reason. It might have been deliberate neglect (since there had been 'excessive focus on the Russian centre' (Suny 1995, p. 105) that ignored the periphery as non-Russian and 'thus, by implication, inconsequential' (Motyl 1994, p. 263); or might have resulted from the Soviet government's restriction of access to the national republics, making them 'one of the most heavily censored, off-limits realms of inquiry, though a number of impressive, empirical works on aspects of nationality problems had been produced nonetheless' (Bonnell and Breslauer 1998, p. 20). While a focus on Eastern European and Russian women continued to dominate post-Soviet Studies (Acar and Günes-Ayata 2000; Heyat 2000), the gradual inclusion of the post-Soviet Muslim Republics signified that scholars were striving to reach a more inclusive paradigm, acknowledging the diversity of transitional experiences in the post-Soviet periphery and their multiple implications for social status and the everyday lives of women.

Women's lives in Azerbaijan and other post-Soviet Muslim republics was often described as puzzling and inconsistent with the official discourse of the Soviet emancipated women, as outlined in the introduction to this volume. Thus, the word 'paradox' has often been used by Western scholars to describe their initial findings about non-Russian women in the former Soviet peripheries (Heyat 2005; Kandiyoti 2007). Within the 'Soviet neopatriarchy' (Voronina 2003) women's subordination continued to be legitimized and normalized, forcing the 'guardians of the nation' (Tohidi 1998) to develop coping strategies that would allow them to reconcile the roles of loyal Soviet citizens and proud, chaste Eastern women (*Şərq Qadını*). To the surprise of Western scholars, women members of the professional *'intelligentsia'* in Azerbaijan, the paramount area of the Soviet emancipation project, were found to be sharing the kind of patriarchal beliefs and values often linked with nationalistic sentiments, thus rejecting feminists' ideas of women's emancipation and empowerment (Tohidi 1997; Heyat 2005).

Moreover, the feminist ideology was deemed 'alien' to Marxism–Leninism and condemned as 'a divisive movement aimed to pit women against men, rather than proletarians against capitalists and bourgeois rulers' (Sperling 1999, p. 65). The myth of the emancipation of the Soviet woman, so unlike the 'oppressed and exploited' Western woman, was omnipresent, at a time when strict censorship and restricted mobility were leaving no chance to explore alternative world-views.

With the fall of communism in Azerbaijan various international organizations and donor foundations[3] tried to address the 'urgency of Azerbaijani women's needs for information, resources, and gender education' (Tohidi 2004, p. 151). The promotion and protection of the rights of women, whose vulnerability increased with the failure of the Soviet social protection system[4] were among their key agenda items. To equip activists with the conventional vocabulary and understanding of the matter, donors organized numerous capacity-building training sessions and seminars under the banner of 'gender education'.

But, eager as local women activists in the 1990s were to stand up for gender equality and proclaim themselves defenders of women's rights, they were unequivocally trying to distance themselves from any associations with 'Western' feminist ideologies. It was not unusual in conferences or round tables to hear an early disclaimer: although the event would deal with issues of equality between the sexes or the protection of women's rights, the organizers did not consider themselves as 'feminists'. For instance, in the directory of the national gender portal (www.gender-az.org) developed in the 2005, only two of the 124 women's organizations and 69 NGOs involved in the implementation of projects related to women's issues and included the term 'feminism' in their description.

In the second half of the 1990s, Azerbaijani academic circles were invited to join various local and regional projects targeting the development of gender studies in the post-Soviet countries. The programmes financed translations of core Western feminist texts into local languages, research on women's issues by local scholars, the organization of gender conferences and the publication of gender textbooks in national languages (Cîrstocea 2010). In 2003 alone, 221 academics in Azerbaijan participated in the four-day training course, *'Methodology of Application of Basics of Gender in Social and Humanitarian Disciplines.'* For the first time, lectures on gender issues were included in an earlier syllabus or appeared as independent courses in seven leading universities in the country,[5] although the curriculum and textbooks often represented a combination of Western feminist and Soviet sex-role theories[6] (Gureyeva 2005).

In 2006, I conducted in-depth interviews with the 'pioneers in the field' and learned with much interest why they had decided to turn to the field of gender studies and what had attracted them in this newly introduced discipline. Their responses can be roughly classified into three groups, with possible overlaps.

1. Many were attracted by the novelty of the discipline and were curious to learn more about it, as the following extract makes clear. *'I heard the term "gender" for the first time during one of the training courses organized by ISAR [approximately in 1996–1997], but I didn't know what it stood for. I tried to find out online, but even my computer suggested that I should replace "gender" by "tender". Once I heard about the opportunity learning more, of course, I wholeheartedly embraced it'* (f., 56, Candidate of Sciences).[7]

2. The monetary incentives for organizational or academic work in the form of grants, honoraria or stipend were not the least stimulus. In

post-Soviet Azerbaijan, academic salaries were extremely low and the possibility of participation in an academic project meant an enhancement not only of one's academic status, but also one's financial well-being.[8] Many respondents confessed that the underlying goal in joining a gender studies programme was to acquire more financial means. As one university professor, a single mother, concludes: *'I'll tell you honestly, I joined because there was money allocated for it, but then I really got interested in the subject ...'* (f., 57, Candidate of Sciences).

3. There were also a few who cherished a hope that the newly acquired knowledge would be practical and would help them to confront the manifestations of gender inequality in everyday life. Professional women shared with me their stories of partner abuse, unequal treatment in the workplace or observations about the constraints that women and girls suffered in their families and communities. *'Violence is dominant in our society. It starts from the very moment that you are taught, "You are a girl! You should not be doing that!"'* (f., 46., Ph.D.).

Whatever the impetus and initial expectations, the acquisition of the new knowledge and skills was not a linear and straightforward experience. Taking on the new role of transmitters of gender scholarship was an uneasy task that required not only building up the expertise, but also finding common ground and reconciliation with one's own preexisting values and presuppositions. Most of the interviewed women scholars considered that the process went far beyond academic practices and made itself felt as 'eye-opening' and psychologically advancing experience that increased their confidence in themselves and awareness of discriminatory practices. As one respondent describes it:

> We were all women working in the office, and when we started we were not 'gender sensitive' at all. We all had different backgrounds in management, finance, or IT. But then we all started to notice that we were now talking to our husbands differently. It's not that we started saying bad things, but we talked differently. And I started to feel I was more confident." (f., 56, Candidate of Sciences)

But many were recalling the mixed feelings of distrust and scepticism during the first encounters with gender studies. One respondent recalls her thoughts after one of the first training sessions she attended:

> I was feeling uncomfortable, thinking: 'Would I be ever able to figure out 'gender problems' and solutions to them or to define 'gender stereotypes'?... To tell the truth I didn't believe that I'd ever manage to produce anything meaningful out of it ... I thought 'Whatever I do, it's going to be alien and superficial..." (f., 57., Candidate of Sciences)

She was not the only scholar to raise concerns over the 'applicability' of concepts and paradigm introduced to the post-Soviet reality. Other respondents emphasized the need critically to access the newly introduced teaching:

> We got introduced to tons of theoretical models from which to select ... What should we borrow from the West? And what should be borrowed from the East? And not many were questioning their input. If we take something in the middle, that again will turn into something that our will doesn't endorse ... But it is all about politics, which Azerbaijanis are not skillful at ... (m., 56, Dr. Prof)

The metaphor of the 'unique' geographical and civilizational location of Azerbaijan at the crossroads between East and West makes for a very strong narrative in the political and academic imaginary. The positive role of the country as the 'bridge between civilizations', is also associated with the discourse of a permanent battlefield or contested area for political and cultural dominance between Eastern and Western ideologies. In this context, the issue of local subjectivity is questionable. For more than seventy years the production of academic knowledge was regulated by the very strict ideological boundaries that cast out any ideas incompatible with Marxism–Leninism. As the quotation suggests, the introduction of gender studies was associated with anxiety about being dragged into another 'ideological trap', in the interests of some certain political force.

The debate whether the essence of gender studies was to be an 'extraneous body' or 'indigenous concept' was not unique to the Azerbaijani context but was taking place across all of post-communist Eastern Europe and the former Soviet Union countries and indeed on a larger international scale. For instance, the complex relationships between the production of knowledge in Western cities and its transmission to the developing world have been extensively discussed in the framework of post-colonial studies. Scholars raised their concern over the unequal power positions between Western and 'Third World Women' and their contrasting representations in scholarship, where the former were constructed as active learners and modernizers and the latter as 'objects' and 'non-feminist others' (Mohanty 1988; Ong 1988). Anti-imperialist critics condemned the Western monopoly over the production of scientific knowledge and engagement of foreign funds in the promotion of Western feminism, putting local women in service to a foreign agenda (Ghodsee 2004). In this scenario, the newly established gender studies programmes in Azerbaijan were playing 'the role of a 'symbolic marker' of Westernization and the compliant incorporation of the Central and Eastern European/former Soviet region into the Western-dominated global system' (Zimmermann 2007, p. 9).

Across the post-socialist space, a camp in opposition was claiming that feminist scholarship provided a useful framework for analysing the existing structural inequalities between the sexes, irrespective of locality, one that created a window for public dialogue concerning such private issues as domestic violence, reproductive rights and sexual harassment (Temkina and Zdravomislova 2003; Barchunova 2000; Funk 2006). This camp considered that, even when gender experts explicitly reject the term 'feminist', 'the work that most of them carry out seems to be feminist in its ethos and implications' (Kamp 2009, p. 3). At the same time, it was also widely acknowledged that some local scholars were misusing or misinterpreting feminist terminology in an attempt to climb on the bandwagon of gender studies as a field of novelty and prestige (Oushakin 2000; Barchunova 2000; Cîrstocea 2009).

Similar trends and public/private debates over them were to be found in Azerbaijan. But conceptually many local scholars were stressing the

10 Exploring Two Generations of Women Activists ... 233

need to develop a local, 'national gender studies', that would consider women's issues through the prism of the 'national mentality': 'We need to develop our own gender studies that would take into account the historical, psychological, mental, ethno-confessional features of the Azerbaijani people, the traditions and norms of historical attitudes towards men and women. In this regard, feminism, in general, had no history in Azerbaijan and therefore is not relevant for domestic Gender Studies' (Zulfigarova 2003, p. 7). This uneasy relationship between 'gender studies' and 'feminism' in Azerbaijani academic discourse cannot be simply classified as a fear of the cultural expansion of the West or hostile attitudes towards 'feminism' dating back to the Soviet legacy. There were other important ontological and epistemological implications concerned with the status of 'feminism' as an ideology and area of epistemic knowledge in the 1990s and 2000s.

First, the respondents spoke of 'the cognitive dissonance' over the understanding of feminist scholarship and described the readings they were exposed to as abstract and detached from Azerbaijani everyday conditions. Those in particular who were looking for practical solutions to gender equality issues were disillusioned to find no references to 'mundane problems' in post-modern feminist theory. As Connell remarks: 'A large part of gender theory in the English-speaking metropole has become abstract, contemplative or analytical in style, or focuses entirely on cultural subversions' (Connell 2009, p. 41), thus losing its connection with the 'ground'. One of the respondents shared with me her impressions of exposure to Western feminist scholarship after taking part in an international conference in Tbilisi on teaching gender studies to political science students:

> They've already lived through it! And that's why everything is on an abstract level ... I can't even explain that to you ... They don't understand what is real to us and I can't understand their teaching. They don't understand us and we don't understand them. We don't understand them since they are far ahead and they're talking about global equality issues, whereas we're flailing around focusing on petty issues. Totally different issues, totally different levels! (f., 32, Ph.D. candidate)

Thus, many were finding themselves comfortable to operate on the level of 'the traditional feminist "biological-social" opposition' (Aghayeva 2012, p. 32), or in other words the level of sex/gender dichotomy that they had been taught in the late 1960s and early 1970s in the US (West and Zimmerman 1987, p. 125), which was reconsidered by feminist scholars in the 1990s and directed towards more attuned interrelations of 'sex and gender'.

Second, the exposure to feminist reasoning on patriarchy and male dominance was taking place in a period of great economic hardship, mass unemployment, low wages and the migration of men to neighboring countries in search of labour opportunities. Economic instability in the 1990s disrupted the power dynamics in the Soviet 'nuclear families' where men were depicted as the main providers for the family, 'breadwinner', with a stable income guaranteed by the employment policies of the Soviet Union[9] and a woman in most cases was regarded as a 'contributor' to the family income, accepting a low-paid job with flexible working hours (for example, teaching and healthcare). In the new market economy, the position of men became far less secure, while the stereotypes and expectations with regard to male and female roles in the family continued to be strong. Thus, men were often portrayed as 'victims' of the transitionary period since 'unemployment resulted in the man's decreasing authority in the household' (UNDP 2007, 23). One of the respondents recalls that some meetings of gender studies scholars focused on men's predicament: '*We need to be doing something to protect our men*' (f., 56, Candidate of Sciences). The feminist framework was considered to potentially exacerbate the existing 'masculinity crises' through the promotion of the 'feminization of men' and 'masculinization of women'. Thus, the locally re-defined framework of 'gender' was justified as a more nuanced socio-biological approach, which was also informed by the Western 'reactive (as well as reactionary) nature of many contemporary representations, the elision of post-feminism with anti-feminism' (Gill and Scharff 2011, p. 4). This is how one of the respondents summarized the history of gender scholarship: '… *Feminism started with the assumption that if women imitated masculine identity they would gain equal rights. But slowly feminism developed, took a turn towards radicalism, and they started to realize that there was a need for a balance in society and that's how "gender" started to emerge ...'* (m., 56, Dr., Prof.). In this sense, 'gender' acts as the all-encompassing theory that can count on the interest of both sexes, whereas 'feminism' presumably discriminated against men.

The third aspect was the relative isolation from global trends of the community of Azerbaijani so-called gender experts. The sporadic conferences and training courses, the rare foreign guests and selective translations of Western feminist literature could not replace inclusion in the academic networks and constant awareness of current issues and debates. The limited knowledge of foreign languages (not counting Russian, which for many academics was either the native or the second language) was a key barrier. Only a few of the interviewed scholars claimed that their intermediate knowledge of English was enough for reading texts with a dictionary, but not for expressing themselves freely. Thus, most of the academic exchanges were with scholars from other post-Soviet countries, who were facing similar problems and challenges. In general, the available printed sources, including books and academic journals, were scarce,[10] mostly donated or purchased through donor funds. Access to digital libraries through local academic centres was made possible only in the second half of 2000.

The fact that the development of gender studies programmes was primarily a 'sponsored project' dependent on foreign funding resulted in the gradual disappearance of the initiatives and the closure of the academic centres.[11] A few initiatives managed to survive, mainly due to the enthusiasm of their founders.[12] The suspension of gender studies in university curricula also began to depend on the personal interest of instructors and the 'open-mindedness' of the administration. Nevertheless, even though controversial in its nature, the academic discourse around gender issues problematized many important aspects of a 'gendered order' in Azerbaijan, including gender discrimination and segregation in the labour market, education and politics, opening up a space for discussing 'taboo' issues, such as violence against women and sexual harassment.[13] One of the respondents recalls how difficult it was to respond to and surmount the negativity that they faced in the early stages of this process: *'There was a concrete wall, which had to be surmounted, which had to be pierced'* (f., 53, Ph.D.). Many pioneers in the

236   Y. G. Aliyeva

field firmly believed that one day Azerbaijan might turn into a more egalitarian society and conveyed their ideals to the younger generation, inviting them to start their own exploratory journey over the field.

Young Activists Seeding a Feminist Movement in Azerbaijan

On a hot and muggy July evening in 2017, one of the small tea-houses in downtown Baku became particularly crowded. All the seats around at the tables were already occupied by the first-comers and young women and men arriving later could only reserve the few places available on window ledges, the entrance stairs or just on the concrete floor. The organizers seemed to be surprised by such a crowd for an event advertised through one of the social networks. They apologized for the inconvenience and started the first 'feminist poetry evening' of its kind in Baku. To address the linguistic diversity of Baku, the poems were presented in three languages: Azerbaijani, English and Russian. Leaving aside a few special guests, such as the teachers and professors of the organizers, the audience was predominantly young and gender-mixed. More than 70 women and men in their 20s or early 30s gathered to hear about the diverse human experiences of what it meant to be female and male across the globe.

Probably the significance of such an event would have been different if it had taken place somewhere outside of Azerbaijan. But in the cultural context of hostility to any kind of feminist ideology and avoidance of it—even if,[14] conceptually, it supported gender equality—everything can be sensed as provocation and incitement: the content, the venue and even the title.[15] The dominance of strict patriarchal attitudes, with the small variance between women and men in Azerbaijan, is a matter of fact. According to a survey by the Caucasus Research Resource Center, most survey respondents believe that women should bear sole responsibility for domestic chores and take care of children, whereas men should have the final word in household decisions. At the same time, 52% believed that gender equality had already been achieved in Azerbaijan, whereas 20% ticked 'do not know' as an answer to this question (The Caucasus Research Resource Center 2012).

However, one can notice how in this patriarchal culture the term 'feminism' has recently begun to be seen on various social platforms. It is often not directly related to gender equality issues, but connected with, for example, English conversation clubs, art groups or educational centres. In the rest of this chapter, I explore how the changing youth culture in Azerbaijan, better integrated into the discursive global streams than before, is seeking to re-direct social attitudes towards a more egalitarian society. I argue that isolated cultural events organized under the banner of 'feminism', such as the feminist poetry reading cited above, are not spontaneous and random occurrences, but rather signifiers of social transformation in the urban spaces of Azerbaijan.

To illustrate my point, I focus on the younger generation of feminist activists in Azerbaijan and discuss their activities around two projects: 'Equals' and 'FEMM'. These groups started their activities at the beginning of 2016 and describe their mission in similar ways to feminist activists in other countries: raising awareness about gender issues and creating a space for public debates. They explicitly claim their association with 'feminism' and feminist ideology and strive to change the negative public perception of feminism. 'Equals' traces its legacy to the early stages of women's activism in pre-Soviet Azerbaijan and '[seeks] to channel that spirit and push for more progress' (see 'Equals' public Facebook page), whereas the FEMM project defines its goal as helping 'Azerbaijani citizens to understand the real meaning of the word "feminism' (see the FEMM project public Facebook page).[16] For instance, the FEMM project films documentaries and conducts interviews with well-known individuals, who publicly address 'sensitive issues', such as gender-based discrimination and traditional attitudes to women, whereas 'Equals' organizes movie nights, featuring documentary and feature films targeting gender equality, followed by discussion. Both groups find it challenging and mostly unnecessary to identify with any particular streams/waves of 'feminism' and prefer to keep the boundaries loose and inclusive. One activist said during our interview:

> It's probably too early for us to define our standpoint conceptually. There are projects that actively promote women's economic empowerment and can be identified as 'liberal feminism'. Our group wants to go beyond that and touch on deeper social tissues, debating and transforming them. (R 1, f., 25. Equals)

It is noteworthy in this context that both groups are well equipped with the feminist lexicon and define 'gender' as informed by contemporary feminist scholarship: '*We consider that "gender" is not strictly defined, but should be treated as fluid ... We just want society to abandon the phrase "Women ought to ... "*' (R 2, f., 25, Equals).

The challenges, in my view, to articulating the standpoints of the two activists' groups are inherently linked to the very nature of the contemporary feminist movement, undergoing yet another shift in paradigm. The divisions in the feminist movement are no longer as straightforward as they used to be in the 1960s during the second wave of feminist activism (Nicholson 1986). The terms 'feminism(s)', 'post-feminism', 'third-wave feminism' and 'new femininities' became widely used yet remained contested in feminist scholarship. In this multiplicity of terms and meanings, the focus moved significantly to the perplexing relationships between feminism and neoliberalism, which prizes an 'active, freely choosing, self-reinventing subject' (Gill and Scharff 2011, p. 7). Scholars argue that, as a political model, '*neoliberalism is always already gendered*' and women are constructed as its 'ideal subjects', since they are 'required to work on and transform the self, to regulate every aspect of their conduct, and to present all their actions as freely chosen' (ibid.).

In response to this neoliberal thinking, some scholars have announced the emergence of fourth-wave feminism, which is based on the critique of neoliberalism and at the same time described as 'fractured and complex, frequently reinforcing the advancement of the individual and centering the seductive notions of "choice", "empowerment", and "agency"' (Rivers 2017, p. 24). Fourth-wave feminism entails a return of the slogan 'the personal is political' and of trouble with declarative equality between the sexes: 'Brought up to know they are equal to men, fourth-wave feminists are pissed off when they're not treated as such, but have more than enough confidence to shout back' (Cochrane 2013).

This post-modern feminist framework, with its strong emphasis on empowerment, individualism, choice, self-invention and self-mastery, combined with a celebration of the body and womanhood, is often mirrored in Azerbaijan's local discourses. Consider, for instance, how an advertisement promoting the initiative by 'Equals' to 'Reclaim the *Hamam*' uses wording which reproduces the image of 'modern self-empowered femininity' to attract more participants: 'A social event to resurrect the *hamam*'s former significance as central to women's lives in Baku and to encourage networking among today's women striving to build independent careers'[17] (Vision.Az 2017). While calling for the reinvention of the *hamam* culture, which had faded with the development of modern housing in the past few decades and turned into a public space that was a male prerogative, young feminists are articulating the need not only to regain its physical presence, but also to celebrate it as a place of independence and solidarity and, of course, the body as a source of pleasure.

The emergence of new global feminist role models promoting the idea of self-empowerment also contributes to wider acceptance of the 'feminist' label, especially among the urban educated young people. The public portrayal of celebrities as 'feminists', such as Beyoncé, Taylor Swift or Emma Watson, signify the shift from perceiving a 'feminist' as a 'man hater' and promoter of 'militant dowdiness' to a more 'desirable' and 'normalized' image of femininity. As one of the activists noted: *'There is no particular way feminists should or should not look... But the expectation is usually that feminists are very masculine, rude, radical, no boyfriends, no husbands, bossy, etc. which doesn't in fact coincide with experience ...'* (R 3, f., 25, Equals).

In this sense, 'being a feminist' becomes an important part of self-identity and the boundary line that distinguishes today's young people from the previous generation(s) of gender activists. In the context of the post-Soviet Azerbaijan, 'feminism' has become a powerful label, symbolizing revolt against social pressure and gender conformity. Coming out as a feminist still requires courage and often meets with strong antagonism in families, verbal abuse (often in virtual, but sometimes in physical space) or benevolent warnings that it might be damaging for one's personal life. One of the respondents initially shocked her colleagues by revealing herself as a feminist. However, their resentment was gradually replaced by curiosity and they started following her group's activities, with a certain level of acceptance and understanding that *'it is not as fearful as was initially anticipated'* (R 1, f., 25, Equals).

The different attitudes to the 'feminist' label are not the only difference articulated by the previous generation of gender experts. One of the key disparities can be found in their 'grass-roots' initiatives, the pillars of these groups, which attract young professionals, who are employed full-time but are ready to volunteer their leisure and effort for the common goal. Their agenda is not in any way pre-determined or shaped by a donor's presence or lacking in 'sustainability', all considered critical issues for local women donors to NGOs in the post-Soviet context (Sundstrom 2002; Kandiyoti 2007). They only ever apply for small grants with which to organize small feasible projects, such as the Azerbaijani version of the children's book 'Rebel Girls' or the FEMM project to film a documentary about gender issues, such as 'Silenced and Lost'. Generally, they do not receive regular remuneration for their efforts and are not under any constant pressure to produce 'winning' projects for the sake of basic income.

'Glocalization'[18] defines yet another essential feature of these feminist grass-root initiatives. Although the 'West' as a metropole of the production of knowledge and practices is still present as a cultural metaphor, the local 'periphery' seems to have moved beyond the limits of 'occidentalist discourse' (Bonnett 2004), debates over the boundaries of Western/Eastern cultures and limits to penetration or resist. This should be largely attributed to the lifestyles of these young professionals, engaged in neoliberal market relationships pre-supposing greater mobility and better interconnectedness with the globalized world. All the respondents declared themselves fluent, at least, in three languages: English, Azerbaijani and Russian; and their use of English as a *lingua franca*, compared to Russian, which used to be vital for professional careers in the Soviet context, is substantially gaining ground. The increased educational mobility of these feminist activists[19] has provided them with the opportunity to experience 'life' in the 'West', represented in the variety of cultural patterns and experiences they recognize, replacing the stereotypical dichotomy of the West as either 'an ideal' or 'a threat'. For instance, one of the respondents recalls his experience during a Summer School in Norway, where at the beginning of the course, he introduced himself as 'a feminist', and was puzzled by the response of the female Scandinavian professor, who not only made this 'act of coming out unwelcome, but strictly pointed out that if he was interested in learning more about feminism he was in the wrong place, since her course focused on issues of gender equality (R 4, m., 20, FEMM project). Although baffled reactions to his revelation in Azerbaijan had already become a norm for him, he was expecting to find more understanding and support in the Scandinavian countries, which are often associated with model practices of equality between the sexes and a strong feminist movement.

Digital technologies and the use of social media in the fourth wave are often invoked as the principal tools for redefining the feminist movement (Cochrane 2013). Access to the Internet provides unprecedented access to information and self-education. It also opens up opportunities for engaging in global causes or campaigns. One of the respondents told me that the global campaign 'He for She' and its 'voice', Emma Watson, the UN Women's Goodwill Ambassador, had inspired him to *start doing something locally* (R 4, m., 20, FEMM project). If generous grants and the expertise of IT professionals were required in the past for developing and maintaining webpages and almost none of the local women NGOs could afford these, now creating a Facebook page is a matter of minutes. Both groups, the FEMM project and 'Equals', actively use their virtual presence to share information and announcements and have hundreds of followers. To ensure better outreach, they publish all posts in several languages ('Equals' in English and Azerbaijani, and the FEMM project in English, Azerbaijani and Russian). While this creates additional challenges, and slows down the regular feed of the page, it helps to ensure inclusivity and escape the criticism of serving the 'interests of certain groups', in a country where language use is a very sensitive issue and is often associated with geopolitical preferences (Shiriyev 2017).

Nonetheless, this virtual presence has its drawbacks. As one of the young activists notes, although it is difficult to gauge the social status of members of the virtual groups, there is a sense of being confined to a circle of urban, well-informed and educated young people. She considers that the most important challenge the group faces now is *'breaking down the barriers'* (R 5, f., 30, Equals), or having better outreach to the communities beyond the virtual space. To engage with the public, both groups are turning to documentary videos. The 'FEMM Project' filmed three documentaries: one about the 'essence of feminism', one about 'violence against women' and the third about 'gender roles/norms in Azerbaijan' which was showcased in Azerbaijan and abroad. 'Equals' are organizing the public screening of 'feminist' movies and poetry readings that attract both supporters and opponents of their views.

Another important aspect is the cooperation between these platforms and creative art initiatives in Baku that explore 'feminist' sentiments. Local artists have recently started to explore unresolved tensions between modern urban lifestyles and traditionally ascribed gender roles. In 2016–2018, exhibitions organized under the label '18+'[20] drew upon psychoanalytic notions of the social fabric of sexualities and social taboos in Azerbaijan and presented a 'female' gaze of women's bodies. The main target of criticism by these creative arts initiatives is the central gender code of the country's patriarchal communities—the cult of 'virginity' and the taboo against premarital sex for women. Such defiance often provokes heated debates and public condemnation.

Thus, certain clusters of urban educated young people in Azerbaijan are increasingly associating themselves with the feminist movement and are interested in promoting the so-called 'emancipative values' that 'give priority to gender equality over patriarchy, tolerance over conformity, autonomy over authority and participation over security' (Welzel and Inglehart 2009, p. 129). However, the groups are shaped in a highly insecure environment, informed not only by the culture of intolerance towards the 'feminist ideology', but also by the ambiguities of the authoritarian regime. The shrinking space for civil activism and employment of various repressive means against dissenters creates an atmosphere of fear and hopelessness in the country (Gogia 2013). Unlike their peers in democratic societies, the local youth activist groups are very cautious with their agenda and political representation, acknowledging their limited means of engaging in political processes in the country. At the same time, as Ilkin Mehrabov (2016) argues, the patriarchal context counterintuitively provides more fertile ground for developing the feminist movement than for other leftist groups in Azerbaijan. He considers that '*the state does not need to extensively invest in the surveillance of women*', since that is the duty of their male relatives (Mehrabov 2016). But this paternalistic treatment of women and girls by their families and the state is precisely the principal target of the young feminists. These young women no longer want to be treated as the 'guardians' of their families and nation but instead to enjoy equal-rights citizenship and be entitled to the normative gender equality frameworks 'guaranteed' by the state.

The powerful rhetoric of such people, grounded in the 'in-your-face' word 'feminism', seeks whatever tools and mechanisms are available to confront the status quo and raise the status of feminist ideology in the public and political consciousness. Without direct linkages to the feminist organizations elsewhere, these groups are still informed and enlightened by the processes that are taking place in the 'metropole', where '… seemingly through the postfeminist glamor, … voices arguing for an openly pro-feminist identity and a "revival" of feminist politics have begun to be heard' (Rivers 2017, p. 25). Still, young feminists cannot be considered as major or mainstream representatives of the youth activist culture in Azerbaijan. They often find themselves confined to the groups of 'intellectually advanced' urban professionals. But as Foucault argues 'one cannot speak of anything at any time…', and 'new objects' do not suddenly 'light up and emerge out of the ground' (Foucault 1972, p. 45). Thus, the mere existence of these young feminist activists is enough to signify slow changes in the power dynamics of Azerbaijani urban life and the development of mindful initiatives to transform the culture into something more egalitarian. It is yet to be seen how the contours of this grass-roots movement will be shaped in the future and how it will position itself in relation to other counter-narratives that are gaining ground among young Azerbaijanis today, especially those related to religious doctrines.

Conclusions

This chapter has explored two cases of pro-gender equality movements in Azerbaijan and elaborated on the way in which they established themselves in a local and highly patriarchal context. I argued that these temporarily sequenced movements used feminist frameworks as reference points but engaged differently with them. As a feminist framework itself, it is not unitary and monolithic, but rather fractured and fragmented, its changing nature setting off varied resonances with the local subjectivities.

In the 1990s and 2000s, gender experts were concerned with the production of 'local gender knowledge', seeking a common ground between the ideology of gender equality and a pragmatic need for the nation to (re)produce and shaping the discourse of national identity. For them the 'feminist' ideology meant the *Western Self*: seductive, intrusive and appropriating. These encounters often resulted in confusion and 'cognitive dissonance', leaving a feeling of not being able to find common ground and 'speak the same language'. Moreover, a so-called identity crisis of the feminist movement in Western 'metropoles', the apparent failure of 'post-feminism' and perception of the 'feminist movement', contributed to the repudiation of the 'feminist' label as inherently wrong and 'outcast' even in the 'West'. But the preferred 'gender framework' was narrow in its scope and methodology, tracing its legacy to Soviet sex-role theory.

The new wave of feminist consciousness in Azerbaijan started to emerge with the new activist groups, such as the FEMM project and Equals in 2010. As discussed, they aim to promote individual subjectivity, emphasizing 'choice' and 'empowerment' and openly criticizing everyday sexism. While not engaged directly in transnational projects, unlike their predecessor, they are more globally propagated through digital networks and could be considered important local signifiers for an emerging fourth-wave feminism. In conditions of a strongly authoritarian regime and strict bounded social heteronormativity, this revived 'feminist' subjectivity seeks creative ways to address societal issues and undermine the central cultural codes of patriarchy: the cult of virginity and subordination to the male members of the family.

Although the impact of gender experts on young feminist activists is limited to individual encounters and their conceptual positions are not continuous but disconnected, both groups share the privilege of belonging to an urban educated professional middle class. What makes the young feminists distinct is not simply the acceptance or rejection of 'feminism' as a label, but their greater confidence in themselves as 'agents' of change that can challenge the normative nature of Azerbaijan's patriarchal society. Such a slow change is already noticeable in this group through the internalization of emancipative values, increased empowerment and personal autonomy.

Notes

1. The first part of this research was conducted with the support of a scholarship programme for young social scientists funded by the Heinrich Boell Foundation—South Caucasus Regional office.
2. The Gender Center at the Western University of Azerbaijan, the Gender and Human Rights Research Union at the National Academy of Sciences, Department of Gender and Applied Psychology at Baku State University and the Azerbaijan Gender Information Center.
3. The most generous donors active in the last decade of the twentieth century included ISAR, OSI, UN agencies, Embassies, Eurasia Foundation, etc.
4. Soviet social insurance benefits provided workers with coverage for maternity, sickness, disability, survivorship and old age, while social assistance benefits were available for those with inadequate employment records to qualify for insurance-based benefits. In addition, many workers received subsidized housing, kindergarten places and annual holidays in 'sanatoriums'. The non-cash benefits also included universal education, university scholarships and free health care (Falkingham and Vlachantoni 2010). Although many of the social insurance benefits were inherited by the Azerbaijani System of Social Protection, the monetary value of these benefits shrank considerably, making them rather symbolic than practical (The Caucasus Research Resource Centers 2011).
5. The Academy of Public Administration, Western University, Baku State University, Khazar University, Baku Slavic University, State Pedagogical University, named after N. Tusi and Odlar Urdu University.

6. 'Soviet sex-role theory, just like its Western counterpart, combines a commitment to the interpretation of 'difference' as a product of social expectations and environment... with an underlying belief that difference is biological and essential' (Pilkington 1996, p. 9).
7. The ages and academic titles of the respondents date back to 2006, the time of the actual fieldwork.
8. Wages in the education sector were significantly lower than the national average wage and the wages in the educational sector, paid from the state budget, remained significantly low, below the national average, which in contrast steadily increased from the beginning of the twenty-first century due to the inflow of oil money to the economy. For example, an average nominal monthly wage in the education sector was 143 manats in 2007 (approx. 170 USD), and the average monthly national salary was 214 manats (approx. 255 USD), while the poverty line was 64 manats (approx. 76 USD) per month per person (UNICEF 2008, p. 22). For further comparative detail on academic salaries in the post-Soviet countries, see for example Yudkevich and Androushchak (2012).
9. There had been no such category as 'unemployed' in the Soviet Union since the 1930s, because the Soviet government guaranteed universal employment for all. Those who tried to avoid 'socially useful labour' were punished by the law as 'parasites' (Trehub 1988, p. 6).
10. For example, the Gender Information Center was offering its readers about 1200 books and editions in three languages (Russian, Azerbaijani and English); of these, 70 publications were in English, largely consisting of reports by International Organizations.
11. Access to external (Western) funding became more problematic in the mid-2000s, because the donors had to reallocate their sparse resources to other 'more problematic' geographical regions when the economic situation in Azerbaijan started to improve. In general, local funding opportunities did not consider the development of Gender Studies and Social Studies to be a priority area. The situation was also aggravated by the introduction of new legislation cracking down on foreign donations to NGOs and raising bureaucratic barriers to registration.
12. These are the Department of Applied Psychology and Gender at Baku State University and the Gender Center at Western University. The Azerbaijan Gender Information Center closed its office, but its web portal still exists online (www.gender-az.org).

13. Undoubtedly the opening up of this public discourse contributed to the adoption of a law on 'Guarantees of Gender (Men's and Women's) Equality' in 2006 and a Law on the Prevention of Domestic Violence in 2010.

14. For instance, Hijar Huseynova, the Head of the State Committee on Family, Women and Children's Affairs (SCFWCA), which is a state institution responsible for implementing the state policy on gender equality, regrets that the 'gender movement' is often confused in Azerbaijan with the term 'feminism'. She explains: 'We are talking about equal opportunities for men and women in the political, economic, social, cultural and other spheres of life in the country, as well as about eliminating all forms of discrimination against women on the basis of gender' (Orujev 2013).

15. Tea-houses in Azerbaijan are closely associated with male culture (Heyat 2005), although a few centrally located downtown tea-houses began to open their doors to women at the beginning of the twenty-first century.

16. Facebook is the most popular social media channel in Azerbaijan, especially among young people. According to data on the social media from December 2017, it has 1.8 million FB users in Azerbaijan, with a penetration rate of 18.1% (https://www.internetworldstats.com/stats3.htm).

17. Since traditional housing did not envision special facilities for taking baths, weekly visits to the public *hamams* were obligatory for all members of the family. *Hamams* were gender disaggregated. Usually people were supposed to wear their best and newest clothes and to perform religious rituals of purification while bathing. Moreover, *hamam*s were considered important public spaces for debates, discussions, rumours and often for brokering deals or negotiating prospective marriages. With the introduction of modern housing in the Soviet era, the culture of the *hamam* started to fade. It is now reviving, along with the introduction of the culture of modern SPA-salons. Notably, young feminists are 're-inventing the tradition' by romanticizing and glamourizing this weekly hygienic necessity, discarded by older generations for its inconvenience.

18. I use the term 'glocalization' to emphasize the interconnectedness between the global and the local and importance of 'creative appropriations' in this process (Roudometof 2015).

19. All respondents are alumni of US or UK educational exchange programmes; some also studied in Continental Europe.

20. The most recently organized events include, but are not limited to the following exhibitions: 'It is what it is', Faig Ahmed, Yarat Contemporary Art Centre, November 2016–January 2017; Group exhibition 'Boys don't cry' at ARTIM Project Space, YARAT Contemporary Art Space June–July 2017; 'My name is Sarah', Vusal Rahim's personal exhibition at ADO, May 2017; Reflector/'virginity test' project by Sitara Ibrahimova, Yarat Contemporary Art Centre, 2016; 'Por que?' photo exhibition by Sultana Ahmadbayli; 'Bakool Arts' underground art fest in Art Villa Baku, September 2017; ESSENCE project by Schachnas Aghayeva, graphic works, ROOM Baku, May 21–June 21, 2018.

References

Acar, Feride, and Ayse Gunes-Ayata. 2000. "About the Book." In *Gender and Identity Construction: Women of Central Asia, the Caucasus and Turkey*, edited by Acar Feride and Ayse Gunes-Ayata, xi–xviii. Leiden, The Netherlands: Brill.

Aghayeva, Khatira. 2012. "Women, Men and Education in Azerbaijan." *Khazar Journal of Humanities and Social Sciences* 2: 26–41.

Azerbaijan Gender Information Center. 2005. *Directory of Women's NGOs and NGOs Implementing Projects on Gender Issues*. http://www.gender-az.org/index.shtml?id_main=27&id_sub=55.

Barchunova, Tatyana. 2000. Ekskljuzijai I nkljuzija soobshchestva gendernykh issledovatelej. In *Preodolenie*, 216–226. Novosibirsk: Sib Novocentr.

Bonnell, Victoria, and George W. Breslauer. 1998. "Soviet and Post-Soviet Area Studies". Working Paper Series, Program in Soviet and Post-Soviet Studies, University of California, Berkeley. https://escholarship.org/uc/item/7rq5g9rc.

Bonnett, Alastair. 2004. *The Idea of the West: Culture, Politics and History*. Houndmills, Basingstoke, Hampshire, and New York: Palgrave Macmillan.

Cîrstocea, Ioana. 2009. "Sociology of a New Field of Knowledge: Gender Studies in Postcommunist Eastern Europe." GSPE Working Paper.

———. 2010. "Transnational Feminism in the Making: The Case of Post-Communist Eastern Europe." In *Exchanges and Correspondence: The Construction of Feminism*, edited by Claudette Fillard and Francoise Orazi, 64–83. Cambridge: Cambridge Scholars Publishing.

Cochrane, Kira. 2013. "The Fourth Wave of Feminism: Meet the Rebel Women." *The Guardian*. https://www.theguardian.com/world/2013/dec/10/fourth-wave-feminism-rebel-women.

Connel, Raewyn W. 2009. *Gender: Short Introduction*. London: Polity Press.

Facebook Page of Equals. https://www.facebook.com/equalsbaku/.

Facebook Page of FEMM Project. https://www.facebook.com/femmproject/.

Falkingham, Jane, and Athina Vlachantoni. 2010. "Pensions and Social Protection in Central Asia and South Caucasus: Developments in the Post-Soviet Era." CRA Discussion Paper No. 1002, University of Southampton, December. https://eprints.soton.ac.uk/173811/.

Foucault, Michel. 1972. *The Archaeology of Knowledge and the Discourse on Language*. New York: Pantheon Books.

Funk, Nanette. 2006. "Women's NGOs in Central and Eastern Europe and the Former Soviet Union: The Imperialist Criticism." In *Women and Citizenship in Central and Eastern Europe*, edited by Jasmina Lukić, Joanna Regulska, and Daria Zaviržek, 265–286. London: Ashgate.

Ghodsee, Kristen. 2004. "Feminism-by-Design: Emerging Capitalisms, Cultural Feminism, and Women's Nongovernmental Organisations in Postsocialist Eastern Europe." *Signs: Journal of Women in Culture and Society* 29 (3, Spring): 727–753. https://doi.org/10.1086/380631.

Gill, Rosalind, and Christina Scharff. 2011. *New Femininities: Postfeminism, Identity and Neoliberalism*. Basingstoke: Palgrave.

Gogia, Giorgi. 2013. *Tightening the Screws: Azerbaijan's Crackdown on Civil Society and Dissent*. New York, NY: Human Rights Watch.

Guliyev, Farid. 2013. "Oil and Regime Stability in Azerbaijan." *Demokratizatsiya* 21 (1): 113–147.

Gureyeva, Yuliya. 2005. "National Status Report on Higher School Reforms and Gender Education in the Country." Open Society Institute-Azerbaijan, Network Women's Program. http://gender-az.org/index_en.shtml?id_main=19&id_sub=67.

Heyat, Farideh. 2000. "Azeri Professional Women's Life Strategies in the Soviet Context." In *Gender and Identity Construction: Women of Central Asia, the Caucasus and Turkey*, edited by Acar Feride and Ayse Gunes-Ayata, 177–201, Leiden, The Netherlands: Brill.

Heyat, Farideh. 2005. *Azeri Women in Transition: Women in Soviet and Post-Soviet Azerbaijan*. London: Routledge.

Kamp, Marianne. 2009. "Women's Studies and Gender Studies in Central Asia: Are We Talking to One Another?" *Central Eurasian Studies Review* 8 (1): 2–12.

Kandiyoti, Denise. 2007. "The Politics of Gender and the Soviet Paradox: Neither Colonised, nor Modern?" *Central Asian Survey* 26 (4): 601–623. https://doi.org/10.1080/02634930802018521.

Mehrabov, Ilkin. 2016. "Azerbaijani Women, Online Mediatized Activism and Offline Mass Mobilisation." *Social Sciences* 5 (4): https://doi.org/10.3390/socsci5040060.

Mohanty, Chadnra Tolpade. 1988. "Under Western Eyes: Feminist Scholarship and Colonial Discourses." *Feminist Review* 30 (1): 61–88. https://doi.org/10.1057/fr.1988.42.

Motyl, Alexandr. J. 1994. "Negating the Negation: Russia, Not-Russia, and the West." *Nationalities Papers* 22 (1, Spring): 263–272.

Nicholson, Linda. 1986. *Gender and History*. New York, NY: Columbia University Press.

Ong, Aihwa. 1988. Colonialism and Modernity: Feminist Re-presentations of Women in Non-Western Societies. *Inscriptions* 3–4: 79–93.

Orujev, Rauf. 2013. *Mnogoobraziye Problem* (Interview with the Head of the State Committee on Family, Women and Children's Affairs (SCFWCA) of the Republic of Azerbaijan, Hijar Huseynova). *Zerkalo Newspaper*, January 12. http://anl.az/down/meqale/zerkalo/2013/yanvar/288647.htm.

Oushakin, Sergey. 2000. "Gender." In (naprokat): poleznaja kategorija dlja nauchnoj kar'ery? *Gendernajaistorija: pro i contra*, edited by M. Murav'eva, 34–39.

Pilkington, Hilary. 1996. "Introduction." In *Gender, Generation and Identity in Contemporary Russia*, edited by Hilary Pilkington, 1–18. London: Routledge.

Rivers, Nicola. 2017. *Postfeminism(s) and the Arrival of the Fourth Wave. Turning Tides*. London: Palgrave Macmillan.

Roudometof, Victor. 2015. "The Glocal and Global Studies." *Globalizations* 12 (5): 774–787. https://doi.org/10.1080/14747731.2015.1016293.

Shiriyev, Zaur. 2017. Betwixt and Between: The Reality of Russian Soft-Power in Azerbaijan. https://ge.boell.org/en/2017/10/16/betwixt-and-between-reality-russian-soft-power-azerbaijanon.

Sperling, Valerie. 1999. *Organizing Women in Contemporary Russia: Engendering Transition*. Cambridge: Cambridge University Press.

Sundstrom, Lisa M. 2002. "Women's NGOs in Russia: Struggling from the Margins." *Demokratizatsiya* 10 (2, Spring): 207–229.

Suny, Ronald Grigor. 1995. "Rethinking Soviet Studies: Bringing the Non-Russians Back In." In *Beyond Soviet Studies*, edited by Daniel Orlovsky, 105–134. Washington, DC: Woodrow Wilson Center Press.

Temkina, Anna, and Elena Zdravomyslova. 2003. "Gender Studies in Post-Soviet Society: Western Frames and Cultural Differences." *Studies in East European Thought* 55 (1): 51–61.

The Caucasus Research Resource Center. 2011. *Social Protection and Social Inclusion in Azerbaijan*. European Commission, Brussels. https://r.search. yahoo.com/_ylt=AwrJS9Zjr9pcLiAAGy4M34lQ;_ylu=X3oDMTByaW1 1dnNvBGNvbG8DaXIyBHBvcwMxBHZ0aWQDBHNlYwNzcg--/RV= 2/RE = 1557864419/RO = 10/RU = http%3a%2f%2fec.europa.eu% 2fsocial%2fBlobServlet%3fdocId%3d6885%26langId%3den/RK = 2/ RS=wyJRo8w960FUywICLR_P7t_xWu8-.

———. 2012. National Survey 'Social Capital, Media and Gender in Azerbaijan'. http://caucasusbarometer.org.

Tohidi, Nayereh. 1997. "The Intersection of Gender, Ethnicity and Islam in Soviet and Post-Soviet Azerbaijan." *Nationalities Papers* 25 (1): 147–167. https://doi.org/10.1080/00905999708408494.

———. 1998. "'Guardians of the Nation': Women, Islam, and the Soviet Legacy of Modernization in Azerbaijan." In *Women in Muslim Societies: Diversity Within Unity*, edited by Herbert L. Bodman and Nayereh Tohidi, 137–162. Boulder, CO: Lynne Rienner Publishers.

———. 2004. "Women, Building Civil Society, and Democratization in Post-Soviet Azerbaijan." In *Post-Soviet Women Encountering Transition: Nation Building, Economic Survival, and Civic Activism*, edited by Kathleen Kuehnast and Carol Nechemias, 149–171. Washington, DC: Woodrow Wilson Center Press.

Trehub, Aaron. 1988. "Social and Economic Rights in the Soviet Union." In *Social and Economic Rights in the Soviet Bloc: A Documentary Review Seventy Years After the Bolshevik Revolution*, edited by George R. Urban, 6–26. Oxford: Transaction Publishers.

UNDP. 2007. *Azerbaijan Human Development Report: Gender Attitudes in Azerbaijan: Trends and Challenges*. Baku, Azerbaijan: Çevik Qrup Publishing House.

UNICEF and Azerbaijan Economists' Union. 2008. *Budget Investments in Health and Education of Azerbaijani Children*. Baku, Azerbaijan: UNICEF and Azerbaijan Economists' Union.

Vision.Az. 2017. *Reclaim the Hamam Event*, January 27. http://www.visions. az/en/whats_on_in_azerbaijan/868/on.

Voronina, Olga. 2003. *Feminism i Gendernoe Ravenstvo*. Moskva: Editorials URSS.

Welzel, Christian, and Ronald Inglehart. 2009. "Political Culture, Mass Beliefs, and Values Change." In *Democratization*, edited by Christian W. Haerpfer, Patrick Bernhagen, Ronald F. Inglehart, and Christian Welzel, 126–144. Oxford and New York: Oxford University Press.

West, Candace, and Don H. Zimmerman. 1987. "Doing Gender." *Gender and Society* 1 (2): 125–151. https://doi.org/10.1177/0891243287001002002.

Yudkevich, Maria, and Gregory Androushchak. 2012. "Quantitative Analysis: Looking for Commonalities in the Sea of Differences." In *Paying the Professoriate: A Global Comparison of Compensation and Contracts*, edited by Philip G. Altbach, Liz Reisberg, Maria Yudkevich, Gregory Androushchak, and Iván F. Pacheco, 21–35. New York: Routledge.

Zimmermann, Susan. 2007. "The Institutionalization of Women's and Gender Studies in Higher Education in Central and Eastern Europe and the Former Soviet Union: Asymmetric Politics and the Regional-Transnational Configuration." *East Central Europe*, 34 (1): 131–160. https://doi.org/10.1163/18763308-0340350102007.

Zulfigarova, Nailya. 2003. *Genderniye aspekti stanovleniya grajdanskogo obshestva v Azerbaijane* (Gender Aspects of Development of Civil Society in Azerbaijan). Dissertation, National Academy of Sciences, Baku.

11

Feminism in Azerbaijan: Gender, Community and Nation-Building

Sinead Walsh

This chapter is a reflection on my encounters with feminism in Azerbaijan, mainly in the context of ethnographic fieldwork related to women's civic activism. It is written in response to a question I am often asked, both inside and outside of Azerbaijan: 'is there any feminism (t)here at all?' The short answer is yes, insofar as there are women and men who identify as feminist, and the concept continues to circulate among others who engage with it more critically. The long answer involves a more nuanced conversation: what are the expectations, prejudices and occasionally desires, that prompt the initial question and its frequent follow-up, 'but are there any *real* feminists?'

The first part of the chapter introduces the field and problematizes the impulse to reduce feminism to a single definition. The remaining parts focus on two sets of constraints affecting the possibility for a broad-based feminist community. To begin with, I consider the ways that gendered power relations limit women's opportunities in the private and public spheres, with a focus on female sexuality as an

---

S. Walsh (✉)
University of Limerick, Limerick, Ireland
e-mail: walshs7@tcd.ie

© The Author(s) 2020
U. Ziemer (ed.), *Women's Everyday Lives in War and Peace in the South Caucasus*,
https://doi.org/10.1007/978-3-030-25517-6_11

253

instrument of repression. After this, the chapter considers how feminism as a form of civic activism relates to the gendered concept of national unity.

This research is based on interviews and participant observation conducted mainly in Baku, but with additional insights from short trips to the north (Sheki, Zagatala, Khachmaz), northwest (Qazakh) and west (Aghdam, Fizuli) of the country. While formal interviews with leaders of women's NGOs provided a general overview of women's activism, much of the detail comes from informal interviews and conversations with younger women, and some men, the majority of whom were urban, middle-class students or professionals. By paying particular attention to the experiences of women in this group who both did and did not identify as feminist, I hope to shed light on the challenges facing feminism in Azerbaijan, but also offer proof of its existence among a small part of the population.

Locating Feminism

When people ask if feminism exists in Azerbaijan, they are usually asking about the existence of an organized movement with a clear manifesto for social change. They want to hear about staged public performances rather than everyday resistance to gender norms. Often what they have in mind are the controversial but widely circulated images of post-Soviet cultural icons such as *Femen* and *Pussy Riot*, whether or not they approve of such sensational tactics. That their questions usually arise from a total lack of knowledge on the subject of post-socialist feminisms indicates the extent to which the former second world has been neglecting in transnational feminist histories (Suchland 2011). Even more disconcerting, however, is the extent to which these questions contain the assumption that feminism follows a linear trajectory—one which will eventually see Azerbaijani women claim a place among the feminisms of the world (Hemmings 2005, see also Pedwell 2010).

This chapter does not use any particular definition of feminism, preferring to give an account based on observation and conversations with women in Azerbaijan. It does, however, separate the categories of women's activism and feminism. While such distinctions have historically proved unimportant compared to the task of advancing women's rights through coalitional movements (Grewal and Kaplan 1994; Moghadam 2005), the distinction evidently matters on a subjective level to the women who identify, and come to identify, as feminist. For Sara Ahmed, feminism is nothing less than a world-building project. It is 'how we survive the consequences of what we come up against by offering new ways of understanding what we come up against' (2017, 22). Ahmed's work gives an insight into the effects of feminism as a scattered, invisible and repeatedly silenced phenomenon, evoking 'wilful subjects' whose persistent tendencies reveal the limits on women's agency and voice in any given context, over and over again (Ahmed 2010).

Taking time to understand the affective properties and emotional appeal of feminism is particularly important at present. While the last five years have seen considerable momentum around women's rights on a global level, in the post-socialist space this has often been experienced as a backlash, and attacks on women's organizations, especially those allied with queer communities, have become commonplace in Hungary, Poland, Russia, Georgia and Armenia (Heinrich Boell Foundation 2015).[1] Although the portrayal of feminists as a fifth column, intent on destroying the nation by attacking traditional values, is recognized as political scapegoating, the prominence of the debate on gender and culture refuels older and to some extent legitimate anxieties about feminism and westernization (Ghodsee 2004; Hrycak 2006). Perhaps the question, 'but are they *real* feminists?' points to the desire to differentiate between an authentic, grass-roots feminism on the one hand, and the reproduction of neoliberal ideology on the other. Yet feminism can be fatally undermined by the imposition of 'cultural differences' on a movement that exists precisely to challenge sexist cultural norms (Narayan 1997, p. 15).

The majority of Azerbaijan's political and civic elite view feminism as divisive, in that it encourages conflict between women and men, and disruptive, in that it goes against traditional gender norms and familial structures. Reinforcing this perception is the official women's policy agenda, which can be seen to advocate reconciliation between the sexes and promote women's rights largely in the framework of traditional gender roles (Gureyeva 2010). Discourses on women's rights draw on a powerful historical narrative: Azerbaijan was the first majority Muslim country where women were fully enfranchised (in 1918), a monument to the unveiled woman has stood in the capital city since the 1950s, and women enjoyed high levels of literacy and employment for decades. These conditions are viewed as the legacy of early twentieth century bourgeois women's activism, later superseded by Bolshevik gender ideology (Kasumova and Kasumova 2006).

There are a number of active women's organizations in the country, at least one of which, the Society for Protection of Women's Rights named after Dilara Aliyeva, pre-dates the country's post-Soviet independence. While the Society for Protection of Women's Rights was created as the women's wing of the Popular Front Party, implying a strong political foundation, the majority of organizations on a list compiled by the Azerbaijan Gender Information Centre were founded to deal with specific social or economic concerns, and as such, claim to be non-partisan.[2] In practice, many of these organizations do not have a continuous presence in public life, but are active for the duration of specific project cycles. However, some organizations have evolved into professional, mainly western-funded NGOs which seek to bridge the gap between civil society, the state and international institutions. For example, the Women's Institute (also known as the Women's Problems Research Union) and Women's Association for Rational Development both advocate for the state's adherence to the Convention on the Elimination of All Forms of Discrimination Against Women (CEDAW) and implementation of its own laws on gender equality (2006) and domestic violence (2010).

There are numerous differences between organizations such as the ones mentioned above in terms of their political outlook, thematic focus, access to resources and contacts in various communities. Nevertheless, these NGOs form part of a recognizable sector, in that they behave according to a similar set of practices, and frequently engage in both competition and cooperation with one another. Previous studies have criticized the tendency of international donors to foster the professionalization of women's NGOs, often to the detriment of grass-roots activism, in post-socialist contexts such as Bulgaria (Ghodsee 2004), Ukraine (Hrycak 2006) and Armenia (Ishkanian 2003). The women who spoke to me on behalf of NGOs in Azerbaijan often pre-emptively raised this issue, stating that donors were an important source of both financial and moral support, but insisting that they set their own agenda independently. Items on this agenda ranged from legal advice and representation for women, to training women as electoral observers and election candidates, to addressing sexual and reproductive health, to supporting women and girls of IDP and refugee background.[3] Interviewees emphasized the importance not just of implementing projects, but of cultivating relationships at a grass-roots level, suggesting that the most meaningful indications of change in society are to be found on an individual or community level, rather than in national policy.

While these NGOs often frame their work in terms of the principles of empowerment and equality, many of the women I interviewed eschewed the word 'feminist', preferring not to refer to themselves as such either publicly or privately. In the course of interviews, it emerged that many established women's rights advocates have a negative view of feminism as being radically anti-men. The discourse of gender equality, on the other hand, is used to invoke notions of balance and choice. The head of one NGO stated:

> When our population hears about women's associations or NGOs, they perceive us as feminist. Whereas in our organisation in particular, we do not apply this word at all. We rather call ourselves gender advocates, rather than feminists. We do not exclude the role of men in any process at all, we do not have this radical, you know, extreme approach. All we want is that women have equal access to all these opportunities, and let her decide whether she wants to marry or not, whether she wants to marry this person or not, whether she wants to get education or not, whether she wants to work or not.

Other women understood feminism as being thoroughly opposed to the traditional display of masculinity and femininity. While arguing for the principle of equality, they emphasized the importance (to them) of biological differences between the sexes, and for the preservation of certain customs arising from the gender binary:

For instance, I want a man to be a gentleman and show me to my place and take my coat – all the same, there has to be some beauty in life, there has to be harmony…You know, there are those pure feminists, the ones who say "how am I any worse than you, why are you giving up a seat for me, why are you carrying that for me?" They want mutual equality in that sense. But gender equality has to be on the societal level, because all that same, there are biological differences.

While this and the previous quote are drawn from interviews with senior figures in the women's NGO sector, similar views relating to feminism were encountered with women of all ages and with varying levels of experience in women's rights activism. An exception to this was found in the Azerbaijani Feminist Group (AFG), which formed in the 1990s and is currently active on the basis of voluntarism and occasional small grants sourced locally and internationally. The AFG stands out for its unapologetic embrace of the word feminist; as one of the founding members said in a workshop address: 'feminism is my religion'. This group has positive relations with the more prominent women's rights NGOs in the country, considering much of their work for gender equality to be 'de facto feminist' (Moghadam 2015, p. 54) and collaborating with them around issues of mutual concern. Speaking with women who took part in some of these wider women's rights campaigns as workers, volunteers or participants, I learned that while some rejected feminism as an ideology, others identified with it on a personal level. Many were simply curious as to the potential meanings of feminism in their context. A quote from a young student illustrates this sense of feminism as a terrain to be explored rather than a system of rigid beliefs:

To tell the truth, I don't have so much information, what is meant under feminism. But I'm coming up with my own understanding of it. And I know that there are radical feminists who are totally against men, and this is for our society something not acceptable, if you are against men, they think that you are crazy, that you are stupid, and that you don't know what you are talking about. This is one way of feminism. But I think that this is like – liberal feminism is more like you say the same thing as radical feminism, but in a softer, more fluffy way. And I think that this is the way, this is something that can change.

In other words, there is potential attached to the word feminism in Azerbaijan, even if only a small fraction of the population choose to identify with it. Feminism is found on the margins, in small communities or widely dispersed networks. It is more frequently expressed in private than in public, and more likely to be the subject of a conversation about meanings than a template for action. Despite the general reticence to be labelled as a feminist, I encountered strong interest in discussing feminist issues—and the term feminism itself—among young women and men who were active in civil society, and who worked in spheres such as education, law, business, media, arts and culture. Almost all the people who identified to me as feminist were living in Baku, but many had moved there for work or study, and retained close ties with family in rural or semi-rural areas, something which informed their understanding of the cultural implications of feminism in Azerbaijan.

The term enjoys greater currency with women who have come of age in the twenty-five years following the collapse of the Soviet Union, and among the urban middle class. However, it is important not to portray this as a simple generational or class divide; associating feminism with youth can provide spurious grounds for its dismissal (Hunt 2013). Some women said that the response to feminism from figures in authority is mostly condescending: self-identified feminists are assumed to be 'good girls' going through a rebellious phase. These women drew attention to a maternalistic rhetoric employed by some established women's rights advocates, who refer to feminists as 'our girls', asserting generational hierarchies in a way that masks the ideological differences which can arise between women of all ages. Meanwhile, young professional women as well as older ones frequently made statements such as 'I am not a feminist, I just defend women's rights', suggesting that there is considerable willingness to comply with the dominant discourse which is sceptical towards feminism, rather than reclaim the word for activist purposes.

Tolerance and subtle patronizing belong at the more benign end of a scale which includes mockery, social ostracism and threatening behaviour. To identify as feminist in Azerbaijan, as in many other places, means to risk being branded as crazy, irrational and unworthy of being taken seriously by others. As noted by bell hooks more than three decades ago, even women who benefit from feminist-generated reforms tend to profess an 'uncritical acceptance of distorted definitions of feminism rather than a demand for redefinition' (Hooks 1984, p. 22). This helps explain why becoming a feminist can be a reluctant process. The social intricacies in Azerbaijan are expressed by the joking manner in which certain women may say '*yes, I'm a feminist – I'm a bad girl*'. While some women prefer to keep their feminist identity to themselves, others think of it as something that exists separately from the self, as an area to be explored rather than a habit to be worn. Yet even to express curiosity about feminism is to acknowledge its potential usefulness as a tool for analysis.

My own position as a western European and Irish feminist complicates this analysis, as it draws post-socialist feminism into a transnational research framework (Suchland 2011; Koobak and Marling 2014; Tlostanova et al. 2016). It is possible that some women identified with me as feminist because they assumed there was something to be gained from it, or to enhance their pro-European credentials. Others admitted that while they could discuss it sympathetically with me, they could not imagine doing so in front of family members. Meanwhile, some of the most acute criticism of gender relations came from women who saw feminism as culturally inappropriate in Azerbaijan. In compositing multiple and contrasting points of view in the following section, I am not claiming to have located a singular feminism underneath it all. Rather, I hope that drawing out some of the recurring patterns in conversations about women, gender and feminism will provide some insight into how feminism is simultaneously present and invisible in contemporary Azerbaijan.

The Politics of Women's Bodies

On one of my trips to Baku, I met a young university lecturer who was dismissive of what she called 'feminist-Amazonians'. Gesturing towards one of her finely plucked eyebrows, she told me to look at the faces of the women sitting near us in the café. Then she told me I should look at the eyebrows of every woman I met during my fieldwork, explaining that this is how to tell, at a glance, if the person you are talking to is a 'good girl' or a 'bad girl' in the eyes of society. In this context, she argued, it was pointless to talk about increasing women's political participation, or enhancing their role in peace processes (a key topic in my dissertation). What was needed was a change in mentality, so that women could pluck their eyebrows if they wanted to, without fear of moral judgement.

It is tempting to argue that this woman was a feminist, even if she did not think of herself as one. She certainly managed to demonstrate how women's lack of agency is connected to socially constructed notions of femininity. By plucking her eyebrows in a certain way she was defying convention, insisting on women's right to control their own bodies, and providing a role model for the students she taught. Nevertheless, as Uma Narayan writes:

An awareness of the gender dynamics within one's family and one's 'culture,' even a critical awareness, does not suffice to make women feminists. Women may be aware of such dynamics but may consider them to be *personal* problems to be dealt with personally, without seeing them as a *systematic* part of the ways in which their family, their 'culture,' and changing material and social conditions script gender roles and women's lives, or without feeling that they must contest them in more formal, public, and political ways. (1997, p. 11)

In Azerbaijan, the word gender is often used interchangeably with the term 'women's problems'. This phrase carries a dual meaning: in addition to the physiological implications, it is widely understood as referring to social issues. This is the result of national political discourse which has, for over a century, used 'the Woman question' to mark the divide between tradition and modernity (Tohidi 1998). The distinction between traditional and modern families is invoked to explain certain practices (such as early or arranged marriages) and to generally absolve society from any collective responsibility for these. Among the middle classes in particular, there is a faith that education will lead to better outcomes for women regardless of changing political and economic contexts.

Deniz Kandiyoti (2007) argues that Soviet policies on gender and national identity led to contradictory outcomes for women, producing what she calls the 'Soviet gender paradox'. She shows how in the majority Muslim states of Soviet Central Asia, high female literacy and labour force participation rates coexisted with high fertility rates and a traditional division of household labour. Although fertility rates were somewhat lower in Azerbaijan, women's emancipation was similarly 'shot through with dilemmas, contradictions and duality' (Tohidi 1997, p. 111), failing to displace the traditional values of 'purity and virginity for girls, and sacrifice and self-denial for wives and mothers' (Heyat 2006, p. 396). Such contradictions were a recurring theme in my fieldwork: particularly how young women whose 'modern' families supported their freedom of education and right to work coped with 'traditional' restrictions in the realm of their own sexuality and personal lives.

Although many families are in favour of women receiving a university education, this goal does not replace marriage and family, or even create the option of an independent life. It merely defers the process by a few years, following in the well-scripted rationale that a woman with an education will make a better mother than one without.[4] A woman who is 25 and single is a cause for familial concern; even women who are younger than this make jokes about being left on the shelf, or traded for a sack of potatoes. While women theoretically have the right to choose their future partner, a potential marriage requires the approval of both partners' families. This need for approval in turn dictates a narrow range of socially acceptable behaviour for unmarried women. 'Good girls' should study hard and get a good degree in a discipline appropriate to their gender. They should maintain a feminine appearance, one which underscores their heterosexuality but also their chastity. They should not smoke or drink, especially in public. They should not frequent bars or nightclubs. They should not engage in multiple relationships (simultaneous or consecutive), and they should abstain from premarital sex (Tohidi 1997, pp. 152–153).

Not all women experience these conditions as oppressive, but many argue that society is overly obsessed with monitoring young women's behaviour. Those from the countryside in particular spoke about how rituals associated with virginity are still preserved: red ribbons are tied to gateposts, brides wear a red scarf while being visited by their parents-in-law. One woman recalled an instance when a gun was fired by a couple on their wedding night to indicate that the marriage had been consummated with honour (see also Aliyeva and Grigoryan 2016). Although some women believed that chastity was a virtue, they were adamant that this should be the private business of the couple involved, not their parents or neighbours. Others said it was a harmful norm, but pointed out the difficulties in changing it. While there are 'open-minded' young men for whom a woman's virginity is not an issue, this can lead to women feeling under pressure to either have sex in order to maintain a relationship, despite the costs to their reputation. Double standards of male and female sexuality ensure that equality in heterosexual relationships remains elusive.

Women's domestic arrangements are rarely conducive to flouting the rules around sexuality. Women are often expected to remain in the family home until they are married. Even if a woman is financially independent, her choosing to live separately would be considered shameful for the family (Heyat 2006, pp. 401–402). There are exceptions, such as young women who move from rural areas to the cities for work or study. However, while some women live together in student dormitories, shared houses or apartments, parents frequently enlist members of the extended family to keep an eye on them, and it is common for women to receive nightly phone calls from their parents. Young men who criticized the honour mentality admitted that they still kept an eye on their younger sisters' behaviour for social reasons. Establishing a relationship can lead to added pressure on women from their new partners: conventional masculinity is associated with jealousy, as demonstrated by possessive behaviour and monitoring of women's private phone calls, emails and social media use (Pearce and Vitak 2015).

Many of the people who spoke to me said that women themselves were to blame for tolerating these restrictions because they remained 'passive' in the face of oppression. This view may locate responsibility exclusively at the individual level, rather than taking structural sexism into account, but it also implies that there is some space for women to negotiate their roles, and that women are perceived as having agency. In her theory of the 'patriarchal bargain', Kandiyoti (1988) argues that women may become invested in upholding repressive conditions if they are likely to derive a future reward—for example, the informal influence a wife may have over her husband, the bond between a mother and her son, or the power of a mother-in-law over her daughters-in-law. Tohidi likewise suggests that older women in Azerbaijan derive pleasure from this gender paradox (1997, pp. 155–156). However, both authors acknowledge that owing to the changing material conditions of society, there is also occasionally room for younger women to alter the rules of the game.

Participation in public life is one area where feminists in Azerbaijan may experience a certain amount of room to manoeuvre. Although the conventional 'good girl' stereotype still prohibits most young women from engaging in social or political activism, there have been expanding opportunities for women in non-formal education and voluntary or charitable work since the collapse of the USSR (Ishkanian 2003; Tohidi 2004). The influence of western educational models, with their emphasis on extra-curricular engagement, provide arguments for why women should do more outside of their studies. Parents who keep a strict watch over their daughter's reputation at home can nevertheless sometimes be persuaded to send them abroad on prestigious scholarships, or allow them to participate in international training or voluntary projects.[5] International companies—and, increasingly, major international sporting and cultural events—create employment opportunities for women who have experience with languages and intercultural communication (Heyat 2006, pp. 400–401).

Women's organizations are among those that have helped to expand the opportunities for women, by conducting seminars which introduce them to the vocabulary of international organizations, training them in areas such as computer literacy and intercultural communication, and by providing links to youth networks and exchanges. This can be seen as a form of targeted socialization: some activists see it as their role to provide younger women with the information, skills and confidence deemed necessary to succeed in an international milieu. Their women-only stance sometimes gives them an additional advantage: they can reach girls whose parents would be even more sceptical of mixed-gender activities.

Potential conflict with family members is one reason, according to some interviewees, why even if you are a feminist, you have to live an irreproachable private life. Women's rights advocates are under pressure to demonstrate to the public that being socially active does not turn you into a 'bad girl' or make you a target for sexual predators. Those who organize and lead international study visits and youth exchanges in particular must show that they are suitable chaperones, capable of protecting young women's reputations. Numerous women I spoke with said that their parents had been very reluctant to agree to their participation in any form of overnight or residential activity, but that they had eventually changed their minds mainly as a result of growing acquainted with the individuals involved as leaders in these projects. While feminists understand that this patient approach has helped to empower countless young women in the short term, they also question the 'trampoline effect'—young women availing of these opportunities for further study or training do not always, or even in most cases, seem to give back to the feminist community on their return home.

Feminism for many Azerbaijani women can thus be understood as part of their personal values system rather than a concerted political movement. However, there are instances when the potential for collective solidarity becomes visible. In May 2015, an 18-year-old schoolgirl called Aytac Babayeva was stabbed to death after rejecting a young man's advances, in what some local media referred to as a 'crime of passion'. Thousands of Azerbaijanis protested online, calling for women not to be silent in face of jealous, vengeful and controlling behaviour (Geybulla 2015). Although the outcry was limited to social media users, it echoed the cries of street protests which took place in Turkey the previous February, following the murder of a 19-year-old student Özgecan Aslan (BBC Azeri 2015). Women and men alike understood the violence as a brutal enactment of society's control over women. It is worth asking, as discussed in the following part of this chapter, why this systematic gender analysis is not more embedded in the civic and political life of the nation.

Gender, Civil Society and Nation-Building

If successive generations of Azerbaijanis have come to believe that national progress is determined by women's role in society, this has been accompanied by the widespread view that the nation's health is determined by the strength of its families. In this way the gender paradox experienced in the family is mapped onto the national landscape. Women's participation in public life is encouraged only insofar as they do not neglect their role in the biological and cultural reproduction of the nation (Yuval-Davis 1997, pp. 22–23). This orthodoxy is reflected in statements made by prominent female politicians, including the first lady (and, as of 2017, vice-president) Mehriban Aliyeva, and Hijran Huseynova, the chair of the State Committee on Family, Women and Children's Affairs since 2006.[6] Consequently, to be accused of seeking to destroy family values is to be accused of undermining both nation and state.

After the dramatic collapse in the numbers of women represented in parliament following the breakup of the USSR, local women's organizations, supported by large international donors such as USAID and various UN agencies, invested time and resources in encouraging women's participation in politics. In 2014, women made up to 35% of elected representatives at the municipal level. From a feminist perspective, there is a fear that this is political tokenism, which serves to reinforce a system that is fundamentally patriarchal, and detract from concerns over other human rights violations (Walsh 2015a). According to many women, gender is not the only obstacle for women seeking a political role. Rather, a lack of connections to influential people is perceived as a major obstacle. The family resurfaces at the core of a system based on patronage and kinship, in which the figure of the late Heydar Aliyev (father to the current president) is venerated as grandfather of the nation (Diuk 2012, pp. 78–79).

Political power is at the heart of feminist politics: without some voice in the system, there is no way to cement whatever gains women are able to make in the private or public sphere. These leaves women dependent on unpredictable factors, vulnerable to change and often without recourse to legislation when they need it most. With vertical movement proving impossible to all but a few, there is a role for a horizontal movement that would create a broad base of women concerned about their rights. However, here we run into the same problems as before. Firstly, few women are prepared to take on the reputational risks that come with political activism, which although it is more egalitarian than formal politics, still calls for personal connections and networks. Secondly, of those who do, only a handful are committed to building a women's movement. Even among women who hold feminist values, the priority appears to be strengthening civil society as a whole, in the face of increasing restrictions on freedom of assembly and expression in recent years.

The idea of women and men standing together in civic unity to defend their human rights is a powerful one, drawing on practices of solidarity in Soviet dissident movements. However, in reality it is mostly men who play a dominant role in political parties and NGOs (Mehrabov 2016). The presence of a few exceptional and outspoken women in public life, from the First Lady and Vice President of the country Mehriban Aliyeva, to those who have faced prison or exile, serves to mask the problem of structural sexism. Ironically, the recognition that women such as Leyla Yunus, former deputy defence minister turned human rights activist, and Lala Shovket, leader of the Azerbaijani Liberal Party (and the only female party head in the country), have received for their individual achievements enables the myth of gender equality to persist, as other women's failure to attain such heights is blamed on personal choices and not structural constraints. This is not to say that all women in the public eye should be obliged to constantly uphold a feminist agenda, but to explain that women's collective activism is also necessary to tackle the root causes of gender injustice.

The women describing themselves as feminists who contributed to this study were aware of these dynamics, citing for example the number of all-male 'expert panels' at conference events, and the tendency for men to dominate during political protests. At the same time, they acknowledged that women were, on the whole, less likely to be targeted by the authorities for arrest and intimidation, and that organizing as women made them feel safer than if they were working in mixed-gender groups. Importantly, many younger women did not feel the need to choose between one way of doing things or the other: they were active in both women's organizations and youth movements. For example, there was considerable participation from young women in the sizeable street protests which took place in 2013 in relation to non-combatant deaths in the army. Whereas youth activism provided an opportunity to stand with their male peers—mostly urban, middle-class students and professionals—on questions of justice and democracy, women's activism created opportunities to tackle systemic gender equality and bridge social divides.

The idea of the nation as a happy family, united around a belief in shared values and the gendered division of labour, has come to the fore in the political discourse of many post-Soviet republics. As well as legitimizing the rule of certain families, it attempts to mask the social unrest that has arisen as a result of deepening wealth inequality and the darker side of globalization (Kandiyoti 2007). Feminists in Azerbaijan who are aware of this divide are concerned by the vulnerabilities faced by women in rural areas and in poorer urban districts. Outside of the capital, women lack access to public space, and social media use is low, especially among women and girls (Pearce and Vitak 2015). As economic problems increase, so do women's vulnerabilities to under age or arranged marriages, casual sex work and human trafficking. Constraints on NGO activities and funding have lowered the capacity of women's organizations to respond to the needs of these communities, reinforcing the perception of feminism as an urban elite phenomenon.

A similar concern with social inclusion pertains to the relationship between feminism and religion. While Islam in the Soviet Union was seen as a general marker of cultural and ethnic identity, the post-Soviet period has seen the rise of 'official' and 'oppositional' variants of religious expression (Bedford 2012). Generally, feminists and women's rights activists agree that it is important to reach out to religious leaders when tackling violence against women, not only because of their influence over men and women in the community, but also to bridge the gap between secular and religious society. They pointed out that while most Azerbaijanis are moderate believers, the public tends to become polarized around certain issues, with veiling being a prime example (Heyat 2008; Najafizadeh 2012; Vazirova 2014). One woman noted that younger women from secular backgrounds are especially prone to be sensitive about the *hijab*, viewing it as a sign of oppression. She saw it as part of her responsibilities as a feminist to help women trust one another and respect each other's choices. Research suggests that such pluralistic alliances may be possible, with some women in online religious forums expressing strong support for the journalist Khadija Ismayil after illegal recordings of her private life were leaked online in an effort to discredit her (Mehrabov 2015).

Finally, the question of gender and nationhood resurfaces in relation to the conflict over Nagorny Karabakh. Although there is a strand of transnational feminism that is concerned with anti-militarism (Cockburn 2007), there is no feminist 'position' on war (Zalewski 1995). My research found that while many women viewed militarization as a cynical tactic used to bolster political power, most also considered themselves 'patriots' and believed that negotiations should be used to bring justice to Azerbaijan. Despite tangible differences in their positions, Azerbaijani women's organizations have worked with their Armenian counterparts to establish dialogue across the divide and to create opportunities for women affected by conflict to meet (Walsh 2015b). While agreeing to disagree on some issues, they are committed to rebuilding trust and to pushing for an inclusive peace process in which women are given a voice on security matters (Freizer 2014).

For some women, the significance of cross-border initiatives lies in the fact that the South Caucasus is a historically diverse region, where ethnic, linguistic and religious minorities have for the most part lived peacefully for thousands of years (Kemoklidze et al. 2014). They pointed to the similarities between patriarchal traditions in Azerbaijan and Armenia, noting that custom rather than religion appears to dictate the most oppressive conditions in women's lives. They also argued that understanding the relationship between culture and gender was crucial to empowering women from minority groups, who are almost invisible across the Caucasus. A case in point is the community of Azerbaijani women in Georgia, who are considered to be one of the most vulnerable groups in Georgian society due to the triple stigma of gendered, ethnic and religious otherness (Peinhopf 2017). Thus, an alternative to rigid ideals of national unity is perhaps to be found in a feminist conception of dialogue across borders (Mohanty 2003)—but is by no means guaranteed in the current climate.

Conclusions

Notions of women's agency in Azerbaijan are mostly connected to widening their space for public participation on the basis of political and economic opportunities that have arisen in the post-Soviet period. However, patriarchal norms continue to restrict women's behaviour and choices in society as a whole, despite the ostensible value placed on women's education. Beneath the surface, there are potentially large numbers of women and men who support a liberalization of gender regimes and encourage respect for women's bodily integrity and sexual autonomy. Their reasons for not adopting a feminist stance in public range from respect for the elder generation and traditional culture, to the belief that sex is best spoken about in private, to the fear that they or their families will suffer shameful consequences for speaking out. While only a small minority therefore consider themselves part of a feminist community, there is a wider appetite for feminist conversation, especially among young people who have already developed an interest in gender issues.

For those seeking to support the spread of feminism in Azerbaijan, it is worth considering how gender issues map onto the terrain of civic and political society. Formal political discourse reinforces the paradox which offers women access to public space in return for their obedience to restrictions on their private lives. Women's ability to participate is contingent on two things: their willingness to address only those gender issues which are deemed to be in the national interest, and their readiness to prioritize the question of national unity above all other issues. However, there is potential for feminist communities to play a bridging role between rich and poor, urban and rural, religious and secular society. In addition, despite the unresolved legacies of conflict, the cultural diversity of the South Caucasus provides a glimpse into the potential for transnational feminist dialogues.

Notes

1. Less attention has been paid to such attacks in Azerbaijan, but they pose no less of a risk for feminist activists. For example, at the time of writing, an article appeared in Azerbaijani media accusing three Azerbaijani

women of being 'feminist grant-eaters'. These women had attended a conference on the future of the Eastern Partnership in Stockholm, where they spoke about restrictions on civil liberties and obstacles to implementing the state's women's rights obligations: https://haqqin.az/news/111648. For the article in the Swedish press, see http://www.forumsyd.org/sv/Media-Opinion/Nyheter/2017/Feminismen-i-Azerbadzjzan/.

2. This list can be accessed at https://www.gender-az.org/index_en.shtml?id_main=10&id_sub=80.

3. There are an estimated 600,000 IDPs, or internally displaced persons, in Azerbaijan, roughly 6% of the overall population. More than twenty years after a ceasefire was signed, it remains unclear whether they will ever return to their homes in and around Nagorny Karabakh. Women's organizations have undertaken initiatives to support economic and political empowerment among IDP women and to encourage their participation in peacebuilding and conflict resolution.

4. The total gross enrolment ratio for tertiary education in Soviet Azerbaijan was at about 25% in the 1980s. By 1997, this had dropped to 17%. This has risen sharply in the last decade, from 19% in 2008 to 27% in 2016. Since 2011, the change has been more pronounced for women than for men. Between 2015 and 2016, the gross enrolment ratio for men rose from 23.64 to 24.99%, while the corresponding jump for females was from 27.48 to 29.69%. This is according to data from UNESCO, available at http://uis.unesco.org/country/AZ.

5. Note that this is still subject to permission: a question I was often asked during my fieldwork, by all age groups, was 'did your parents agree to let you come and do this?'

6. Thank you to Leyla Jafarova for sharing her translation of some of these statements with me in her unpublished report on the scale of domestic violence in Azerbaijan.

References

Ahmed, Sara. 2010. "Feminist Killjoys (and Other Willful Subjects)." *The Scholar and Feminist Online* 8 (3). http://sfonline.barnard.edu/polyphonic/print_ahmed.htm.

———. 2017. *Living a Feminist Life*. Durham and London: Duke University Press.

Aliyeva, Lala, and Ani Grigoryan. 2016. "Virgins, Doctors and Traditions." *Chai-Khana*, May 5. https://chai-khana.org/en/virgins-doctors-and-tradition.

BBC Azeri. 2015. *#BBCAzeriTrending: Aytac Babayeva üçün kampaniya genişlənir.* May 5. http://www.bbc.com/azeri/azerbaijan/2015/05/150505_aytac_babayeva_campaign.

Bedford, Sofie. 2012. "Oppositional Islam in Azerbaijan." *Caucasus Analytical Digest* 44 (20): 9–11.

Cockburn, Cynthia. 2007. *From Where We Stand: War, Women's Activism and Feminist Analysis.* London: Zed Books.

Diuk, Nadia. 2012. *The Next Generation in Russia, Ukraine, and Azerbaijan: Youth, Politics, Identity, and Change.* Lanham, MD: Rowman & Littlefield.

Freizer, Sabine. 2014. "Twenty Years After the Nagorny Karabakh Ceasefire: An Opportunity to Move Towards More Inclusive Conflict Resolution." *Caucasus Survey* 1 (2): 109–122. https://doi.org/10.1080/23761199.2014.11417295.

Geybulla, Arzu. 2015. "From Emancipation to Restraint: Violence and Gender Inequality in Azerbaijan." *OpenDemocracy*, June 8. https://www.opendemocracy.net/od-russia/arzu-geybulla/violence-and-gender-inequality-in-azerbaijan.

Ghodsee, Kristen. 2004. "Feminism-by-Design: Emerging Capitalisms, Cultural Feminism, and Women's Nongovernmental Organisations in Postsocialist Eastern Europe." *Signs: Journal of Women in Culture and Society* 29 (3, Spring): 727–753. https://doi.org/10.1086/380631.

Grewal, Inderpal, and Caren Kaplan, eds. 1994. *Scattered Hegemonies: Postmodernity and Transnational Feminist Practices.* Minneapolis: University of Minnesota Press.

———. 2010. "Policy Attitudes Towards Women in Azerbaijan: Is Equality Part of the Agenda?" *Caucasus Analytical Digest* 21: 5–7.

Heinrich Boell Foundation. 2015. *Anti-gender Movements on the Rise? Strategising for Gender Equality in Central and Eastern Europe.* Volume 38 of the Publication Series on Democracy, February. Berlin.

Hemmings, Clare. 2005. "Telling Feminist Stories." *Feminist Theory* 6 (2): 115–139. https://doi.org/10.1177/1464700105053690.

———. 2006. "Globalisation and Changing Gender Norms in Azerbaijan." *International Feminist Journal of Politics* 8 (3): 394–412. https://doi.org/10.1080/14616740600793010.

———. 2008. "New Veiling in Azerbaijan." *European Journal of Women's Studies* 15 (4): 361–376. https://doi.org/10.1177/1350506808095275.

Hooks, Bell. 1984. *Feminist Theory from Margin to Centre.* Boston, MA: South End Press.

Hrycak, Alexandra. 2006. "Foundation Feminism and the Articulation of Hybrid Feminisms in Post-socialist Ukraine." *East European Politics and Societies* 20 (1): 69–100. https://doi.org/10.1177/0888325405284249.

Hunt, Theresa. 2013. "Transcending Polarisation? Strategic Identity Construction in Young Women's Transnational Feminist Networks." *Women's Studies International Forum* 40: 152–161. https://doi.org/10.1016/j.wsif.2013.06.004.

Ishkanian, Armine. 2003. "Gendered Transitions: The Impact of the Post-Soviet Transition on Women in Central Asia and the Caucasus." *Perspectives on Global Technology and Development* 2 (3–4): 475–496. https://doi.org/10.1163/156915003322986361.

Kandiyoti, Deniz. 1988. "Bargaining with Patriarchy." *Gender and Society* 2 (3): 274–290. https://doi.org/10.1177/089124388002003004.

———. 2007. "The Politics of Gender and the Soviet Paradox: Neither Colonised, nor Modern?" *Central Asian Survey* 26 (4): 601–623. https://doi.org/10.1080/02634930802018521.

Kasumova, Yelena, and Irada Kasumova. 2006. *Traditsii Zhenskoi Aktivnosti v Azerbaidzhane: Konets XIX – Nachalo XX Veka*. Baku: Açıq Cämiyät İnstitutu - Yardım Fondu.

Kemoklidze, Nino, Cerwyn Moore, Jeremy Smith, and Galina Yemelianova, eds. 2014. *Many Faces of the Caucasus*. Abingdon and New York: Routledge.

Koobak, Redi, and Raili Marling. 2014. "The Decolonial Challenge: Framing Post-Socialist Central and Eastern Europe within Transnational Feminist Studies." *European Journal of Women's Studies* 21 (4): 330–343. https://doi.org/10.1177/1350506814542882.

Mehrabov, Ilkin. 2015. "Gendered Surveillance and Media Usage in Post-Soviet Space: The Case of Azerbaijan." *Baltic Words* 8 (1–2): 44–48.

———. 2016. "Azerbaijani Women, Online Mediatized Activism and Offline Mass Mobilisation." *Social Sciences* 5 (4). https://doi.org/10.3390/socsci5040060.

Moghadam, Valentine. 2005. *Globalizing Women: Transnational Feminist Networks*. Baltimore: John Hopkins University Press.

———. 2015. "Transnational Feminist Activism and Movement Building." In *The Oxford Handbook of Transnational Feminist Movements*, edited by Rawwida Baksh and Wendy Harcourt, 53–81. Oxford: Oxford University Press.

Mohanty, Chandra. 2003. *Feminism without Borders: Decolonizing Theory, Practicing Solidarity*. Durham, NC: Duke University Press.

Najafizadeh, Mehrangiz. 2012. "Gender and Ideology: Social Change and Islam in Post-Soviet Azerbaijan." *Journal of Third World Studies* 29 (1): 81–101.

Narayan, Uma. 1997. *Dislocating Cultures: Identities, Traditions and Third World Feminism.* London: Routledge.

Pearce, Katy E., and Jessica Vitak. 2015. "Performing Honor Online: The Affordances of Social Media for Surveillance and Impression Management in an Honor Culture." *New Media & Society* 18: 1–18. https://doi.org/10.1177/1461444815600279.

Pedwell, Carolyn. 2010. *Feminism, Culture and Embodied Practice: The Rhetorics of Comparison.* Abingdon and New York: Routledge.

Peinhopf, Andrea. 2017. "Ethnic Minority Women in Georgia—Facing a Double Burden?" European Centre for Migration Issues, Working Paper 74, February. http://www.ecmi.de/uploads/tx_lfpubdb/Working_Paper_74.pdf.

Suchland, Jennifer. 2011. "Is Postsocialism Transnational?" *Signs: Journal of Women in Culture and Society* 36 (4, Summer): 837–862. https://doi.org/10.1086/658899.

Tlostanova, Madina, Suruchi Thapar-Bjorkert, and Redi Koobak. 2016. "Border Thinking and Disidentification: Postcolonial and Postsocialist Feminist Dialogues." *Feminist Theory* 17 (2): 211–228. https://doi.org/10.1177/1464700116645878.

Tohidi, Nayereh. 1997. "The Intersection of Gender, Ethnicity and Islam in Soviet and Post-Soviet Azerbaijan." *Nationalities Papers* 25 (1): 147–167. https://doi.org/10.1080/00905999708408494.

———. 1998. "'Guardians of the Nation': Women, Islam, and the Soviet Legacy of Modernization in Azerbaijan." In *Women in Muslim Societies: Diversity within Unity*, edited by Herbert L. Bodman and Nayereh Tohidi, 137–162. Boulder, CO: Lynne Rienner.

———. 2004. "Women, Building Civil Society, and Democratization in Post-Soviet Azerbaijan." In *Post-Soviet Women Encountering Transition: Nation Building, Economic Survival, and Civic Activism*, edited by Kathleen Kuehnast and Carol Nechemias, 149–171. Washington, DC: Woodrow Wilson Center Press.

Vazirova, Aysel. 2014. "Freedom and Bondage: The Discussion of Hijab in Azerbaijan." In *Changing Identities: Armenia, Azerbaijan, Georgia*, 148–176. Tbilisi: Heinrich Boell Foundation.

Walsh, Sinead. 2015a. "Representation, Reform and Resistance: Broadening Our Understanding of Women in Politics in Azerbaijan." *Caucasus Analytical Digest* 71: 6–9.

———. 2015b. "One Step Forward, Two Steps Back: Developing a Women's Peace Agenda in Post-Soviet Armenia and Azerbaijan." In *Gender and Peacebuilding: All Hands Required*, edited by Maureen P. Flaherty, Tom Matyok, Jessica Senehi, Sean Byrne, and Hamdesa Tuso, 139–155. Lanham, MD: Rowman & Littlefield.

Yuval-Davis, Nira. 1997. Gender and Nation. London: Sage.

Zalewski, Marysia. 1995. "Well, What is the Feminist Position on Bosnia?" International Affairs 71 (2): 339–356.

Index

A

Abkhazia 4, 9, 10, 14, 155–160, 163, 211

Activism
feminist activism 12, 13, 77, 225, 238
street activism 8, 74, 88, 267
women's activism 11, 77, 89, 90, 237, 254, 256

Agency 2, 8, 51, 59, 73, 74, 80, 81, 83, 88, 180, 194, 238, 255, 261, 263, 270

Armenia 1, 2, 4–6, 8–10, 12, 14, 15, 72, 73, 76, 77, 80, 81, 83, 85, 90–92, 129, 131, 132, 137, 139, 140, 143, 144, 146–149, 183–185, 195, 255, 257, 269
Armenian society 10, 71, 74, 75, 78, 85, 88, 89, 121, 130, 131, 133–136, 140, 146, 185

Authoritarian
authoritarian government 71, 72
authoritarianism 73
authoritarian regime 72, 80, 227, 242, 244
hybrid regime 14
semi-authoritarian 1, 71

Azerbaijan 2, 4–7, 9, 10, 12–14, 24–26, 30, 31, 34, 38–40, 73, 74, 129–139, 144–146, 148, 183–185, 195, 225–229, 231, 232, 235–237, 239, 241–247, 253–255, 257, 259–262, 264, 268–271
Azerbaijan society 10, 11, 13, 23–25, 27, 37, 134, 236, 237, 245, 259, 261, 265, 268–270

© The Editor(s) (if applicable) and The Author(s) 2020

U. Ziemer (ed.), *Women's Everyday Lives in War and Peace in the South Caucasus*,

https://doi.org/10.1007/978-3-030-25517-6

278 Index

B

Baku 7, 10, 23–27, 29–35, 37–40, 130, 132, 134, 135, 137, 139, 140, 142–146, 148, 149, 226, 236, 239, 242, 254, 259, 260

Belonging
citizens' belonging 53, 160
ethnic belonging 158
national belonging 7, 185

Body(ies) 74, 103, 147, 148, 163, 239
active bodies 80
women's bodies 81

C

Challenges 10–12, 14, 84, 107, 130, 146, 183, 193, 194, 211, 235, 238, 241, 254

Children 10, 12, 28, 32, 33, 49, 55, 64, 85, 86, 104, 106, 107, 109–111, 113–115, 117, 121–123, 133, 139, 142, 162, 164, 168–172, 181, 185, 187–189, 191, 192, 196, 211, 236, 240

Control 14, 34, 187, 213, 261
social control 34, 35, 81, 142, 182, 188, 191, 192
societal control 182, 188

Crisis 11, 143, 147, 159, 161, 168, 172, 211, 244

D

Discourse
political discourse 156, 157, 205, 261, 268, 270
public discourse 7, 12, 207, 215–218, 247

societal discourse 189

Displacement 9–11, 129, 130, 141, 155, 157, 159–161, 163, 171–173, 181

E

Employment 5, 10, 76, 78, 139, 145, 146, 208, 234, 242, 245, 246, 256, 264

Ethnic groups 132, 156
diverse ethnic groups 269
ethnic minority groups 269

Ethnography 158, 173
ethnographic study 73, 182

Everyday
everyday activism 13, 80
everyday challenges 2, 11
everyday life 25, 44, 46, 63, 65, 136, 193, 210, 220, 230

F

Family 3, 6, 10, 12, 15, 24, 32, 35, 36, 45–47, 49, 50, 55, 57, 58, 62, 75, 79, 85, 105, 106, 108, 109, 111–113, 115, 116, 118, 121, 134–137, 139, 142, 144–146, 149, 158, 160, 162, 165, 167, 169, 170, 185–192, 209, 212, 213, 216–218, 234, 244, 247, 259–264, 266, 268

Femininity 51, 85, 134, 135, 185, 239, 257, 261

Feminism 11–13, 28, 38, 79, 134, 225, 229, 232, 233, 235, 237–239, 241–245, 247, 253–255, 257–260, 265, 268–270

Feminists 3, 12, 13, 25, 39, 60, 72–74, 79, 80, 83, 86, 119, 158, 163, 217, 225, 226, 228, 229, 232–245, 247, 253–255, 257–261, 264–270

G

Genocide 74, 104, 106, 108, 109, 119–122
The Armenian Genocide 105
Georgia 1, 2, 4–6, 8, 9, 12, 14, 15, 43, 45, 46, 49, 50, 56–58, 65, 79, 89, 145, 155–158, 160, 161, 164, 169, 207, 208, 212, 213, 215–217, 219–222, 255
Georgian society 44, 46, 48, 51, 52, 54, 64, 205–207, 209–212, 218, 269
Globalization 268

H

Hate speech 12, 206, 213, 214
Husband 6, 9, 10, 15, 29, 31, 58, 63, 103, 106, 107, 109, 112–123, 133–137, 139, 142–145, 149, 162, 168, 169, 180, 186–193, 195, 213, 230, 264

I

Internally Displaced Persons (IDPs) 6, 9, 130, 147, 157, 160, 164, 167, 169, 172, 173, 271

L

Labour
labour force 3, 5, 14, 262
labour market 5, 14, 235
labour market participation 4
Lesbian, gay, bisexual and transgender (LGBT) 12, 60, 206–211, 213–215, 217–220, 222
LGBTQ x

M

Marriage 10, 28, 35, 40, 46, 62, 105, 106, 113, 115–120, 123, 133, 139, 182, 185, 189, 190, 192–194, 209, 211, 212, 215, 220, 222, 247, 261–263, 268
Masculinity 8, 51, 234, 257, 263
Mass media 90
social media 226, 241, 247, 263, 265, 268
Men
Armenian men 88, 112, 118, 133, 149
Azerbaijani men 23, 233, 236, 265
Georgian men 5, 66
traditional men 3, 8, 24, 28, 36, 44, 45, 50, 51, 55–57, 63, 65, 66, 75, 88, 89, 233, 255
working men 56, 234
Migration
forced migration 139
labour migration 234
Modernity 7, 23–27, 31, 37–39, 45, 65, 261
Modernization 6, 8, 26, 27, 44, 46, 51, 52, 64

280   Index

Mother 8, 24, 28, 56, 59, 62, 64, 65,
   73, 85, 86, 89, 104–107, 110,
   122, 158, 159, 162, 190, 230,
   262, 264
   motherhood 46, 50, 74, 75, 85,
      133, 185, 188
Movement
   feminist movement 236, 238
   political movement 72, 265
   social movement 13, 72–74, 78,
      79, 84, 89, 217
   women's movement 267

N

Nagorny Karabakh 2, 4, 9, 14, 91,
   130, 147, 179, 184, 186, 193,
   195
   Karabakh men 74, 190, 191
   Karabakh women 6, 11, 29, 74,
      180–183, 185, 191, 193–196
Nation 7, 28, 39, 50, 73–75, 82, 85,
   104, 108, 116, 122, 123, 185,
   215, 228, 243, 244, 255, 265,
   266, 268
Non-governmental organizations
   (NGOs) 73, 205, 206, 209,
   210
   women's NGOs 13, 15, 60, 77,
      217, 220, 229, 240, 241, 254,
      256–258, 267, 268

P

Post-socialism
   post-socialist 8, 72, 79, 164, 180,
      182, 232, 254, 255, 257
   socialism 3, 4, 76

Private 4, 6, 8, 15, 32, 45, 54,
   56–58, 60–65, 75, 76, 85,
   133, 137, 146, 158, 166, 208,
   212, 232, 253, 263, 264, 266,
   269
   in private 36, 51, 259, 270
Protests
   Armenian protests 78, 89
   social protests 141
   street protests 8, 71, 84, 89,
      265
Public 3, 4, 7, 13, 15, 27, 32, 33, 36,
   38, 39, 45, 48, 51, 54, 56–58,
   60, 61, 63, 65, 71, 72, 75,
   76, 84, 85, 87, 91, 134, 163,
   173, 206, 208, 209, 211–214,
   216–218, 232, 237, 239, 242,
   243, 247, 253, 254, 261, 264,
   266, 268, 270
   in public 34, 35, 81, 133, 134,
      146, 193, 210, 220, 256, 259,
      262, 264, 266, 267, 270
   public speeches 91

Q

Quotas 77

R

Refugees 6, 9, 111, 118, 129–131,
   135–149, 160, 170, 172, 257
Revolution
   Coloured Revolutions 79
   Orange Revolution 79, 90
   Rose Revolution 1, 8, 44, 51–53,
      79, 90, 213, 221
   Velvet Revolution 71, 73, 80

S

Social change 2, 3, 6–8, 13, 14, 45, 80, 86, 194, 254
South Caucasus 1–7, 9, 12, 14, 15, 62, 90, 179, 180, 183, 220, 269, 270
South Ossetia 1, 4, 9, 14, 155–157, 211
Supra 8, 43–45, 47–51, 53–60, 62, 63, 66
Survival 4, 7, 117, 157, 163, 168–170

T

Tbilisi 14, 28, 29, 46, 50, 56, 60, 216, 218, 220, 233
Tradition(s) 7, 8, 24, 26, 28, 30, 31, 33, 35–37, 39, 45, 46, 50, 54, 60, 61, 63, 65, 75, 77, 132–134, 173, 182, 185, 187, 188, 190, 192, 220, 247, 261, 269

U

Unemployment 4, 5, 76, 131, 195, 234
Union of Soviet Socialist Republics (USSR) 4, 7, 12, 76, 148, 212, 264, 266

V

Violence

domestic violence 6, 15, 24, 35, 36, 91, 232, 256
physical violence 209, 218
sexual violence 6, 209, 210, 219, 232, 235

W

War 1, 2, 4, 9, 10, 14, 36, 73, 74, 104, 107, 108, 110, 111, 113, 117–121, 123, 130, 131, 143, 145, 147, 156, 157, 160, 161, 163, 165–168, 170–173, 179–182, 184, 186–190, 193, 194, 196, 211, 213, 227, 269
Widow 113, 116, 134, 141, 168, 186–190, 192–195
widowed women 180, 181, 191
widowhood 11, 180, 181, 183, 186, 191, 192, 194
Women
Armenian women 9, 10, 15, 75, 103–111, 114, 118, 119, 121, 123, 130, 131, 133–135, 144, 147, 185
Azerbaijani women 13, 24, 39, 40, 228, 254, 265, 269, 271
Georgian women 8, 44, 45, 54, 63
independent women 63
widowed women 180, 181, 191
women's organizations 77, 255, 264, 266, 267, 271